Mrs. W. E. Lawrence (neé Smither) (1801 – 1880)

1823 - BEFORE
and AFTER
(2021 edition)

. . . The story of William Effingham Lawrence,
Tasmanian pioneer, and his family

E. FRANK LAWRENCE

With much valued assistance from
John L. Lawrence, and Diana E. Targett

*The land both gifted to, and purchased by, William Effingham
Lawrence and his family stood on the ancestral lands of the Stoney
Creek nation comprising Tyerrenotepanner, Leterremairrener and
Panninher clans.
We acknowledge and pay respect to the Tasmanian Aboriginal
peoples as the traditional custodians of this land for thousands of years,
and to the elders both present and emerging.*

Cover Photograph: Outbuildings at *Formosa*, Cressy, Tas., mostly
built with convict labour in the 1830s (c. J.D.L. Heard, 2021).

Kol Sasson Press, Kingston, Tasmania

ISBN: 978-0-646-84361-2

CONTENTS

Introduction

This book is the completion of a sixty-five year life journey that began with my father in the 1950s regaling me with stories of his great-grandfather closing his business in London, England, loading his family and goods onto his 71 ton cutter and embarking on a nine month voyage to Van Diemen's Land, arriving in February 1823.

This sparked a deep-seated abiding interest in the history of our family which has led to contact with many interesting people in many parts of the world who have a common interest in our family heritage.

The sesquicentenary of the arrival of William Effingham Lawrence (WEL) (1782-1841) and his family, fell in 1973 and the occasion was marked with a major family reunion and the publication of "1823 – Before and After", 1973 edition.

The bicentenary is in 2023 and the occasion is likely to be marked in some fashion. The 2021 edition of the family history contains detail of change in the family since 1973 and much more detail on the family in earlier years, especially prior to the early 1800s.

The early chapters cover the origins of the family and the years spent in North America. Chapter 4 is the life and times of WEL, the subsequent chapters are devoted to each of the offspring of WEL, and the final chapters cover other items of family interest. Inclusion of extensive references, cross-referencing within the book, and a comprehensive index are changes since the 1973 edition.

Generation numbers continue to be used
- the early generations are Nos. 1-8, starting with Robert Lawrence (1490-1527) (p. 11) in England.
- the generation of WEL restarts the numbering at number one (p. 55) and continues to generation No. 8 with some of the family lines.

Inaccuracy of information (especially dates) is a potential problem with a book of this type and we have been constantly aware of this. Errors can be present with any data – whether it is official records, cemetery headstones, verbal history, even *Ancestry.com* – and we have tried wherever possible to confirm independently material received. Any feedback concerning corrections or additions, preferably in writing, would be most welcome. Any errors in the material published in this book are the responsibility of the author.

It is a real pleasure to acknowledge the interest and support I have received from many members of the family, and other people, during this project, and I am happy to receive further information on family matters, as desired, in years to come.

My brother John Lawrence and his daughter Samantha (p. 150) have been responsible for the 1973 book becoming an electronic manuscript. John, and later Diana Targett (p. 179) my researcher for the early family information in the first three chapters and much other work, have since provided much support over a long period of time. They are largely responsible for the fact that the manuscript for this book has progressed towards a "print ready" form. Ruth Amos of Kol Sasson Press (Kingston, Tas) has provided the conduit to the printer's office, has assisted greatly with formatting the book and has shown skill and willingness to tolerate my funny ways! Many thanks to all concerned.

Finally, my wife Beatrice deserves a big vote of thanks for her support in many ways including her tolerance of my tendency to find relatives in all sorts of unexpected places.

EFFINGHAM FRANK LAWRENCE
fb_lawrence@yahoo.com

November, 2021

Chapter 1

ORIGINS OF THE FAMILY
(1490-1635)

The family of William Effingham Lawrence has its origins in England with some accounts suggesting a kinship with Robert Lawrence who accompanied King Richard Coeur de Lion (Richard I) on his famous expedition to Palestine in the late 12th century.[1] He is notable in the siege of St Jean d'Acre in 1191, by being the first to plant the banner of the cross on the battlements of that town, for which he received the honours of knighthood from King Richard, and also a coat of arms (this coat of arms is still preserved, impressed on the seal appended to a document of William Lawrence 1680, and also Richard Lawrence 1711, preserved in the Surrogate's Office, New York City.)[*]

The arms "argent, a cross raguly gules" were granted in A.D.1191.[1] Verification of the above connection is very difficult because of inadequate records and conditions in Europe at the time.

The historical backdrop during the 14th-16th centuries in England was marked by political turmoil and repeated outbreaks of Bubonic Plague, also known as the Black Death,[2] which had arrived in England through the port of Weymouth in August

---

[*]In 1858 Thomas Lawrence compiled an account[1] of the three Lawrence brothers and their descendants, to which he appended a number of full transcripts of important documents, which were on file in the office of the Secretary of State, Albany NY, some of which were lost in the Albany fire of 1911. The purpose of this book was to prove genealogy for a claim on the Townley estate believed to be held in Chancery in England (p. 48-49).

1348. The plague is caused by infection with the bacterium yersinia pestis, which is highly contagious, and was responsible for the death of at least 50 million people in Europe, Asia and Africa. The highest mortality was in the 14th century but cases of this disease still occur and need to be combated with stringent public health measures.

Henry VIII was crowned in 1509 and his mother died in the same year of the plague of 1508/1509.[3] By 1529 Henry VIII declares himself head of the newly formed Anglican Church which started the Reformation and the destruction of the monasteries.

Between 1543-1558 small outbreaks of the plague were recurring yearly in London, during which time King Edward VI is crowned in 1547, then Queen Mary in 1553 when Catholicism is returned as the State religion and 300 protestants were burned at the stake. In 1558 a protestant Queen Elizabeth I was crowned. In 1563 a plague outbreak in London killed a quarter of the population then spread to outlying counties with a 20% estimated death toll.[3] By 1578, Elizabeth I issued *The Orders*, whereby sick persons were not allowed to work or leave their homes, and burials, took place only at night.[3] The social conditions of this time reflected the changing political and religious chaos, the standard of living fell as the tax burden increased, compounded with poor harvests. Towards the end of this period, the Spanish Armada was destroyed in 1588.[4] In 1603 Queen Elizabeth I dies and James I (VI of Scotland) inherits the English throne.[3]

The Great Plague of London in 1665, which killed 100,000 people, was the last major outbreak, and after the Great Fire of London which started 1st Sept 1666 lasting for 6 days, it does not reappear in Britain[2] until the 19th century (according to current research as broadcast on SBS Australia 28/3/2021 with archaeologist Raksha Dave).

Against this backdrop, finding original accurate records of forebears is difficult. It is not until 1539 that regular parish records started to be kept,[3] which was dependent upon the diligence (and health) of the pastor. This is also reflected in online databases. Baptisms (bp.) were recorded but not the birthday of the child, and occasionally the father's name is given, but not all children were recorded in burial records from this period.

The parents and grandparents of the Lawrence family that migrated to the American colonies are well recorded as being members of the parish of The Abbey, St Albans, Hertfordshire, but earlier than 1539 many records may be lost, destroyed, not yet transcribed, or may not even exist, as many persons with the exact same name appear in burial records with no further information as to age or kinship.[5] In the St Albans district in Hertfordshire the grave records showing deaths due to the plague increase in the years 1578, 1592 and 1609.[5]

Much of the next information is from secondary sources, notably Find a Grave Memorial,[5] but some of the birthdates as given have not been found or verified in other sources. The reasonably accurate family tree begins with Robert Lawrence (1490-1527) of St. Albans, Hertfordshire, England.

Genealogy

1. **Robert Lawrence** (1490-1527).[6] He wrote his will on 20/6/1527, and probate a month later on 8/7/1527, naming his wife Avis and son John, and although he made a bequest to the Abbey Church, he had requested to be interred in the graveyard at St Peter St Albans. Married Avis _____ (-1527) whose burial date was 20/6/1527, yet was still mentioned in her husband's will; had issue.

2. **John Lawrence** (1514-5/1578),[7] Mayor of St Albans 1567-1568, 1575-1576, Principal Burgess of St. Albans, who also owned a number of tenements. Married Cecily Steward (1518-9/1578)[8] 1539, both of whom died during a plague outbreak; had issue.

   3. Avis Lawrence (c.1540-10/1625) married John **Clark**.

   3. Joan Lawrence (c.1542-   ) married John **Bishop**.

   3. William Lawrence (c.1544-   )

   3. Elizabeth Lawrence (c.1548-   ) married Roger **Shad**.

   3. Thomas Lawrence (c.1550-1573) age 22, buried 10/9/1573 Abbey Church

   3. **John Lawrence,** chandler (c.1554-1609)[9] married Elizabeth Bull (bp. 4/8/1563-1609)[10] 9/11/1579 at St Andrew, Hertford.[11] John and Elizabeth died within 2 months of each other during the 1609 plague; had issue[12]

      4. William Lawrence (bp. 4/12/1580-   )

      4. Edward Lawrence (bp.18/6/1582-   )

      4. John Lawrence (bp.1/1/1584-18/6/1675)[13] married Joane Roe (-5/7/1656) 18/6/1620;   had issue.

         5. Eleven children.

      4. Elizabeth Lawrence (bp.10/2/1585-   )

      4. Frances Lawrence (bp.22/5/1586-   )

      4. Richard Lawrence (bp.26/7/1587-   )

      4.**Thomas Lawrence** (bp.2/2/1588/89-20/3/1625)[14] one of the Principal Burgesses of St Albans 1622-1623. Married Joan Antrobus (bp.25/6/1592-c.1662)[15] 3/10/1609; had issue. Records in America show the family lived in Hertingfordbury, Hertfordshire, prior to emigrating.

      After Thomas' death, Joan married John **Tuttle** (c.1596-30/12/1656)[16] 1627 and migrated with her mother Joan Antrobus (née Arnold), her second husband John with their children, also the four youngest Lawrence children, to America on the *Planter* arriving 1635. John later emigrated to Ireland 1651, followed by Joan in 1654. She signed a letter-of-attorney to her son, Simon Tuttle in New England 29/1/1661 from Carrickfergus, died c.1662 and was buried at Carrickfergus, Antrim, Ireland[16]; had issue[17]

5. Joan Lawrence (bp. 8/1610, buried 8/1610)
5. Jane Lawrence (bp.18/1/1614-1680) married George **Giddings** (1609-1676) 16/2/1634 in St Albans, Hertfordshire, England, died in Ipswich, Massachusetts; had issue.
   6. Eight children.
5. Marie Lawrence (bp. 17/11/1616- buried 28/11/1616)
5. John Lawrence (bp. 26/7/1618-1699) (p. 18) migrated to North America 1635, married and died in New York; had issue.
   6. Seven children.
5. Thomas Lawrence (bp. March 1620-1703) (p. 20) migrated 1635, married twice, died in New Town, Queens County, NY; had issue.
   6. Eight children.
5. **William Lawrence, Captain** (bp. 27/7/1622-14/3/1680) (p. 23) migrated 1635, married twice, died at Tews Neck, Flushing Town, Long Island; had issue.
   6. Ten children.
5. Marie (Mary) Lawrence (bp. 10/4/1625-1715) (p. 46) migrated 1635, married Thomas **Burnham**

(1623-1694) c.1645, apparently lived and died in Ipswich, Massachusetts; had issue.

      6. Fifteen children.

   4. Anne Lawrence (c.1593-   )

   4. Mary Lawrence, (bp.26/4/1601-1602) burial not recorded.

   4. Mary Lawrence (bp.6/3/1603-   )

  3. Agnes Lawrence (c.1558-   ) married Thomas **Holden**.

2. William Lawrence, yeoman (c.1518-1580)[18] (second child of Robert Lawrence 1490-1527, p. 11) married Joan _____ (-); had issue

  3. Richard Lawrence (1550-1616)

  3. Bray Lawrence (1554-1611) married Joan Lowen (-); had issue

   4. Seven children; four died of the plague in 1592, and one more in that of 1609.

  3. John Lawrence (-)

  3. Alice Lawrence (-)

2. Ellen Lawrence (c.1520-1578) married – **Harrison** (-)

2. Alban Lawrence (c.1522-   )

2. _____ Lawrence (c.1526--/2/1572) married 1550 to Robert **Shrimpton** (-). Burial records as Mrs Lawrence Shrimpton.

Chapter 2

THE FAMILY IN NORTH AMERICA
(1635-1780)

Before commencing this chapter, it is important to note that dates given in original documents can be accurate "according to that time frame" but may not translate exactly to the format as used in the 21st century. From 1620 until 1752 the **calendar year, as used in England and the American colonies**, began on the **25th day of March** (Lady Day), and that month called "the first month". This was "the old style" or Julien calendar, (for example, 27/1/1631 is actually 27th March 1631, and 27/10/1631 is actually 27th Jan 1632), but some sources have left the original intact. Others have corrected the original. In 1752 the Gregorian calendar was enacted. The switch to the Gregorian calendar starts on the 1st January, but in the changeover, 11 days had to be omitted from September, so Wednesday 2nd September was followed by Thursday 14th September. Therefore, in this Chapter dates are shown as c. (meaning circa or approximate).

The Puritan Migration (*1620-1640*) from England to the developing American colonies for many migrants was originally a chance for religious freedom. However, the reasons for the Lawrence family migration may have been largely economic as Charles 1 had dissolved Parliament from 1629-1640 and after 1640 the emigration numbers decreased dramatically. The colonists to New England were mostly families with some education who were leading relatively prosperous lives in England, but up to 10% of colonists returned to England after 1640.

The Great Migration Study Project[*] records three brothers[1] John Lawrence age 17 (1618-1699), Thomas Lawrence (1620-1703), William Lawrence age 12 (1622-1680), and sister Marie Lawrence age 9 (c.1625-1715) who migrated with their grandmother Joan Antrobus age 65, stepfather John Tuttle, their mother Joan Tuttle (Antrobus) age 42 (the widow of Thomas Lawrence (1588/89-c.1624) (p. 12), with their four half-siblings[2] leaving St. Albans Hertfordshire and arriving in Massachusetts Bay 1635 on the *Planter*.[2] It is now believed that Thomas was omitted from this passenger list and is now included in the 1635[1] arrival.

The American records of the origins of the Lawrence family published by Thomas Lawrence in 1858,[3] indicate the emigrant Lawrence/Tuttle family lived in Hertingfordbury, Hertfordshire, which may have been correct in the lead-up to their departure in 1635 from St. Albans.

Their uncle, Henry Lawrence,[3] the Lord President of Oliver Cromwell's Council was also an early patentee (c.1632) of a large estate on the Connecticut River,[4] and it was he who sent out his Lawrence cousins[3] John, William and Thomas Lawrence, whether to protect his estates or as an opportunity for them (although there are some sources disputing this relationship with Henry).

In context, their arrival is fifteen years after the Plymouth colony (approx. 50 km south of Boston) which was established by the Pilgrims from the *Mayflower* which became part of New England.

Abutting this region, the Dutch West India Company (WIC)

[*]'The Great Migration Study Project' is an ongoing scholarly project, since 1988, to create an accurate database derived from many sources, of immigrants to New England from 1620 to 1640.[1]

established in 1621 New Netherland,[5] with a fort/trading post for the fur trade named New Amsterdam* in 1626[5] with a population of 270 persons. New Sweden established 1638 on the Delaware River was incorporated by the Dutch into New Netherland in 1655. In that same year, two thousand Susquehannock Indians and members of allied tribes attacked several settlements killing 100 people and took 150 prisoners (Peach Tree War). The territory of the north-western end of New York was also under dispute from the French and English, and the Iroquois Confederacy.[5]

Europe during this period was wracked by overlapping wars, and England was in political and religious turmoil culminating in the Civil War (1642-1651) and the execution of King Charles I on 30th January 1649.

Charles II ascended the throne 1660 and in 1664 deeded New Netherland[5] to his brother, the Duke of York, so four English frigates sailed into New Amsterdam harbour and successfully demanded surrender. This started the second Dutch-Anglo War (1665-1667) which concluded with the Treaty of Breda 1667[5], ceding New Netherland to the English. New Amsterdam under the English was renamed New York in 1665, with a population of 2500. The Dutch briefly re-took New York in the third Dutch-Anglo War (1672-1674), but at its conclusion, the Dutch gave up any claim to Manhattan and the Treaty of Breda was reinstated.

In 1675 the New Netherland population estimate was 7,000-8,000 comprised of European colonists (only half of whom were of Dutch descent), American Indians and imported African slaves.[5]

---

*Dutch West India Company purchased Manhattan from the Native Americans in 1626.

Genealogy

5. **John Lawrence** (1618-1699) (son of Thomas Lawrence 1588-
   1624 and Joan Antrobus 1592-1662)[6] baptized 26/7/1618
   at St Albans Hertfordshire.[1] At age 17 he emigrated on the
   Planter, landing in 1635 at Plymouth, Mass.[2] The family
   moved to Ipswich, then to Long Island and in 1644 John
   became one of the patentees of Hempstead on that island
   under the Dutch governor of New Amsterdam.[5] In 1645,
   along with his brother William and sixteen others, including
   John Adams,[3] obtained a Dutch patent (title) for Flushing. In
   1655 the three brothers[7] obtained a Dutch title to a large tract
   in Newtown, Long Is, and in 1689 received an English patent
   for their estates. John owned a small trading vessel called
   the *Adventurer*, trading both sides of Long Island.[8] In 1658,
   as a resident of New Amsterdam and with a country house
   near Flushing,[7] he was appointed Boundary Commissioner
   (1663) by the Dutch to negotiate the boundaries between
   New Netherland and New England. The English confirmed
   the Dutch Flushing patent of 1645 in 1665, the same year
   as New York was incorporated as a city.[1] At that time he was
   the first alderman (1665-1667)[8] appointed under the English
   government to the city council, twice Mayor of New York
   1672-1674 and 1691, appointed to His Majesty's Council
   1672-1698, and Supreme Court judge 1692-1698;[9] he died
   in 1699.[10] In his Will[11] he declared "he was a patentee in
   Hempstead and Flushing and the only survivor in both" and
   his wife (who survived him) and son-in-law Gabriel Monveille
   were appointed as executors.[8] Married Susanna N. (-1698)
   1642[1] Hempstead, Long Island; had issue.
   6. John Lawrence (c.1642[1]-   ) married[1] Sarah Cornell (-)

18

1682 by licence, widow of (i) Thomas Willett and (ii) Charles Bridges; no issue[3]

6. Mary Lawrence (c.1645[1]-1671) married Rev. William **Whittinghame**[12] (c.1640-<1672) 1664, son of John and a divinity graduate Harvard University 1660;[3] Mary died during childbirth[13] with her fifth child; had issue.

(The next generation dropped the "e" from their surname)

   7. Elizabeth Whittingham (-) Married . . .

   (i) Rev Edward **Payson** (-) 1683; had issue.

   (ii) Col. Samuel **Appleton III** (-); had issue

   7. Richard Whittingham (-) married _____ Bulkley; issue unknown.

   7. Martha Whittingham (-9/3/1759)[14] married[14] Rev. John **Rogers** (7/7/1666-28/12/1745) 4/3/1691, a graduate of Harvard 1684; had issue.

   7. Mary Whittingham (1665-1730) had a distinguished literary career, and at her death bestowed gifts to Harvard and Yale colleges; Married[8] . . .

   (i) William **Clarke** (-c.1712); issue unknown

   (ii) Gurdon **Saltonstall** (1666-1724) 1712,[13] the governor of Connecticut (1708-1724)[15]; had issue.

   7. William Whittingham (9/11/1671-)

6. Joseph Lawrence (c.1648-)[1] married - ; who died a widower, leaving one daughter who died young.[3] He was made an ensign 1684[1] (not to be confused with younger cousin Joseph, son of William[1]).

6. Thomas Lawrence (c.1651-)[1] died unmarried[3]

6. Martha Lawrence (c.1653-)[1] married Thomas **Snawsell**[1] (-) 1675; no issue.[3]

6. Susanna Lawrence (c.1655-c.1738)[1] married twice and survived both husbands.

(i) Gabriel Monbeille[1]/**Minvielle**, Mayor, (c.1644-1702) emigrated from France 1673, a merchant and trader, the fifth mayor of New York City;[16] married c.1676 by licence;[1] no issue.

(ii) William **Smith**, alderman, (　-　) 1702 by licence;[1] no issue.

6. (possibly)[1] William Lawrence (c.1657-　) baptised 25/4/1657 New York Dutch Reformed Church, no further record[1]

5. **Thomas Lawrence** (1620-1703) (son of Thomas Lawrence 1588-1624 and Joan Antrobus 1592-1662)[6] was baptised 8th March 1619/20 St. Albans Abbey, Hertfordshire,[1] and his gravestone is the first one installed in the Lawrence Cemetery New York[17] but inscribed incorrectly as 1625-1703.[*]

Thomas is reported as arriving in New England after the rest of his family.[3] In 1635 he would have been fifteen, so unless he was an apprentice or in school, and arrived later (with no immigration records found to support this[1]), it is now believed he is an unrecorded member with the rest of his family on the *Planter* arriving Ipswich 2nd April 1635,[2] recorded in 1645 as resident of Long Is, and died at Newtown.[1†]

---

[*]Major Thomas Lawrence is buried in his own family burial ground founded in 1703 with his own burial, together with his descendants (the "Newtown branch" of the Lawrence family) and the last grave is dated 1956. It is a half-acre block in the centre of a residential block housing 89 graves in present-day 20th Road/35th Street, Astoria, Queens County, New York. The plaque depicted was erected 1976 outside this cemetery.

[†]There are two Lawrence cemeteries surviving, the 3rd has disappeared. One is located 20th Road/35th Street, Astoria, Queens County, NY and in use from 1703 to 1956. The second Lawrence cemetery is on the corner 216th Street/42nd Ave in Bayside NY, and was in use from 1832 to 1939. The third cemetery, that is now obliterated, was located at Ditmars Boulevard and 37th Street in Astoria.

He, together with his two brothers in 1655 obtained a tract of land in Newtown, Long Island.[1] Thomas later bought the whole of Hell Gate Neck.[1] When the Glorious Revolution* began in 1668 he supported the (rebel) protestant cause. He was listed as Captain Tho. Lawrence on tax-list 1678.[1] He received a commission 24/12/1689[1] as Major of horse in Queens County, NY, during the Leisler Rebellion† (1689-1691).

Thomas was listed as head of the Newtown branch of the family.[7]

Married . . .

(i) Mary -   (-   ) c.1646;[1] had issue

   6. Thomas Lawrence[1] (c.1646-   ) married widow Francina Smith (née Berry) (-   ) 2/8/1685 in Bergen Dutch Church; had issue.

      7. Four children

   6. Sarah Lawrence[1] (c.1648-   ) Married . . .

   (i) Joseph **Winslow** (-   ) c.1668; issue unknown.

   (ii) Charles **LeBros** (-   ) <1679; issue unknown.

   6. William Lawrence[1] (c.1650-   ) married Annetje Edsall (-   ) by licence; issue unknown.

   6. Mary Lawrence[1] (c.1652-   ) Married . . .

   (i) Thomas **Walter** (-   ) 16/12/1671; issue unknown.

---

*The Glorious Revolution 1688-1689 in England** was the overthrow of the Catholic King James II by his Protestant daughter Mary and her Dutch husband, William of Orange. This political and religious unrest was mirrored in the American colonies.

†**Leisler's Rebellion** was an uprising in colonial New York in which German American merchant and militia captain Jacob Leisler seized control of the colony's south and ruled it from 1689 to 1691. The rebellion reflected colonial resentment against the policies of deposed King James II.

LAWRENCE FAMILY GRAVEYARD

In this private cemetery are buried members of one of America's most distinguished families. The first Lawrence to be buried here was Major Thomas Lawrence in 1703 and the last was Miss Ruth Lawrence in 1956. The roster of family notables includes Major Jonathan Lawrence, patriot, statesman, and soldier in the American Revolutionary War, and twelve other military officers of successive generations from Dutch Colonial days to the Civil War period. Seven of the Lawrences interred here held major government posts. This small cemetery is a reminder of over two and a half centuries of family history.

Plaque provided by the New York Community Trust, 1976

(ii) John **White** (-) <1704; issue unknown.

6. John Lawrence,[1] Captain (c.1655-17/12/1729) married Deborah Woodhull (1654-1740) c.1690, became High Sheriff of Yorkshire,[7] Long Island. In 1686 Gov. Dongan issued a English patent naming John (c.1655) and his older brothers Thomas (c.1646) and William (c.1650) as patentees[20] of Newtown, but John was the only one who remained in Newtown;[21] had issue.

7. Three sons.[7]

6. Jonathan Lawrence[1] (c.1658-) married Mary (-); issue unknown.

6. Daniel Lawrence[1] (c.1660-) married Geesje Theunis (-) 23/5/1696; issue unknown.

6. Elizabeth Lawrence[1] (c.1663-) married John Saunders (-) by licence 26/7/1683; issue unknown.

(ii) Mary Ferguson[1] (-) (2nd wife to widower Thomas Lawrence 1620-1703) (p. 20) married 9/11/1692 in the

New York Reformed Dutch Church;[1] no issue

5. William Lawrence, Captain (1622-14/3/1680), (son of Thomas Lawrence 1588-1624 and Joan Antrobus 1592-1662)[6] was baptised 27/7/1622 St. Albans Abbey, Hertfordshire,[6] England, migrated aged thirteen[2] with the extended family on the *Planter* 1635, and became a Dutch patentee at age twenty two with brother John and sixteen others[3] in 1644 of Long Island New York. He was a magistrate under the Dutch government, later a Captain under English government[1], a Justice of the Peace [Judge[3]] for the North Riding of Yorkshire, Long Is. 1675, 1676, and 1679 as Captain W. Lawrence.[1] He died a wealthy merchant 1680 on his own land at Tews Neck, Flushing Town, Long Island, New York.[*]

---

[*]The **William Lawrence Family Burial Ground** was located on the property of William Lawrence (1622 - 1680) on Tew's Neck, renamed Lawrence Point, now called College Point, in Queens County, New York.[23]

At the time of the arrival of the William Lawrence from Massachusetts in 1645, the area was known as Vlissingen, New Netherland. Under the British in 1664, it became Flushing, NY.

William Lawrence came to own all 900 acres of Tew's Neck via his patent with the Dutch in 1645. At the time, the peninsula was separated from the remainder of Flushing to the south by a swamp (presently filled in). It had been named for Michael Tew, the first settler, but it became known as Lawrence's Neck during the family's tenure. Although he also owned land elsewhere in Flushing, William Lawrence made his home on Tew's Neck. The peninsular property as a whole remained in the hands of the descendants of William Lawrence for its first century, with the Lawrences having been the only white inhabitants. Beginning in the mid 18th century, however, portions of the Lawrence property were gradually sold off. Knowledge of the exact site of the family cemetery on Tew's Neck has been lost to time, but it was operational from approximately 1645-1795. Although it may have been located on the former farmlands of Gilbert Lawrence in the northeastern portion of College Point, there are no remaining signs of it, with the former peninsula now covered by the modern city grid. [23]

His holdings in Bayside were extensive. His will lists ten properties valued @ £1,617, merchant stock, etc. valued @ £2,815, and names seven young children for guardianship;[1] Married . . .

(i) unknown[1] (-   ); had issue.

   6. Elizabeth Lawrence (1650-1683),[1] married Thomas **Stevenson** (-   ) 1/2/1672 in Newtown; had issue

   6. William Lawrence, Major (1656-1720).[1] William's grave marker 1645-1720[23] is either another William, or the family "guesstimated" his birth year to coincide with his father's move to Tews Neck.[24] However, Major Lawrence's will details of 1719 are recorded correctly, which lists wife Deborah, daughter Elizabeth, sons Joshua, Caleb, Stephen, Obadiah, Daniel, Adam, and son-in-law Joseph Rodman, and was proved 16 March 1720.[25]

William, Richard and Samuel died in his lifetime. Married Deborah Smith (1658-1743) 1680, the youngest sister of his stepmother[7] (Elizabeth Smith, 1643-1712, p. 25); had issue.

   7. William Lawrence (c.1682-1719) died before his father and without issue.[20]

   7. Richard Lawrence (c.1684-1719) married;[20] had issue.

      8. William Lawrence[20] (-   ) married Charity Cornell (-   ) 1740; had issue.

   7. Obadiah Lawrence (c.1685-1732) married Sarah[20] (-   ); had issue.

      8. Dr. William Lawrence[3] (-   ) moved to Oyster Bay, Long Island.

   7. Daniel Lawrence (c.1687-1757) married Mary[20](-   ); had issue.

   7. Samuel Lawrence (c.1690-<1720) married Mary[20] (-   ); had issue.

7. Joshua Lawrence (1691-1776) unmarried, died in Young, Texas

7. Adam Lawrence (c.1692-<1780), High Sheriff of Queens County, a leading churchman and an elected member of State Legislature;[7, 44] married Sarah Willett (-) 1717; had issue.

7. Deborah Lawrence (1693-1773) married John **Willett** (-) 1734; had issue.

7. Sarah Lawrence (-1757) married Joseph **Rodman** (1685-1769)[26] 1709; had issue

7. Caleb Lawrence (1697-1723) died West Nimba, Liberia (West Indies).[21]

7. Stephen Lawrence (1700-1781) married Amy Bowne (1715-1780) 1734; issue unknown

7. Elizabeth Lawrence (1706-1776)

6. John Lawrence (c.1657-1714)[1] (son of immigrant Captain William Lawrence 1622-1680) (p. 23) married Elizabeth Cornell (-) 1680; had issue[21]

7. William Lawrence (-)

7. John Lawrence (-)

7. Richard Lawrence (-)

7. Elizabeth Lawrence (-)

7. Mary Lawrence (-)

7. Deborah Lawrence (-)

7. Benjamin Lawrence (-)

7. Sarah Lawrence (-)

7. Charity Lawrence (-)

(ii) Elizabeth Smith (1643-1712) 4/3/1664 at Long Is. NY. (the 2nd wife to Capt. William Lawrence 1622-1680, p. 23). Elizabeth's second marriage on 26/3/1681 to Sir Philip Cartarett (1639-1682) Governor of New Jersey[27] lasted until his death a year later.[28][*] It was in her honour he named Elizabeth New Jersey, Eizabethtown NJ, and Elizabeth port NJ.[7] She then married for the third time 6/3/1685, to Col. Richard Townley (-1711)[29] who had migrated with Lord Effingham to Virginia in 1683. Col. Townley also held political office in both the New York Provincial Council and New Jersey Provisional Council for the Eastern Division until 4 weeks before his death in 1711. Elizabeth raised the seven younger Lawrence children.[18] Unusually, Elizabeth managed both Townley and Lawrence[1] estates, both of which she willed to her heirs.[3] Elizabeth Townley died in New Jersey 1712; had issue[1]

6. Mary Lawrence (c.1665-   )[1]
   Married . . .
(i)   James **Emmott** (-   ) 1682; issue unknown.
(ii) Rev. Edward **Vaughan** (-   ) 1714; issue unknown.
6. Thomas Lawrence (c.1667-1687),[1] age 19.
6. **Joseph Lawrence** (1668-18/4/1759)[1](sixth child of
   immigrant Captain William Lawrence 1622-1680)
   married Mary Townley (1670-1758) in 1690. Mary's
   sister Dorothy married Francis Howard[†] (later 1st Earl

[*]Philip Cartaret (1639-1682), was the Proprietary Governor of New Jersey 1665-1673 and 1st Governor of East New Jersey 1674-1682 when NJ was divided. "The New York Governor Edmund Andros attempted to seize power in East Jersey. When Philip Carteret refused to give up his position as Governor, Andros sent a raiding party to his home and had him beaten and arrested to New York. Carteret was placed on trial, but aquitted by the jury. The attack caused permanent injuries to Carteret, and he died in 1682."
[†]Francis Howard (1683-1743), 7th Baron Howard of Effingham 1725; a prominent military commander, created 1st Earl of Effingham in 1731.

of Effingham) who commanded a British frigate which moored in Long Is. Sound in front of Joseph's mansion.[7] Dorothy (Joseph's sister-in-law) mostly lived with Joseph and Mary so as to see her husband when he was in port. Joseph, who owned his own sloop, was also a close friend of Francis.[7] In honour of this friendship Joseph's grandson was named Effingham.[7]

Joseph Lawrence (1668-18/4/1759) married Mary Townley (1670-1758) 1690; had issue.

7. **Richard Lawrence** (1691-1781)[30] married Hannah Bowne (1697-1748)[31] 1717; had issue.[*]

   8. Mary Lawrence (3/4/1718-1776) married Ebenezer **Burling**[33] (1717-1758) 23/3/1736; had issue.

      9. Eleven children

      Rebecca their firstborn, who died young, arrived four months after the wedding. The parents were placed "under dealings" for "undue familiarity before marriage" by their church. The births of their next two children were recorded at the Friends' Meetings, but Mary and Ebenezer withdrew thereafter from Quaker society and moved from Long Is. Sound to Westchester County.

   8. Elizabeth Lawrence (14/6/1719- <1776) Elizabeth's

---

[*] The next two generations living in New York, and other coastal areas, had to deal with regular **yellow fever** epidemics (1790-1820), but the New York 1798 epidemic was one of the worst when 2760 persons died, thereby reducing the population to 15,300.[32]

parents were condemned[†] by their local Friends Society for "giving so much way to the marriage of daughter Elizabeth" who apparently married "out of meeting"[‡] to John Embrie [**Embree**][36] (-   ) 3/2/1740; had issue.

    9. Effingham Embree (1759-1817) married cousin Mary Lawrence (1763-1831); had issue

    9. Lawrence Embree (-   )

    9. George Embree (-   )

    9. Elizabeth Embree (-   )

    9. Hannah Embree (-1798)

8. Joseph Lawrence (10/11/1721-died young)[8]

8. Caleb Lawrence (10/2/1724-19/11/1799), (fourth child of Richard Lawrence 1691-1781, p. 27) admitted freeman to New York City 1745/46, a Quaker, and merchant in NY until 1774. In 1772 he was a brewer in business with brother-in-law Thomas Burling and John and Joseph Lawrence.[37] He moved to Westchester County during Revolutionary War (1775-1783) until 1790. He is listed in [Revolutionary War] Patriot

---

[†]"The close knit nature of the **Society of Friends** presented problems. The families of the NY Quaker colony were soon to intermarry so that by the 3rd and 4th generations, cousins married second and third cousins many times over. Friends were disowned for marrying out of the Society, but were also condemned for marrying first and second cousins... Many acknowledged fault and were accepted back in the community, but others not wishing to condemn themselves simply left a demanding culture".[34]

[‡]**Marrying out** – marrying a non-Quaker, being married by a priest, or marrying 'contrary to discipline'.[35]

Index (067108); served in two regiments, first as a Lieutenant, second time as Captain of 1st Westchester Militia 12/1777-3/1778.[38] He was back in New York by 1797. Caleb's will proved in 1799, listed his wife and all his living children, including those of his deceased son Richard. Married Sarah Burling[33] (-) 1754[8], cousin to Ebenezer Burling;[31] had issue.

9. Richard Lawrence (29/7/1755-<1799) married Mary Lawrence (1755-) 5/10/1780, the daughter of Dr. William Lawrence (p. 24); had issue.

   10. William Lawrence (-)

   10. Caleb Lawrence (-1847)

   10. Mary Ann Lawrence (-)

   10. Elizabeth Lawrence (-)

   10. Jane Emma Lawrence (-)

   10. Richard Lawrence (4/3/1788-12/4/1855) born in NY and died in Lafayette, Indiana. Married cousin Sarah Matilda De Zeng (16/4/1797-) 15/2/1818 in NY; had issue.

   10. Sarah Lawrence (22/4/1793-24/11/1872) married her cousin, Richard Lawrence **De Zeng** (3/10/1788-17/6/1848) 12/9/1815; had issue.

9. Elizabeth Lawrence (-<1799) not named in father's Will.

9. Sarah Lawrence (-)
   Married . . .

(i) _____ Green (-);

(ii) Caleb **Newbold** of Burlington (-1799); had issue.

9. Charlotte Lawrence (-06/12/1798) unmarried.

9. Hannah Lawrence (8/7/1758-   )
9. Mary Lawrence (11/11/1762 – infant death)
9. Mary Lawrence (11/9/1765-   ) married Major Frederick Augustus **De Zeng** (-   ); had issue 10. Nine children
9. Phebe Lawrence (24/2/1771- infant death)
9. Esther (Hester) Lawrence (12/05/1775-   ) married Captain John Gilbert **Clark** (-   ) 1796 and "was dismissed for marrying out" on 1/2/1797;[34] had issue.
8. Hannah Lawrence (02/4/1726-25/5/1806) (fifth child of Richard Lawrence 1691-1781, p. 27) married Abraham **Willett** [Willet] (-   ); had issue.
8. Lydia Lawrence (29/7/1728-1790) married Steppanus **Hunt**[30] (1721-1790), a highly respected and wealthy farmer,[3] 1745; had issue.
9. Joseph Hunt (1746-   ) married Martha Cursor (-   )
9. Hannah Hunt (1749-died young)
9. Josiah Hunt (1751-1829) married Elizabeth Palmer (-   ); had issue.
9. Gulielmo Hunt (1753-   ) married Martin **Burling** (1755-   ); issue unknown
9. George Hunt (1755-   )
9. Stephanus Hunt (1758-   )
9. Lydia Hunt (1760-   ) married Beriah **Hartshorn** (-   ) 1782; had issue
9. Richard Hunt (1762-   ) married Mary Pell (1762-   ); had issue
9. Lott Hunt (1764-1838) married Esther G. Hunter (-   ); took over the family farm and regularly

sent fruit to Capt. Effingham Lawrence in London;[3] had issue.

9. Mary Hunt (c.1766-   ) married Caleb **Bell** (-   ); issue unknown.

9. Effingham Hunt (1768-died young)[3] named in honour of his uncle Capt. Effingham Lawrence, London.

8. John Lawrence - lived nine days.[8]

8. John Lawrence (22/1/1732-26/7/1794) (eighth child of Richard Lawrence 1691-1781, p. 27)* did business with son-in-law[39] Jacob Schieffelin. Married Ann Burling (24/9/1735-14/2/1821) 1755,[37] cousin to Ebenezer Burling (p. 27); had issue.

9. Edward Lawrence (1756-1831) married Zipporah Lawrence (-   ) daughter of Dr. William Lawrence (p. 24); had issue.
   10. Six children

9. Hannah Lawrence (1758-1838) married Lieut. Jacob **Schieffelin** (1749-1835) 1780,[37] who resigned from the British army to marry a Quaker.[39] He was involved in shipping and a co-partner with John, his father-in-law as "Lawrence & Schieffelin, druggists".[39] Jacob bought John's share in 1799, but they continued in partnership buying tracts of land laying out *Manhattanville*[39] in which Manhattan St

---

*John Lawrence (1732-1794) was buried at Little Green Street Burial Ground of the Society of Friends (Quakers) which was located under the NE corner of the present-day site of Liberty Place & Maiden Lane, Manhattan, NY.

was renamed in 1920 as West 125th St, and Lawrence St[*] was renamed West 126th St.;[40] had issue.

10. Seven children

9. Effingham Lawrence (1760-1800) married Elizabeth Watson (-   ); had issue.

10. Five children

9. Mary Lawrence (1763-1831) married cousin Effingham **Embree**[36] (1759-1817); had issue.

10. Six children

9. Catherine Lawrence (-   ) unmarried.

9. Jane Lawrence (2/10/1768-6/8/1854) married Isaac **Livesay** (-   ) 1791 in New York; no issue.

9. Phebe Lawrence (24/12/1770-2/7/1771)

9. Anna Lawrence (1772-1846) married Thomas **Buckley** (-1846) 1793;[33] had issue.

10. Seven children.

9. **John Burling Lawrence** (31/10/1774-8/10/1844)[41] (son of John Lawrence 1732-1794 and Ann Burling 1735-1821, p. 31) a noted abolitionist of slavery; married Hannah Newbold (23/6/1782-2/9/1832) 15/2/1804;[41] had issue.[42]

10. Edward Newbold Lawrence (12/2/1805-21/10/1839) married Lydia Ann Lawrence (12/11/1811-7/2/1879) (daughter of Judge Effingham Lawrence, 1779-1850, and Ann Townsend, 1787-1845); had issue

---

[*]'Lawrence Street Manhattan' is now in Brooklyn New York, and - [40] 'Lawrence St BMT subway train station' was renamed in 2011 as Jay St/Metrotech.

(Lydia married (ii) Cornelius van Wyck Lawrence (1791-1861) and had issue.)

11. Frederick Newbold Lawrence (1834-1916) was assigned a general guardian at his grandfather's probate proceedings,[43] and later became President of the New York Stock Exchange 1882-1883.[44] Married Elizabeth Boyce (-1894) 1855; had issue.

10. George Newbold Lawrence (20/10/1806-17/1/1895) married Mary Ann Newbold (1808-1895); had issue.

11. Emlen Newbold Lawrence (1837-9/8/1925) died in New York

11. Amelia Lawrence (1841-)

11. John B. Lawrence (1846-1929)

10. Mary Newbold Lawrence (31/10/1808-15/11/1808)

10. Newbold Lawrence (23/10/1809-12/10/1885) lived in New York, married Anna Hough Trotter of Philadelphia[45] (25/5/1821-18/7/1893)[46] 21/10/1851; had issue

11. Caroline Trotter Lawrence (25/8/1852-1/6/1937) the family record keeper, published a record of the New York family history in 1931. Never married, took over the family affairs after the death of her brother.

11. Annie Trotter Lawrence (1853-12/10/1931) married Harold **Herrick** (26/11/1853-28/5/1933) lived in Lawrence, Nassau, NY; had issue.

12. Anna L. Herrick (1879-1963)

12. Newbold Lawrence Herrick (1885-1976)

12. Harold Edward Herrick (1890-1975)

11. Newbold Trotter Lawrence (8/6/1855-14/8/1928) a real estate operator in New York, but died in Belgium whilst visiting his son.[47] Married Isabel Gillet of Baltimore (-/6/1860-18/10/1904) an artist who painted life size family portraits; reputed to be descended from William Brewster who led the pilgrims to America on the *Mayflower* in 1620; 6/12/1887; had issue.

12. Isabel Gillet Lawrence (-/2/1890-24/8/1890)[48]

12. Newbold Lawrence (1892-1892) died in infancy

12. Newbold Trotter Lawrence II, (9/1/1893-18/11/1968)[49] worked in Belgium, then manager of United States Line in Germany retiring as vice president in charge of operations,[50] latterly a longshoreman's mediator in New York; married Mary Evelyn Cromwell (11/8/1893-6/11/1968); had issue.

13. Newbold Trotter Lawrence III, (3/9/1922-23/3/1970) born in Baltimore, Mass.[51] 'Boldy' as he was affectionately called, was one of the early ski paratroopers of the US army in action in the Italian Alps during the war, 1942-1943. He was the only member of his unit to return home. He was multilingual and later taught languages at the State Univ. of New York.

13. Richard Cromwell Lawrence (19/10/1933-21/3/2016) born in Hamburg Germany[52] and died in North Carolina. Known as Dick, he managed a construction company in the Virgin Islands and throughout the Caribbean. Married Suzanne Were (25/5/1935-   ); had issue.

14. Anne Evelyn Lawrence (1956-   ) is a graduate of Boston Univ., trained as a jeweller, worked in law and government for many years and served as city commissioner, and Mayor of Oakland Park, Florida, 2008-2012. Married ...

(i) Christopher **Wray** (-   ) 17/6/1977; had issue.

15. Morgan Elizabeth Wray (1980-   ) graduated Vaughn Aeronautical Univ. and works as an air traffic controller. Married Andrei **Muresan** (-   ) 2016; had issue.

16. Evelyn Maria Muresan (2019-   )
16. Sorina Elize Muresan (2021-   )

15. Charlotte Anne Wray (1983-   ) graduated from Univ. Central Florida and works as an implementation manager for Experian Health, married Navid **Nowakhtar** (-   ) 11/10/2014; had issue.

16. Alice Simine Nowakhtar (2015-   )
16. Alden Navid Nowakhtar (2017-   )

15. Christopher Alden Wray Jnr.
(1985-   ) an electrical engineer
and musician, guitarist and writer
for the technical metal band "Into
the Moat", married Lisa Ann
Bauman (-   ); had issue.
16. Ashton Jaymes Wray (2017-   )
(ii) Stephen **Sallee** (-   ) 11/8/2003
14. Richard Cromwell Lawrence Jnr.
(1958-   ) multi-talented with a love
of fishing. Licensed sea captain in the
Caribbean, married Pamala Yee (-   );
had issue.
15. Bryan Lawrence (1988-   )
sommelier, restaurant manager in
Miami, Florida; partnered Sandy
Nieves (-   ); had issue.
16. Jade Isabella Lawrence
(15/7/2018-   )
16. Gianni Liam Lawrence
(3/3/2020-   )
15. Rebecca Alice Lawrence (1990-   )
14. Elizabeth Were Lawrence (1960-   )
worked in oil and gas banking with
Chase Manhattan/J P Morgan Chase;
Married ...
(i) Miguel **Alvarez**, Dr. (1957-1983); had
issue.
15. Ricky Rene Johnson (1988-   )
legally changed his name to his
stepfather's last name.

(ii) Chuck **Johnson** (-) 1996.

14. Robert Newbold Lawrence (1961-) worked in shipping in the Caribbean, married Mary Kate Rich (1956-2015); had issue.

    15. Kristopher Lawrence (17/6/1989-)
    15. Jason Lawrence (5/10/1990-) married Sarah _____ (-) 2019; had issue.
       16. Leia Kathleen Lawrence (16/5/2020-)

14. Mark Trotter Lawrence (1963-2019) worked in Fort Pierce, Florida, married Robin _____ (-); had issue.

    15. Mark Trotter Lawrence Jnr (8/10/1993-)

14. Denise Gillet Lawrence (14/9/1971-); no issue.

11. Susan Newbold Lawrence (27/7/1856--/7/1923) married James William **Walsh** (1852-1908); had issue.

    12. Margaret Ruth Lawrence Walsh (1883-1948)
    12. James William Walsh (7/4/1887-27/10/1973)

11. Mary Gertrude Lawrence (27/5/1860-23/7/1941) married Francis Wisner **Murray** (-); had issue.

    12. Francis Wisner Murray (-)
    12. Caroline Lawrence Murray (-)

10. Alfred Newbold Lawrence[42] (7/10/1813-20/4/1884)[43]

10. Caroline Augusta Lawrence (18/8/1815-
20/4/1841) buried in the Lawrence Burying
Ground, Bayside, Queens County, NY; married
William Effingham **Lawrence** (13/12/1813-
19/1/1871) 18/6/1840; had issue.
  11. Edward Newbold Lawrence (c.1841-)
  assigned a general guardian, William Ripley, at
  his grandfather's probate proceedings.[43]
10. John Burling Lawrence Jnr (30/12/1817-
13/3/1887)[42]
10. Thomas Newbold Lawrence (15/1/1820-
9/7/1889)[42]
9. Cornelia Lawrence (17/3/1778-27/3/1778)
9. Phebe Lawrence (17/3/1778- 8/8/1780)
8. **Effingham Lawrence, Captain**[3] (**11/2/1734-
17/5/1806**) (ninth child of Richard Lawrence 1691-
1781, p. 27) returned to England and married Catherine
Farmar/Farmer (born in New York)[53] (c.1750/51-
<>1803) 18/3/1781[54] in London; had issue.
9. Five children (p. 51)
8. Norris Lawrence (6/1/1737-10/7/1769) married Ann
Pell[31] (-   ) 1765;[8] had issue.
  9. Norris Lawrence[30] (c.1768-   ) was apprenticed to
  Robert Bowne 1786.
8. Joseph Lawrence, Captain (23/8/1741-5/11/1813).
Joseph was a merchant captain and inherited *Bayside*
the family mansion[3] of his grandfather Joseph (p. 26)
at Flushing, Long Island, New York, and at one time
was employed by Samuel Townsend, the son of one
of the first settlers. Townsend built the brig *Aubrey*
at Oyster Bay, Long Island, which, before the War of

Independence, was commanded by Joseph's brother Capt. Effingham Lawrence.

Joseph was Captain of the sloop *Wheel of Fortune* and was given a passport on 19th July in 1763 for Cuba, with a letter from Lt Governor Colden of New York to the Spanish Governor demanding the release of Capt. Effingham Lawrence[3] and other prisoners held in Cuba c.1763. Married Phebe Townsend (13/9/1740-17/9/1816) 1764 by license; had issue.

9. Elizabeth Lawrence (1765-   ) married Silas **Titus**; had issue.

   10. Six children

9. Henry Lawrence (1767-1824)
   Married . . .

(i) Harriet van Wyck (1771-1812); had issue.

   10. Ten children, seven lived.

      ... *1st child* - Cornelius van Wyck Lawrence[8] (1791-1861) merchant, Member of Congress,[*]

---

[*]A brief overview of the background is that "King Charles II in 1674 appointed the New York's royal governor 1674-1681, who reintroduced the English form of government with English as the official language".

The 1st New York elected General Assembly 1683-1686 was suspended 1686-1691 during the Leisler Rebellion. The 1st permanent New York General Assembly 1691-1769 re-enacted the 1683 "Charters of Liberties and Privileges', and from 1769-1774 the English Parliament passes laws without American representation, which results in the 1774 First Continental Congress.

Subsequently, the American Revolution, or The Revolutionary War 1775-1783, takes place. In 1776 the 2nd Continental Congress adopted 'Declaration of Independence' and in 1787 New York sends delegates to Philadelphia's Constitutional Convention when a National Constitution was adopted. The newly formed United States of America government was activated in 1789.[55]

Mayor of New York, President of the Bank of the State of New York, Collector of the Port of New York, married three times.

... *4th child* - Joseph Lawrence[8] (1797-1866) merchant, President of Bank of State of New York, Treasurer of City of New York, President of United States Trust Company, married once.

(ii) Amy Pearsall (-   ); no issue

9. Phebe Lawrence (1770-1839) married Obadiah **Townsend** (-   ); had issue

   10. Joseph Townsend (-   )

9. William Lawrence (c.1771-   ) married Mary Frame (-   )

9. Lydia Lawrence (1773-1837) married Joseph W. **Corlies** (-   )

9. Effingham Nicoll Lawrence, Judge (1779-1850) a judge in Queens County in early 19th century, lived in the family homestead *Stone House* in Bayside,[3] married Anne Townsend (1787-1845); had issue.

   10. Solomon Townsend Lawrence (1808-9/11/1839) died in Vicksburg Mississippi, buried Bayside Queens.

   10. Henry Effingham Lawrence (24/5/1810-17/8/1875) born in Bayside, lived in New Orleans, died New Jersey and buried in Bayside Queens. Married Frances E. Bresher (10/5/1819-17/3/1895) 20/8/1844, born in Kentucky, died in New Jersey, buried Bayside, Queens; had issue.

   11. Robert Brashear Lawrence (2/1/1847-8/11/1929) born in Louisiana, died in Georgia. Married Marion Eugenia _____

(18/3/1853-1945); had issue.

    11. Townsend S. Lawrence (-/4/1848-7/7/1908) born in Mississippi, died Bayside Queens.

    11. Lydia Lee Lawrence (8/12/1853-6/6/1925) born in Louisiana, died Bayside Queens; had issue.

        12. Henry Effingham Eccles (31/12/1898-14/5/1947) born in Bayside, died in Vermont.

  10. Lydia Ann Lawrence (12/11/1811-7/2/1879) Married ...

(i) Edward Newbold **Lawrence** (1805-1839) (son of John Burling Lawrence 1774-1844, p. 32); had issue.

    11. Frederick Newbold Lawrence, Colonel (1834-1916), Married Elizabeth Anne Boyce (-1894) 1855; had issue.

        12. Lillee Lawrence (1857-1920) married _____ **McKinstry** (-)

        12. Elizabeth Lawrence (1862-1906) married _____ **Alexandre** (-); had issue.

        12. Virginia Lee Lawrence (1864-1891), married Louis **Howland** (-); had issue

          13. Hortense Howland (-), married Courtland Palmer **Dixon I** (-) ; had issue

            14. Courtland Palmer Dixon II (-30/11/2006), married Penelope Harrison (-); had issue.

              15. Penelope Dixon (-), married Evan Randolph (-); had issue.

              15. Courtland Palmer Dixon III,

(-) inducted into Boulder County Business Hall of Fame 24/3/2013. Married Brenda _____ (-); had issue.

(ii) Cornelius van Wyck Lawrence (28/2/1791-20/2/1861) (second husband of Lydia Lawrence, p.41), had issue.

11. James Ogden Lawrence (1826-1904)
11. Van Wyck Lawrence (1822-1886)
11. Mary Lawrence (1831-1893)

10. William Effingham Lawrence (1813-1871) Married ...

(i) Caroline August Lawrence (1814-1841) 1840

(ii) Rachel Augusta Mickle (1828-1863) 1846; had issue.

11. Caroline Lawrence (1849-1925)
11. Andrew Lawrence (1853-1908)
11. Effie Lawrence (1856-   )
11. William Effingham Lawrence–Jnr (1857-1902)
11. Grace Lawrence (1859-1927)
11. Louisa Lawrence (1863-1876)

10. Robert Townsend Lawrence (1817-11/11/1842) died in New Orleans, buried Bayside Queens, NY.

10. Effingham Nicoll Lawrence[56] (1820-1878) moved to Louisiana in 1843. He was involved in the sugar industry and served in the State House of Representatives. After the 1872 elections he served the shortest term in congressional history, being one day in the US House of Representatives.[56] Lawrence had unsuccessfully sought election to the US Congress in 1872 but appealed the result on

the grounds of "electoral irregularities". This appeal was eventually successful and he took his seat in Congress on 3rd March 1875.

In the meantime however, the 1875 election had taken place and Lawrence was unsuccessful; his replacement assuming the seat on 4th March 1875. Married ...

(i) Jane Lucretia Osgood (1829-1863); had issue.

    11. Annie Townsend Lawrence (1847-1942)

    11. Jane Lucretia Lawrence (1847- <1877)

    11. Isaac Osgood Lawrence (1850-1870)

    11. Jeannie Osgood Lawrence (1851-1934)

    11. Adele Lawrence (1853-1860)

    11. Effingham Lawrence (9/6/1856-26/11/1899) born Louisiana, died in Bayside, NY.
Married Janet M. Campbell Mickle (1857-1939) 1877; had issue.

        12. Effingham Lawrence (8/9/1878-9/9/1956) married Dorothy Quincy Gookin (1881-1969); had issue.

            13. Dorothy Quincy Lawrence (22/9/1908-22/4/1981) Married ...

            (i) George Hopper **Fitch** (1909-) 1934

            (ii) Blinn Sill **Cushman** (1907-1980)

        12. Anne M. Lawrence (1881-1887)

    11. Bessie Amelia Lawrence (1858-1937)

    11. Helen Lawrence (1860-)

(ii) Gertrude Cammack (1839-1870)

    11. Horace Claiborne Lawrence (1868-1874)

    11. Gertrude Lawrence (1869-<1877)

The 1877 will of Eff. Lawrence (1820-1878, p. 42)

names Effingham Jr, Annie T, Jenny, Bessie and Helen only.

10. Mary Nicoll Lawrence (9/1/1822-12/8/1896) born & buried Bayside Queens. Married Andrew Hutchins **Mickle** (1805-25/1/1863) 1851; had issue.

    11. Anne L Mickle (1853-1880), married Samuel **Willets, Jnr** (1849-1877)

    11. Janet M Campbell Mickle (19/1/1857-19/11/1939) married Effingham **Lawrence** (9/6/1856-26/11/1899) 31/10/1877 in Douglaston, Queens. Buried Bayside Queens; had issue.

        12. Effingham Lawrence (1878-1956)

        12. Anne M Lawrence (29/3/1881-22/9/1887) buried Bayside Queens.

    11. Mary Lawrence Mickle (20/12/1860-   )

10. Joseph Effingham Lawrence (1824-14/7/1878) buried Bayside Queens.

10. Cornelius Lawrence (3/5/1826-18/1/1896) born and buried Bayside Queens.

10. Edward Arthur Lawrence (1831-1883); Democrat politician, NY State Senate, buried at Bayside.

10. Hannah Townsend Lawrence (22/3/1833-20/10/1898), born and buried Bayside Queens.

7. John Lawrence (1703-10/11/1781) (second child of Joseph Lawrence 1668-1759, p. 26) emigrated to Elizabethtown, NJ, where he inherited an estate,[7] later moved to and was buried at Rhode Island.[57] He was an extensive ship owner with other mercantile interests, and built the vessel *The Three Brothers*[58] (named after John,

William & Thomas) which departed on a voyage for
Europe and was lost at sea;
Married . . .
> (i) Mary Woodbury (1705-1760)[57] 1728; had issue.
> > 8. Eight sons, three daughters.
> (ii) Elizabeth Little (1705-   ) 2/12/1761 in Warwick,
> > Rhode Is.;[57] no issue.[7]

7. Elizabeth Lawrence (1695-   )[57] (third child of Joseph
   Lawrence 1668-1759, p. 26) married John **Bowne** (-)
   1737, moved to Westchester County; had issue.
   8. Eleven children.
7. (possibly) Sarah Lawrence (c.1697-   )
7. Hannah Lawrence (1699-1785)[57] (daughter of Joseph
   Lawrence 1668-1759, p. 26) married Moses Millenux/
   Mullineaux[59] (1693-1748) 1746; had issue.
   8. Three children
7. Abigail Lawrence (1701-   )[57] married Major Alexander
   Forbs/**Forbes** (1703-1781) of the British army; issue
   unknown.
6. Richard Lawrence[1] (c.1671-   ) (seventh child of immigrant
   Captain William Lawrence 1622-1680, p. 23) married
   Charity Clark (-   ) 24/9/1699 by licence; issue
   unknown.
6. Samuel Lawrence (c.1673-9/8/1687)[1] age 15.
6. Sarah Lawrence (1675-   )[1] (possibly married* James **Tillett**
   in 1705; or unmarried.[60])

*There is some confusion whether "Sarah Lawrence (b.1675-) married James Tillett
in 1705, or Sarah Lawrence (b.1679-) daughter of William, grand-daughter of
immigrant Thomas made this marriage" [60]

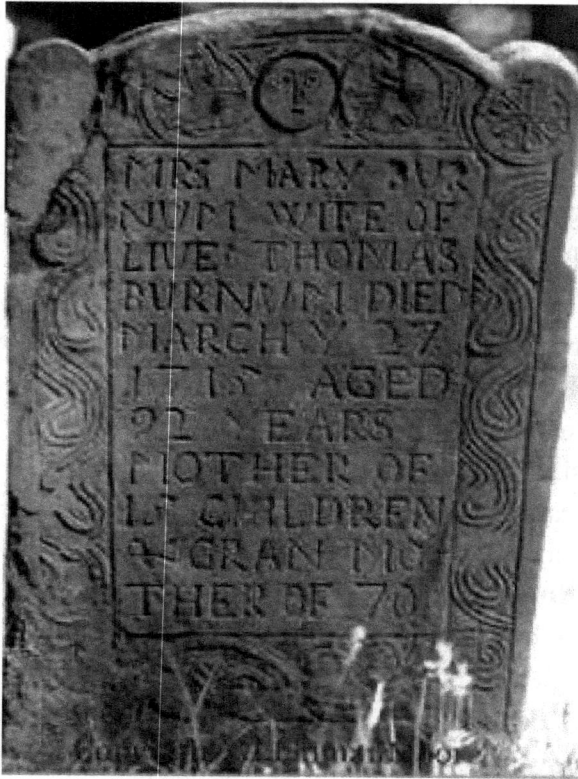

Mary (Lawrence) Burnham's gravestone
Plot D-171, 'Old North Burying Ground' cemetery, Ipswich, Essex,
Massachusetts.

6. James Lawrence (c.1677-   )[1] named in the guardianship
   papers,[1] but no further record.
5. **Mary Lawrence (1625-1715)**[1] (daughter of Thomas Lawrence
   1588-1624 and Joan Antrobus 1592-1662, p. 13)[6] at St.
   Albans, Hertfordshire, England, baptized 10th April 1625,[6] and
   sister to John, Thomas and William Lawrence. In migration
   records to America, she is listed as Marie Lawrence, age nine, as
   passenger[2] with her brothers, maternal grandmother, mother,

46

step-father and their children on the *Planter* arriving 1635[2] in Ipswich, Massachusetts.

Her husband, Thomas Burnum (1623-1694), was born in Norwich, Norfolk, (although this information has been disputed).[61] Some records show he migrated with his two brothers in charge of their maternal uncle Captain Andrews, the master of the *Angel Gabriel*.[62] One of the first records for Thomas Burnum is the grant to him, and others, by the town of Ipswich in December 1643 of monetary compensation "for their service to the Indians."[62] Mary's headstone reads "Mrs Mary Burnum wife of Lieut. Thomas Burnum died March 27th, 1715 aged ninety two years mother of fifteen children and grandmother of seventy."[63] The gravestone indicates two additional children who presumably died before 1694, as they were not mentioned in her husband's will of January 1694. Married[64] Thomas **Burnum** [**Burnham**][65] (c.1623-19/5/1694) c.1645; had issue.[62]

6. Thomas Burnham (c.1644-1728)
Married . . .
(i) Lidia Pengry (-   ) c.1685/9
(ii) Hester/Esther Bishop (née Cogswell) (-   ) 1728
6. John Burnham (1647-1703/4) married Elizabeth Wells (-) 1669
6. Mary Burnham (c.1651-c.1723) married John **Clark** (-   ) 1702.
6. James Burnham (c.1653-1729) married Mary – (-   ) 1676.
6. Johanna Burnham (c. 1654-   )
Married . . .
(i) John **Newmarsh, Jr.** (-   ) 1671.
(ii) Erasmus **James** (-   ) 1682.
6. Abigail Burnham (c.1655-   )

6. Ruth Burnham (1657-1657) lived one month.

6. Ruth Burnham (1658-1724) married John **Carter** (-   ) 1678.

6. Joseph Burnham (1660-<1694)

6. Nathaniel Burnham (1662-<1694)

6. Sarah Burnham (1664-   ) married Mesheck **Farley** (-   ) 1684.

6. Hester/Esther Burnham (c.1665-1749) married Matthew **Perkins** (-   ) 1686.

6. Phebe/Pheby Burnham (1667-<1694)

The Lawrence-Chase-Towneley Claim[66]

The source listed in References, Chapter 1:1 and elsewhere, is a publication titled - *Historical genealogy of the Lawrence family: from their first landing in this country AD 1635 to the present date July 4th 1858* by Thomas Lawrence; published by E. O. Jenkins, New York, NY, 1858, which was originally written to prove the Lawrence genealogy in America, and to enable the Lawrence family to claim monies that were apparently held in Chancery in England from the Towneley estates. However, further research has shown that this was a "scam" and that there were no monies held in Chancery.

"'The Lawrence-Chase-Townley Association' made claims that were put forth by the descendants of Mary Towneley and John Lawrence. Various Family Associations were formed in the mid- and late-1800s, and as late as 1920, in many places within the United States and Canada. Members of some schemes would subscribe $20 and receive certificates stating that their share would be $1000 when the claim was successful. These organizations were incorporated and consolidated in order to gather funds to hire lawyers and take their claims back to England. At stake were estates in

48

Lancashire, the Ashton Hall in Lancaster, and Towneley Hall in Burnley. Other claims have also identified Corby Castle.

One such case was heard in the House of Lords in April 1890, the case of 'Lawrence vs. Lord Norreys and others'. The American claimants of the Lawrences were represented by Col. Joseph Fraser Jacquess, who was subsequently charged with 'fraud' in 1894."

The original case was brought by English High court solicitor named Howell Thomas which was heard 17th June, 1887, and had been thrown out of court for being "frivolous". The Appeal submission to the Court of Appeal failed, the case was then presented to the House of Lords in 1890. The result of this Appeal was that the case was again thrown out of court, and in 1894 Howell Thomas was in Central Criminal Court defending the charges of "forgery, perjury and fraud". By one account, he had "scammed" $80,000 from his clients.[66]

Further information of the scam had been available since 1888, when Frank Alden Hill, after making basic genealogical research which showed that Mary Towneley did not exist, had published a book titled - *The Lawrence, Chase, Towneley Estate: The Mystery Solved*. However, this did not stop the hopeful, and another scheme was generated in 1920.

Notes

Chapter 3

EFFINGHAM LAWRENCE
(1734-1806)

Effingham Lawrence was born in New York and became involved in the commercial maritime trade, becoming a merchant captain as did his brother Captain Joseph Lawrence.

He captained the *Aubrey* also *Earl of Dunmore* (1771), and in June 1773 ferried General Gage and others to England, but when the Revolutionary War (1775-1783) broke out, the Admiralty Agency in New York chartered his vessel as a Naval Store Ship, and it served throughout the war.[1] He was involved extensively with local trade, also to Cuba, as witnessed when his brother Joseph carried a letter to the Spanish Governor demanding the release of Effingham and other prisoners in 1763[2] (p. 39).

The War of 1775-1783 was a challenging time from many points of view, including the effects on business and the disruptive effects on families. Effingham was a British loyalist and his brothers appear to have supported the other side (the "colonists", or "patriots"). He clearly found it advantageous to move his business from New York to London, England in 1780 where he managed the English side of the merchant shipping business[1] at Tower Hill, London.

He was elected as one of the elder brethren of Trinity House* (for

---

*Trinity House is the 'Lighthouse & Principal Pilotage Authority' for Great Britain, formed by Royal charter in 1514. The board consists of 10 elected former ships' masters. Capt. Effingham was a member 1796-1806, and his son WEL 1821-1826. The building was later bombed in WWII so many records have been lost.

the years 1796-1806).[3]

The following letter was found in the Trinity House records:

> To Robert Preston Esq Woodford:
> Sir,
> I am informed it has been objected to me by some gentlemen in the Corporation of Trinity House that I am an alien and have sail'd under American colours.
>
> I think it a duty incumbent on me Sir, to state to you that such reports are ill founded.
>
> I was born in New York, and brought up in the Sea Service from early life in the year 1767.
>
> I succeeded my late worthy friend Mr. Davis in the command of a ship in the trade between London and New York and continued in that line of business until the commencement of the unfortunate war with that country; during which, I commanded an arm'd ship with a Letter of Marque against all his Majesty's enemies, belonging to Messrs. Davis, Shenham and Co. and myself, and was constantly employed in supplying the British garrison in America; and had several other ships in the same service, since which I have been settled here in business, except that I have been twice out to America since, to adjust and settle an extensive business there, and returned home passenger in an American ship, the only time I ever sailed under American colours, and so far from being an Alien here, I am a proscrib'd[*] person there.
>
> Some of my friends in the Corporation advis'd me to trouble you Sir, with this vindication of my loyalty and attachment to this country, which I hope will plead my excuse for so doing.

---

[*]'proscribed' means "forbidden, especially by law" *Oxford Dictionary of English*.

I am with gratitude and respect.

Sir, your faithfull and most obedient Servant.

Eff. Lawrence

Tower Hill   12 Nov. 1796

Both he and his eldest son were still extensively engaged in maritime business at the time of his death.

Effingham Lawrence died in London 17th May, 1806, and left a considerable estate as attested by his request on 14th November, 1803 (also in Trinity House records).

> "All his houses, farms, plantations, lands and tenements whatsoever situated in any part of the United States of America in trust to his son William Effingham Lawrence, John Masterman of White Hart Court, Lombard Street, London, Banker, and Amos Hayton of Mark Lane, London, Merchant, on trust to sell and dispose of the same together or in parcels by public auction . . .
>
> His dwelling house on Tower Hill with all plate, china, books and furniture, to his son William Effingham Lawrence and his brothers and sister. His business and trade to be carried on by his son William Effingham until his son Edward attained the age of twenty-one when he was to be taken into partnership."[5]

It was also requested that his funeral should not exceed fifty pounds. His will written 1803, was proved in 1806.[5]

At the end of the Napoleonic Wars (1803-1815) almost 1000 ships were laid up including all their men, most to never sail again, so the family business could have been in difficulties. Before E.L's death, the two middle sons were admitted to the East India Company in 1799 and 1804. W. E. L. was in business with his father until the latter's death, then, as the youngest was not yet 21, and in accordance with their father's will,[5] W.E.L. managed the business solo[6] until E.B.L. was of age. The W.E. & E.B. Lawrence business is listed from 1814-1823[6] by which time W.E.L. had left for the colonies.

Lawrence's wife-to-be was Catharine Farmar, the ninth child of Major Thomas Billopp[7] (1711-1750)[*] and Sarah Leonard (-1770). Her father, Major Billopp was the fourth child[8] of Thomas Farmar and Anne Billopp, who changed his name to Billopp to enable him to inherit the Billopp family property *Bentley Manor*[8] on Staten Island, New York, under the will[9] of his maternal grandfather, Captain Christopher Billopp, RN, (c.1650-1725).

The main house on the property became known as *Conference House*[10] as it was the site of an abortive peace conference on 11/9/1776 between the American patriots and the British authorities. The conference was not successful and the Revolutionary War (April 1775-1783) continued until its final conclusion in 1783.[9]

Eight of Major Thomas Billopp's children resumed the surname Farmar after his death,[7] and one son Thomas (-27/8/1822) served in the war as a patriot. The eldest son[8] and heir, (the great-grandson of the original Captain Christopher Billopp), Colonel Christopher Billopp (1738-29/3/1827) retained the name Billopp and, serving in the war as a loyalist, was known as the "Tory Colonel". He and other loyalists subsequently moved to New Brunswick, Canada, after the War in 1785. *Bentley Manor* was confiscated from the Billopp family after the War.

[*]The Gravestone of Thomas Billopp reads - "Here Lyes ye body of Thomas Billopp, Esq. son of Thomas Farmar, Esq. Dec'd August yᵈ 24 1750. In yᵉ 39th year of his age" buried at 'Old Billopp House' on Bentley Manor.

Of interest is that two rocky islets, seven km south east of Portland, Victoria, Australia, were mapped on 5/2/1800 by Lieut. James Grant, on the survey brig *Lady Nelson*. He named them the Lawrence Rocks for Captain Lawrence, whom he had sailed with previously. Lawrence had at no time travelled to Australia.

Genealogy

8. Effingham Lawrence, Captain (11/2/1734-17/5/1806[4]) (son of Richard Lawrence 1691-1781 and Hannah Bowne, p. 27) born in New York, married Catharine Farmar (c.1750-<>1803) 18/3/1781 after the move to London.[11] Catharine's dates are uncertain, but she is registered as Katherine Farmar (ninth and youngest child of the 2nd marriage of Major Thomas Billopp, 1711-1750, and Sarah Leonard , n.d.- 1770))[7] born after her father's death, c.1750.[8] She is not mentioned in her husband's will, so may have died earlier than 1803;[5] although other sources record her death as 1806;[9] had issue.[*]

1. William Effingham Lawrence[†] (5/3/1782[12] -18/4/1841) operated his father's business solo (1806-1814)[6] then as W. E. & E. B. Lawrence (1814-1823)[6] London, a listed member of Trinity House (1821-1826),[3] before emigrating to Van Diemen's Land 1822 in the vessel the *Lord Liverpool*,

---

[*]William Effingham Lawrence, currently Generation 9, now reverts to Generation 1 (as do his siblings). W.E.L. was the first generation of his family to live in Australia.

[†]The year of birth of W. E. Lawrence is noted as 1781 in various sources, however, his baptismal records at All Hallows, Barking by the Tower, London, show the date of his birth as being 5/3/1782.

arriving Launceston in 1823. Married Mary Ann George (née Smither) (1799-1880) in 1826 in Van Diemen's Land;[13] had a large family, and currently (in the year 2021) has many descendants throughout the world (p. 65).

1. John Curson Lawrence (23/9/1783[14]- [15]) is recorded in the East India Co. Penang Civil Service[16] from 1804-1821; listed in Penang 1805 as writer,[17] Commissioner for recovery of small debts also Assistant Secretary by 1810,[19] as a clerk 1804 (at home)[17] sailed 1805 from England,* later as Superintendent of Company's lawsuits,[20] and Malay translator. In 1816 he was the Co. Resident at Magelang,† 1819 pay master and merchant,[22] and in 1820[19]-1821[23] listed as senior merchant "at home" in East India Company records. His first postings were Prince of Wales Island (later the name reverted to Penang)‡ and he is mentioned in histories of Java[24] and Sir Thomas Raffles, Kt., F.R.S.[25] The Dutch East India Company and [English] East India Company had conflict of territory§ throughout Java during this period so much source material is not available in English. Details of his wife and other details of JCL are unknown at this time; had issue.

---

*John Curson Lawrence "sailed late April 1805... on vessel *Ganges* with numerous officials of the new Presidency government of Prince of Wales Island in a large fleet of 18-22 East Indiamen including Governor and family on the Cumberland departing Portsmouth".[18]

†Magelang, is located in Central Java, Indonesia.[21]

‡Penang's modern history began in 1786, and formed part of the Straits Settlements in 1826, and became a British crown colony in 1867.[23]

§Political reforms that had begun under the Dutch Governor Daendels (1808-1810) continued under the British administration (Sir Stamford Raffles) (1811-1816), during which the British authorities annexed the Sultanate of Banten (1813). Control of central Java then reversed in 1816 to Dutch East Indies.[26]

2. Alfred Curson Lawrence (1807-   ) baptised 28/7/1817 at St Olave Hart St London.[27]

2. Horatio Curson Lawrence (1811-1847) baptised on 28/7/1817 at St Olave Hart St London.[27] Article clerkship 29/12/1836 at Meaburn Tatham,[28] and buried on 9/8/1847 at Brompton Cemetery[29] London.

1. Effingham Calvert Lawrence (2/5/1785[30]-15/5/1824) joined East India Co. Bengal Civil Service admitted in 1799, as the Register of the Zillah at Midnapore,[31] and active service up to 1824[32]. He served in Bauleah, Rungapore, Jelalpore, Rajeshahye, lastly as a Provincial Court of Appeal and Circuit Judge and Magistrate at Benares before dying 15/5/1824 on return passage from India on the *Commodore Hayes* and "Mrs Lawrence was landed at Mauritius."[32]

His 1823 will[33] registered in England 1826, and proved in 1837, named brother JCL of London, brother-in-law Lt. Col. John T. Jones of Royal Engineers, and Charles Monro, lawyer, as executors, also his agent in Calcutta, Charles Sutherland from East India Co. to convert property in India to the trustees in England.[33] He was married by special license[34] to Caroline Monro (1790-22/12/1858)[*] 27/3/1815[36] London; had issue.

2. Effingham John Lawrence (1816[37]-5/2/1888), eldest son of ECL,[37] born in Bengal, East Indies.[37] He attended Tonbridge School, Kent, 1827-1832,[38] Matric. Michs. Trinity College Cambridge 1835, a Smythe Exhib. Scholar, BA 1839, MA 1842, and Fellow of Trinity College 1841. Admitted Lincoln's Inn 1841, called to the Bar 1845, died aged 71 in London.[39]

---

[*] "At Blackheath, aged 68, Caroline, widow of Effingham Calvert Lawrence, esq., of the Bengal Civil Service, and dau. of the late Charles Monro, esq."[35]

Married[40] Sarah _____ [41] (1817-1877[42]), had issue

3. Agnes Elizabeth Lawrence (1858[41] -   ), executor[42] of her father's will in 1888, and the following year an executor[43] for Caroline Effingham Elizabeth Lawrence's (c.1824-1889) will of 17/12/1889, spinster, age 65.[44]

3. John Effingham Lawrence (1860[41]-   ) married Evangeline Gertrude Cardon (1860[45]-   ) 28/7/1887[46] at All Saints Church, Kensington; issue unknown

2. Charles Harding Lawrence (1818-1847), second son of ECL, baptised[47] 5/7/1818 Dacca, Bengal, East Indies, attended Tonbridge School,[38] Kent 1827-1833 (as Harding Charles Lawrence).

He was gifted a silver watch in his father's will in 1824.[33]

In 1846 admitted to Sussex House* London and his death registered in 1847.[50]

Presumed unmarried and had no issue.

2. (possibly) Caroline Effingham Elizabeth Lawrence† (c.1824-

---

*Admission CHL on 17/8/1846, died a year later 5/8/1847.[48]
Sussex House Asylum, London, (1846-1884), privately licensed and only for gentlemen (a social status not a gender status), and in 1846 had 12 patients. Later it became Fulham Hospital and is now the site of Charing Cross Hospital. Note that epileptics and homosexuals could be incarcerated in this period.[49]

†Caroline Effingham Elizabeth Lawrence (1824-1889) – possibly the daughter of ECL (1785-1824) and Caroline Monro, with both parent's first names, likely born on Mauritius after her father's death, but no records found in East India Company Select Births & baptisms, nor London birth/baptism records. Possibly executor Agnes was her niece. "The will of Caroline Effingham Elizabeth Lawrence late of Hendon-grove Hendon in the County of Middlesex, Spinster who died 3/11/1889 at Hendon-Grove was proved at the Principal Registry by Agnes Elizabeth Lawrence of 52 Landbroke-Grove-Road Notting Hill in the said County spinster one of the executors. Estate value £1,832 19s. 1d." [51]

3/11/1889). Her death notice describes her as "spinster, 65 years old"[44] which presumes her birth year to be 1824. One of the executors of her will was Agnes Elizabeth Lawrence, which presumes a relationship; unmarried; no issue

1. Catherine Maria Lawrence (17/8/1786[52]-1/12/1859) (fourth child of Captain Effingham Lawrence (1734-1806) married John Thomas Jones (25/3/1783-26/2/1843)[53] of Felixstowe, Suffolk, England; ADC to the Duke of Wellington[7] and afterward to Queen Victoria.[7] Chief of Engineers on the staff of the Duke of Wellington,[7] active in at least six sieges during the Napoleonic Wars (1803-1815)[54] and based on those experiences he published extensively including the standard work "Sieges of the Peninsular War".[1]

   In recognition of his services he was created Baronet Jones of Cranmer Hall,[53] Norfolk, England 30/9/1831,[54] promoted to Major General in 1837, and died 25/2/1843[7] at his residence Pittsville, Cheltenham. After his death a memorial was carved by William Behnes and can be found in St Paul's Cathedral, London.[54] The marriage took place on 20/4/1816;[1] had issue.[55]

   2. Lawrence Jones (10/1/1817-7/11/1845) **2nd Baronet**,[53] murdered by robbers at Macri, near Dalman, Turkey.

   2. Willoughby Jones, magistrate, (24/11/1820-21/8/1884) **3rd Baronet**,[53] married his cousin[7] Emily Jones (1832-23/6/1917) 15/4/1856; had issue.

      3. Lawrence John Jones (16/8/1857-21/10/1954) **4th Baronet**,[55]

         Married . . .

      (i) Evelyn Mary Bevan (1853-17/1/1912) 13/4/1883; had issue.

         4. Hester Catherine Jones (1883-1/11/1918)

         4. Willoughby John Jones (19/3/1884-11/8/1898)

4. Lawrence Evelyn Jones, barrister and author,
   (5/4/1885-6/9/1969) **5th Baronet**,[55] married Lady
   Evelyn Alice Grey (14/3/1886-15/4/1971) 23/11/1971;
   had issue.
   5. Nancy Lawrence Jones[55] (7/10/1913-) married
      David Vivien Morse (-1993) 12/11/1941; had
      issue.
      6. Jonathan Patrick Morse (7/10/1940-); issue
         unknown.
      6. Annabel Harriet Morse (27/9/1944-); married
         Alexander **Urquhart** (-) 1972; had issue.
         7. Two daughters.
      6. Oliver Jones Morse (14/3/1949-)
   5. Dinah Evelyn Lawrence Jones (11/6/1916-
      25/12/1942).
      6. Debra Vera Lawrence Jones (27/8/1920-
         10/4/1927).
   5. Vivien Lawrence Jones (30/8/1923-) married
      Simon Anthony Roland **Asquith** (20/8/1919-
      18/12/1973) 1/10/1942; had issue.
      6. Conrad Robin Asquith (10/10/1945-) married
         Patricia Sproston (-) 1977; had issue.
         7. Daisy Asquith (16/6/1976-)
         7. Lily Asquith (12/4/1978-)
      6. Ivon Shawn Asquith (26/12/1946-)
         Married . . .
      (i) Pauline R. Murray-Jones (-) 6/2/1982,
          divorced 1985; had issue.
          7. Thomas Asquith (12/12/1982-)
      (ii) Katherine Tanya Jury (-); had issue.
          7. William Asquith (1985-)

7. Rosamund Eloise Asquith (1991-   )
6. Rosalind Lucy Asquith (2/5/1948-   ); partnered John **Fordham** (-   ); had issue.
7. Frederick Simon Asquith-Fordham (1985-   )
7. Leo Robin Asquith-Fordham (1989-   )
5. Lavinia Lawrence Jones (21/7/1925-) (daughter of 5th Baronet Lawrence Evelyn Jones 1885-1969, p. 60). married Frank John **Monaco** (-   ) 25/10/1980; issue unknown
4. Bertram Edward Jones (1/10/1886-16/4/1958) (son of 4th Baronet Lawrence John Jones 1857-1954, p. 59), Married . . .
(i) Gwendolen Mary Goodall (-   ) 13/2/1913, divorced 1938; had issue.
5. (a son) (20/12/1928-20/12/1928)
(ii) Margaret Louise Cookson (-   ) 16/11/1938; had issue.
5. Christopher Jones (19/1/1940-   ) **6th Baronet**[55] married Gail Pittar (-   ) 3/2/1967; had issue.
6. Mark Christopher Jones (28/12/1968-   ) married Susanna Jane Bantick (-   ) 2004; issue unknown.
6. John Alexander Jones (23/1/1971-   ) (*surname change **Lawrence-Jones** from 2/2/1969*).
4. Maurice Herbert Jones (18/12/1888-8/9/1915)
5. Two daughters.
4. Rachel Margaret Lawrence Jones (-   )
(ii) Paula Shuster (-23/2/1956) 2/3/1916 (second wife of 4th Baronet Lawrence John Jones 1857-1954, p. 59); no issue.
3. Mary Florence Jones (1859-31/1/1956) (daughter of 3rd

Baronet Willoughby Jones 1820-1884, p. 59)

3. Catherine Jones (1860-26/11/1879)
3. Herbert Edward Jones, M.A., D.D., Bishop Suffragan of Lewes, 1914-1920; (6/4/1861-19/2/1920) married Madeline Long Fox (1862-18/5/1928) 18/7/1888; had issue.
  4. Edward Lawrence Jones (7/8/1891-14/8/1948). Married . . .
  (i) Kathleen Nairne Scott (-   ) 1915, divorced 1922.
  (ii) Mary Senior Williams (-<1943) 15/2/1923; no issue.
  (iii) Elinor Wren (1906-3/7/1944) (second daughter of John Wren,* Studley Park, Melbourne, Vic.) 1/1/1943 in London,[58] and died in London; no issue.
  4. Violet Madeline Jones (1894-1989) British artist.
3. Gertrude Isabel Jones (1863-1/3/1941) married Edward **Fuller-Maitland**, artist [59] (7/5/1859-31/7/1944) 4/8/1889; issue unknown.
3. Willoughby Jones (18/5/1864-1889)
3. Maud Emily Jones (1867-   )
3. Harry Daniel Jones (6/8/1868-30/8/1869)
2. Herbert Walsingham Jones, Rev. (10/10/1826-9/2/1889) (son of 1st Baronet John Thomas Jones 1783-1843, p. 59) an Anglican Curate of Rentam in 1851 then rector of Sculthorpe by 1861, the family seat in Norfolk, England.[59] Married Catherine Rachel Gurney (1829-   ) 23/4/1850;

---

*John Wren (1871-1953) was an "infamous tote tycoon" well known for his multifarious business activities in Melbourne and elsewhere in the early 1900s.[56] Married Ellen Mahon (-1968) 1901; had issue.
Nine children (two deaths in infancy, and three daughters married in Europe).[57]

had issue.

3. Bertram Jones (18/5/1862-1868)

2. Emily Florence Jones (1831-1891) married William **Franks** (1820-1879) 27/12/1849, barrister-at-law and executor to Edward Billopp Lawrence's will[64] in 1861; had issue.

3. Florence R. Franks (1862-   )

1. Edward Billopp Lawrence (29/7/1790[60]-20/08/1861) (fifth child and fourth son of Captain Effingham Lawrence 1734-1806 and Catherine Farmer, p. 55). He was 16 when his father died in 1806,[5] so according to his father's will, brother William operated the business until Edward came of age, and by 1814 W.E. & E.B. Lawrence[6] were listed as merchants until 1823. After WEL departed for Van Diemen's Land in 1822, he remained in London until his death in 1861 at 8 Baker St, Portman Sq., London, transacting business in both land and lease with family members Effingham John Lawrence (1816) and Charles Monro father and son.[61] He died on 20/8/1861[62] at his home in Tower Hill and was buried on 24/8/1861 at Sculthorpe,[63] Norfolk, England, the home of Willoughby Jones (1820-) 3rd Baronet. His executors, nephews William Franks[64] and Effingham John Lawrence (both barristers-at-law) stated in November 1863 that "his estate was under £25,000"[64] and the estate in Ireland as at 9/9/1861, did not exceed £1,500.[65] A letter from Downing Street, London dated 1821 and sent to the governor of NSW writes that - "Edward Bellopp Lawrence, brother of William Effingham Lawrence, recommended as free settler"[66] and vouching   for "his good character", but this move did not eventuate. Unmarried, no issue.

Notes

Chapter 4

WILLIAM EFFINGHAM LAWRENCE
(1782-1841)

William Effingham Lawrence was born in London, soon after his father Captain Effingham Lawrence, having served on the loyalist side in the Revolutionary War of 1776-1783, moved his business and family from New York, in 1780. William and his brother Edward carried on the family business from 9 Trinity Square, Tower Hill, London after their father's death at least until the late 1820's as there are entries in the London Directory of 1821 (and several subsequent years) under "W. E. and E. B. Lawrence, Merchants". Family legend has it that, with British Government approval, one of their vessels was supplying munitions to dissidents in Spain's South American colonies, and was confiscated, and that in compensation W.E.L. was granted land in the Australian colonies.

Other sources suggest that it was for reasons of health that he, at the age of forty years, uprooted his family to make a new life in the colonies. In any case, he had a sloop (later described as a cutter) named the *Lord Liverpool* of 71 tons (p. 268), built and sailed for Van Diemen's Land, leaving England in May 1822 and arriving at the mouth of the Tamar River in Van Diemen's Land on 10th February, 1823. Not until six weeks later however, did the vessel sail up river to Launceston but when it did, a record was set for the speed with which this trip was accomplished (as recalled in the Launceston Examiner of 10th February, 1923).

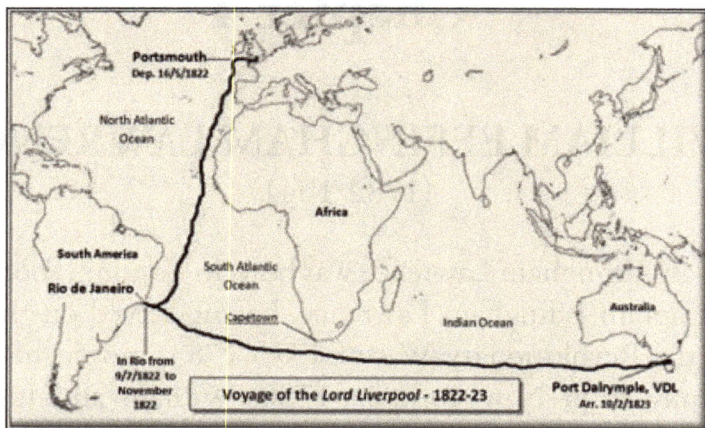

Voyage of the *Lord Liverpool* - 1822-23

Lawrence brought with him his future wife, two children (probably Charles and Mary Ann) a carpenter and blacksmith and two apprentices. The crew consisted of Capt. George Coulson (1778-1862) (whose descendants to this day live near Windermere, on the East Tamar, Tasmania) a Mate (Samuel Budge) and four seamen all of whom intended to settle in the colony. He also brought a large quantity of merchandise including furniture, agricultural implements and tools. On arrival, he visited Lieutenant-Governor William Sorell in Hobart Town and was granted tracts of land in Northern Tasmania, in proportion to the capital in goods and money he had brought to the colony.

William Sorell[1] (1775-1848) was Lt. Governor of Van Diemen's Land from 1817-1824 and was largely successful in restoring public order and improving administration in the chaotic colony he inherited in 1817. Control of the menace of bushranging and establishment of the penal colony at Macquarie Harbour occurred during his term of office.

The following notes are quoted from the Australian Dictionary of Biography, 1788-1850.[2] The entry concerning W. E. Lawrence is the result of research by the late Bruce Wall from *Lake House*, Cressy, Tasmania. Much of this information came from original family documents subsequently lost in a fire in his library at his home in the 1960s.

"Lawrence, William Effingham (1782-1841), landowner, was the eldest son of Captain Effingham Lawrence, merchant and one of the corporation of the elder brethren of Trinity House, London, and his wife Catherine, née Farmer. With his brother Edward Billopp, Lawrence continued his father's business, mainly in shipping, with houses in London, Liverpool and New York.

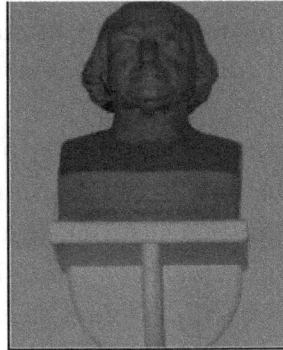

This bust of Jeremy Bentham came to Van Diemen's Land with W. E. Lawrence and is still in the possession of the family.

He was highly educated and deeply interested in scientific and constitutional developments. He was a close friend of Jeremy Bentham:* when Lawrence, due to ill health and

*Jeremy Bentham (1748-1832) was a well-known English philosopher, economist, and theoretical jurist, who was born and lived in London and was a graduate of Queen's College, Oxford. Bentham founded and promoted utilitarianism based on the premise that ideas, institutions and actions should be judged on their utility (usefulness). This led to some 60,000 pages of writings in his lifetime and many significant reforms, e.g. in operation of parliaments, the law courts and the prison system. Some of his ideas on 'Model Prisons' were used in the design of the Port Arthur penal colony, Tasman Peninsula, Tas., operating from 1833-1853.[3 & 4]

also for economic reasons, decided to emigrate, Bentham wrote to Buenos Aires: "Our excellent friend, on his way to Australia, is not without thoughts of touching at Rio de Janeiro: a worthier man, a more benevolent cosmopolite, never left any country; and very few better informed or more intelligent".

Having arranged satisfactory terms with the British government for an Australian land grant in lieu of a treasury payment in compensation for the loss of a ship, Lawrence had the vessel the *Lord Liverpool* (71 tons) built and eventually sailed for Australia in May 1822. Putting in at Rio de Janeiro for provisions and water, Lawrence found a political situation most attractive to his intellectual pursuits. Under the regent, Dom Pedro, Brazil was struggling for its independence from Portugal.

Instead of remaining just a few days Lawrence stayed for months and became a confidant of the chief minister, the distinguished Paulista, José Bonifacio Andrada, who wanted him to settle permanently in Rio.

However, Lawrence sailed in November 1822, and arrived at George Town, Van Diemen's Land, next February. He carried instructions to Governor Brisbane that 2,000 acres be granted to him and a similar area to his brother. Their lands were to adjoin, with provision for a reserve of 4,000 acres to be given within five years upon cultivation and improvement of the original grant. Lieut-Governor Sorell authorized the grants and stipulated that they were to contain 8,000 acres exclusive of waste land. Through this stipulation and the negligence of the deputy-surveyor-general, Lawrence's grant amounted to 12,000 acres, independent of a further 2,000 acres reserved for his son. In 1824 Lieutenant-Governor Arthur questioned his right to acquire so much land and relations between them were strained until Arthur's recall."

Lord Bathurst on Gov. Arthur's recommendation reduced the grant to 4,000 acres, and WEL was not appointed a magistrate nor a member of the Legislative Council until Arthur returned to England.*

Lawrence's grant, known as *Formosa*, was on the Lake River, south of Cressy. At an early date, WEL had obtained from Lieut. Gov. Sorell thirty acres on the south-west of Launceston running from the banks of the Tamar near the end of Margaret Street along the base of Cataract Hill as far as (what is now) the junction of Balfour and Upton Streets. He fenced this and planted two acres of vines, but the local inhabitants deemed this grant to be an infringement on town housing sites. The Crown resumed the land and WEL in compensation was granted a strip of land running north-eastward in a rectangular strip from Wellington Road to the left bank of the North Esk River opposite Killafaddy an area known as *Lawrence's Paddocks* (164 acres) through which Lawrence Vale Road now runs.[5]

> "He owned much more land in and around Launceston including a town residence, *Vermont* (310 acres), *The Punchbowl* (924 acres) and *Penquite* (1,832 acres). Later he bought more properties: *Billopp* (2,000 acres) near *Formosa*, *Point Effingham* (9,651 acres) and *Danbury Park* (3,500 acres) on the Tamar River. At his death he was one of the colony's largest and wealthiest landowners.

---

*George Arthur (1784-1854)[3,4] was a British Army Serviceman and later Colonial Administrator who served in that capacity in Honduras, Van Diemen's Land (1824-1836), Canada and India. He was created a Baronet in 1841 and gazetted Lieutenant-General in 1842. He was an able administrator, a high-minded autocrat and in his term further significantly tightened administration in the colony of Van Diemen's Land.

With his varied interests Lawrence was a prime mover in many schemes that benefited the north of Tasmania. In 1824 he, with Thomas and Joseph Archer, were granted land on the marsh land at Launceston on the condition that they drained, embanked and improved it. They abandoned this project and withdrew their claim to the marsh, after there were complaints to the Governor.

By 1826 when many landowners had surplus stock for sale, a market was instituted at Ross Bridge, with Lawrence as chairman, for the disposal of stock and grain; it was similar to the fairs in English country towns. From this small beginning developed the Midland Agricultural Association, operators of the Campbell Town Show.[*]

Lawrence was also prominent in the field of education. In June 1826 he drafted a plan for establishing the Cornwall Collegiate Institution for the liberal and scientific education of youth, first in the school and later by lectures and physical experiments; the plan also included a botanical garden, chemical laboratory and a valuable and extensive library with a reading room for adults. Arthur granted fifty acres at Norfolk Plains[†] and the institution was opened on 1st March 1828.

Unfortunately it was not a success and soon became a private grammar school, but Lawrence did not lose interest in higher education. In 1838 he formed a committee, with William and James Henty and P. A. Mulgrave to establish in

[*]In its 183rd year in 2021 and the premier sheep show in Tasmania.

[†]Norfolk Plains is the fertile farming district surrounding Longford and Cressy. It was so named as the last group of settlers to leave Norfolk Island, when this penal settlement was closed in 1814, were granted land in the area.

Launceston, a school based on the principles of the Church of England, and under its supervision. He did not live to see this plan culminate in the opening of the Launceston Church Grammar School in 1846.*"

Lawrence played an important part in 1828 as one of the foundation directors of the Cornwall Bank. In 1832 the Cornwall Bank was in confusion and they sought aid from a branch of the Van Diemen's Land Bank in Launceston to support their note

Third and fourth generations at Grammar, 1957

The author (far right, centre row) and two of his four siblings,
Ian (third from the right, front row) and John (far left, front row)
Lawrence, at Launceston Church Grammar School.
(E.F. Lawrence, personal collection.)

*The family has continued to maintain a close relationship with the school and many descendants have attended it. In 1998 the W. E. Lawrence Memorial Scholarship was established and is still available to students in Years 11 and 12.

issue, so in 1834 Charles Henty, another of the founders, took over the books and in 1835 declared a 15% half-yearly dividend. Meanwhile, they were negotiating in England with the newly formed Bank of Australasia, and in 1836 the Bank of Australasia took over the Bank's affairs and began business in the old premises of the Cornwall Bank with WEL as one of the directors where he remained until his death.[5]

"In 1832 he was a founder of the Tamar Steam Navigation Co. which bought the steam tug *Tamar* for use with sailing vessels on the Tamar River, and the *Steam Packet* (formerly the *Governor Arthur*) for passengers and cargo between Launceston and George Town. Later they acquired the river steamer *Gipsy*. Until 1846 these ships were important in developing the Tamar valley.

Official recognition of Lawrence's merits was long in coming. However, Sir John Franklin quickly appreciated Lawrence's high character, great worth and commanding talent. R. C. Gunn considered him the cleverest and richest gentleman in the colony. In 1837 Lawrence was appointed a justice of the peace and next year a member of the Legislative Council. He retained his seat until his death at Launceston on 18 April 1841. According to his obituary,[6] "Mr. Lawrence, in his seat in the Council, was foremost in advocating popular rights. He had a mind which soared above all petty notions of party politics or political maneuvers. The colonists have lost a valuable friend; an able advocate; a disinterested patriot; by whom, through the constant and consistent exercise of independent principles – by pursuing an honest and honorable course of public life, aided by the possession of superior talents and abilities – he had rendered himself greatly prized and esteemed". In 1826 Lawrence married a widow, Mary Ann George, née Smither, and he was survived by five sons and four daughters. His eldest son, Robert William (d. 1833) was Tasmania's first distinguished botanist.

Three sons continued in pastoral activities at *Formosa*, *Billopp* and *Point Effingham*; another held a commission in the 7th Dragoon Guards, and the youngest entered the medical profession, practiced in Melbourne and was closely associated with the Melbourne Hospital from 1868 to 1878."

FORMOSA was the original land grant to W. E. Lawrence, 8,000 acres, authorised by Lieut. Governor William Denison. Details of the grant reads – "Lake River District – Bounded on the **West** side by a Run of Water commonly called Brumby's Creek commencing at the junction of the Deep Creek with it on the **North** side by grants to Williamson, Brumby, and Hammand on the **East** side by the Lake River surrounding a thirty acre grant to W. Taylor and on the **South** side by an East line to the Lake River again commencing from the before mentioned Junction of the Deep Creek with Brumby's Creek."

Following is a map of *Formosa*, with paddocks named, from a survey by James Scott in 1848.

The northern boundary of the grant is an east-west line from a point on the Lake River approximately 1.5 km north of the present day Westmore bridge west to Brumby's Creek.

Formosa has been owned by members of the family since 1823, some resident and some non-resident.

1823	Original grant
1824	First house built, wooden slab, near Brumby's Creek
1826	February; homestead and a significant acreage of crops burnt by Matthew Brady and his gang of bushrangers (value of property destroyed, est. £3,000)

Survey of *Formosa* 1848
Archives Tasmania. AF396-1-1257

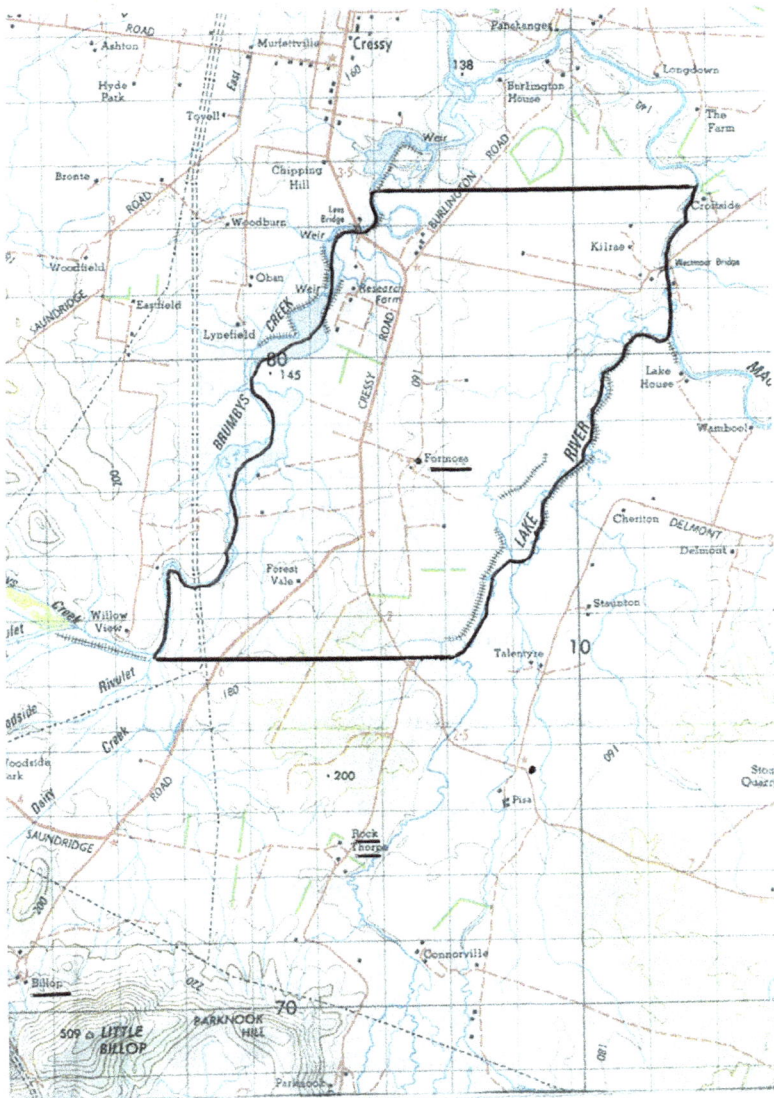

Recent map showing some Lawrence properties and Pisa Church; also
the boundaries of the original grant.
Tasmap, South Esk. 1:100,000, 1976

1827	Development of Formosa garden commenced
1832	Second house of mud walls, built on higher ground overlooking the Lake River flats
1832-33	Robert William Lawrence (p. 91), manager
1830-1840s	Farm buildings, built with convict labour (still standing)
1833-1841	John G. Robertson, manager
1841-1898	William Lawrence (p. 113), owner (lived in N.Z.)
1841-1881	R. C. Gunn (p. 91), executor (from Launceston with a succession of local lessees)
1878	15th January, second house burnt
1880-1885	Third house built of bricks made on *Formosa*
1885-1905	Effingham Billopp Lawrence (p.143), manager, of *Billopp*
1898-1900	Alfred William Lawrence (p. 114), owner, lived in Vic.
1900-1940	Cornelius Henry Lawrence (p. 114), owner, resident 1905-1914, the first resident owner since 1833
Early 1900s	Third house partly burnt
Before 1905	Fourth house built utilising part of the third house, weatherboard.
1906	Commencement of breeding Polwarths (based on Carr's Plains sheep)
1914	Cornelius Henry Lawrence, owner, retired to live in Geelong, Vic.
1914-1923	Leonard Linley Lawrence (p.175), manager, but lived at *Wetmore*, then *Charlton*, Ross
c.1918	The Soldier Settlement Scheme begins in Tasmania and reduction in size of *Formosa* from 12,000 acres to 4,000 acres takes place over the next 30 years.
1923-1926	Cecil Effingham Lawrence (p. 115), manager
1926-1945	Leonard Linley Lawrence, manager, resident at *Formosa* from 1928.
1929	Fourth house rebuilt for family of Leonard Linley

Lawrence, to become the fifth house.

1940-1945	Estate of Cornelius Henry Lawrence, owner
1945-1967	Leonard Linley Lawrence & Sons, owners
1945-1947	Purchase of *Rockthorpe* near Cressy, and *Gees Runs* (in 2021 called *Nosswick*) at Bracknell, Tas.
1966	Fifth house extensively remodelled to become the sixth *Formosa* house, brick and weatherboard.
1967	The L L Lawrence & Sons partnership was split to be equal value between the brothers and Geoffrey Linley Lawrence (p.175) owned most of the acreage of *Formosa*. Richard Effingham Lawrence (p.177) owned *Rockthorpe*, *Gees Runs* and several hundred acres of *Formosa*, renamed *Rockmore*, which adjoined the Lake River & Cressy Road. All three properties were sold after Dick's death in 1995.
1967-1984	Geoffrey Linley Lawrence (p. 175), owner
1974-1991	The era of the Australian Wool Corporation and the ill-fated guaranteed minimum reserve price scheme for wool. This led to over-production and ultimately to the collapse of the wool market in February 1991 with catastrophic financial loss for many businesses. The stockpile of nearly five million bales took ten years to be sold. Times were very difficult for many Polwarth breeders particularly as finer wooled merinos were also replacing Polwarths as the preferred breed in many areas. Polwarth Stud animals became worthless.
1984-	Estate of Geoffrey Linley Lawrence, owner
1984-1987	Charles Wilson, manager
1987-1988	Michael Blake, manager
1988-1992	Donald V. Telfer (p. 121), manager
1993-1999	Brian W. Lawrence (p. 151), manager

1999-2016   Robert Henry, manager
13/12/1999   Complete dispersal sale of the Formosa Polwarth Stud
2016-   John D. L. Heard (p. 176), grandson of G. L. Lawrence, manager
c.2021   Internal remodel of sixth house planned.

Following the death of William Effingham Lawrence in 1841, an inventory of his assets was made by Theodore Bartley, Valuer, on behalf of the executors.

The details for **FORMOSA**, 8,000 acres, are as follows –

CATTLE	£	FARM EQUIPMENT	£
78 working oxen @ £12	936	set of blacksmith's tools	20
115 steers @ £8	920	set of carpenter's tools	10
312 cows @ £5	1560	set of plasterer's tools	2
135 yearlings @ £3	405	set of sawyer's tools	10
172 calves @ £2	344		
3 bulls @ £20	60		£42
815	£4225		

HORSES			£
		19 bullocks chains	6
9 breeding mares - loose	400	2 timber chains	3
4 breeding mares -stabled	200	16 pr. Bullock bows	4
22 yearlings @ 2yr old	500	16 yokes	4
7 foals	105		£17
42	£1205		

GRAIN			
1000	bushels – wheat (abt)	350	
600	bushels – oats, threshed	110	
500	bushels – oats in straw	90	
600	bushels – cape barley	120	
35	tons of hay (about)	140	
		£810	

SHEEP

560	fine woolled ewes	
134	half-bred Leicester ewes	
2514	ewes (general flock)	
3208	breeding ewes	
454	ewes for meat	
647	wethers	
40	ram slags	
95	rams	
2242	lambs	
9894 @ 12/-		£5936

PIGS

80	£100

POULTRY

80	turkeys	20
50	ducks	6
60	fowls	6
27	geese	8
217		£40

HOUSEHOLD FURNITURE

1 couch	3
6 hair bottomed chairs	6
6 cane bottomed chairs	2
2 dining tables	7
3 dressing tables	3
1 fender & fire irons	2
1 Brussels carpet	3
1 hearth rug	1
1 Fent bedstead & hanging	6
1 French bedstead	5
1 feather bed	6
3 wool mattresses	6
1 palliass	2
2 chest of drawers	10
1 wardrobe	3
2 wash stands & furniture	3
3 looking glasses	3
bedroom carpeting	1
window curtains	3
	£75

FARMING IMPLEMENTS

3	bullock drays	45
1	bullock cart	15
1	horse cart	15
1	wagon	35
1	horse dray (old)	8
1	water truck	10
4	wooden ploughs	12
2	iron ploughs	8
4	pr. harrows	8
1	roller	3
1	winnowing machine	15
1	wheat screen	2
1	wool press	5
		£181

TOTAL VALUE = £12,631

Shearing shed and barn, Formosa (c.1830s) with Great Western Tiers in the background. Photo c. J. D. L. Heard, 2021

BILLOPP, 2,000 acres, 50% hill country and closer to the Western Tiers, was purchased from the Crown by William Effingham Lawrence in 1835 and initially used as an upper sheep "run", in conjunction with *Formosa*.

1835	Purchased by William Effingham Lawrence
1841	Estate of W. E. Lawrence; R. C. Gunn, executor. *Billopp* was not listed as a separate entity in the inventory of 1841.
1856-1865	Leased to C. H. G. Fletcher
1865-1896	Owned and operated by Effingham Billopp Lawrence (p. 143)
1896-1908	Leased from E. B. Lawrence and operated by Effingham Dryburgh Lawrence (p. 145)

1908-1948	Owned and operated by Effingham Dryburgh Lawrence
1948-1967	Owned and operated by Effingham Lambert Lawrence (p. 145)
1967-2014	Owned and operated by Ian Martin Lawrence (p. 149), then his son, Samuel Ian Effingham Lawrence (p.149)
2014	Sold outside the family after 180 years

PENQUITE, 1,832 acres, on the southern edge of Launceston, was the home of Octavius Vernon Lawrence (p. 181) for some years, prior to his move to Melbourne in the early 1860s for completion of his medical degree, his entry into medical practice, and living permanently in Victoria.

The 1841 inventory shows –

CATTLE

8	cows (dry) @ £8	64
7	cows in milk	56
9	heifer calves @ 50/-	23
4	bull calves	10
16	working oxen @ £25	200
3	working bulls	40
47		£393

SHEEP

At the farm . . .

104	ewes	
17	rams	
22	wethers	
12	lambs	
	At the Run . . .	
20	lambs	
788	ewes	
44	rams	
50	wethers	
1057	@ 12/-	£6342

FARM IMPLEMENTS

1	horse wagon	35
1	horse cart	15
2	bullock carts	32
1	rollers	4
4	ploughs	12
5	harrows	10
2 sets – plough harnesses		4
2 sets – cart harnesses		5
1	water truck & cask	3
		£120

TOOLS

12	hay forks	1
4	scythes	1
1	Xcut saw	1
4	pr. Mall rings)	
11	wedges)	1
4	augers)	
	sundry other tools)	5
		£9

HORSES				SUNDRIES		
1	plough horse 4yr old	60		49	milk tins	8
1	plough horse, aged	50		3	cream pans	2
1	entire cart horse, aged [stallion]	80		3	sail cloths (1 new)	10
1	chestnut saddle horse, 3yr old	40		1	fowling piece [gun]	2
1	roan saddle mare, 3 yr old	40				___
3	fillies, 3yr old, handled	100				£22
1	bay saddle horse, aged	30				
___		___				
9		£400				

GRAIN, etc.

SWINE					
			1 stack of wheat about		
1	white boar	5	500 bushels	175
3	sows	12	-- unthreshed wheat in barn	
18	young pigs	5	-- threshed wheat in barn	
___		___	1 stack of oats, say 500 lb	100
22		£22	2 stacks hay, say 45 tons	220
			2 ½ acres potatoes-say 4 tons	30
				___
				£525

POULTRY			
21	turkeys	6	
70-80	fowls	8	
		£14	TOTAL VALUE = £2129

POINT EFFINGHAM, 9,651 acres, situated on the east side of the Tamar River near the present Bell Bay, was owned by John Effingham Lawrence (p. 131) and family, and was eventually sold to the Archer family in 1900.
The inventory shows –

HOUSEHOLD FURNITURE				
1 dining table	3	6 bedroom chairs	3
2 small tables	2	3 dressing tables	2
1 sofa	5	2 looking glasses	2
8 chairs	8	4 wash stands	8
1 carpet	2	1 wardrobe & drawers	16
2 fenders & fire irons	2	1 bedroom carpet	1
1 pr. Candlesticks	2	2 kitchen dressers & kitchen utensils	5
2 bedsteads & bedding	20	7 bedsteads & bedding for 7 men	5
			___
			£86

STOCK, ETC.

170 head of horned cattle on the whole estate		800 - wool @ 1/-	40
chiefly cows & calves @ £4	680	10 turkeys @ 6/-	3
20 working bullocks @ £10	200	9 geese @ 7/-	3
803 sheep & lambs @ 7/-	281	7 pigs	4
1 mare	25	2 bullock drays	20
	£1186	1 old cart	3
		1 plough	6
		3 harrows	4
50 bushels barley & oats	10		£113
sundry tools & family implements	20	TOTAL VALUE = £1385	

DANBURY PARK, 3500 acres, on the west Tamar River, north of Riverside, inherited by Edward Effingham Lawrence (p. 89) in England who bequeathed it to Effingham Billopp Lawrence (p. 143) in Tasmania.

Valuation taken 30 April, 1841

1000 ewes @ 10/-	£500	
2 bullocks	20	
2 cows	9	
30 tons Hay @ £4	120	
3 bullock chains &		
12 bows	3	TOTAL VALUE = £652

15 BRISBANE STREET, known as *Sunnybanks*, was built by WEL in 1824 as his town house and was diagonally opposite Government Cottage at the end of Brisbane St. This property was demolished in 1890 when Brisbane St. was extended to the junction of Elphin Rd. and High St.

The WEL town property originally extended from York St. down through Brisbane St. to the end of City Park, which at that time was nothing but a marsh. Lawrence St is found along the north east boundary of the current City Park.

Sunnybanks was originally a stucco and brick, full verandahed bungalow, with a hip roof, accessed via a battleaxe drive. By 1867 the block had been divided between *Koorong* and *Sunnybanks*. The

Brisbane St house was sold from the WEL estate in 1868 and bought by Mr David Ritchie (owner of Ritchie's Mill), occupied by him and then by his son Mr Frank Ritchie. The advertisement in the Cornwall Chronicle 14 August 1867 describes "the house as being near Government Cottage, overlooking the Horticultural Gardens. The house contains 15 rooms with a large verandah and cellars in the basement. There are also domestic offices comprising dairy, kitchen, washhouse, besides a substantial brick stable, coach house, granary, and other out-buildings. The garden has choicest fruit trees, shrubs. The land was listed as 1 acre, 1 rood, 25 perch." A large paddock once adjoining the property (it is now unclear whether this is to the West or East) was used as "rounding up" ground for aboriginal persons immediately prior to transportation to the islands.

Black & white copy of painting of 15 Brisbane St c.1930s
now held in private hands

The current wing extensions and roofline changes to the house were done by David Ritchie c.1886 with stone from the Nunamara Ironstone quarry. The house was sold again in 1955 and altered in 1957, the most notable of which was the removal of the French doors on the front verandah replacing them with windows, leaving the original front door in place. Further alterations took place in 1979.

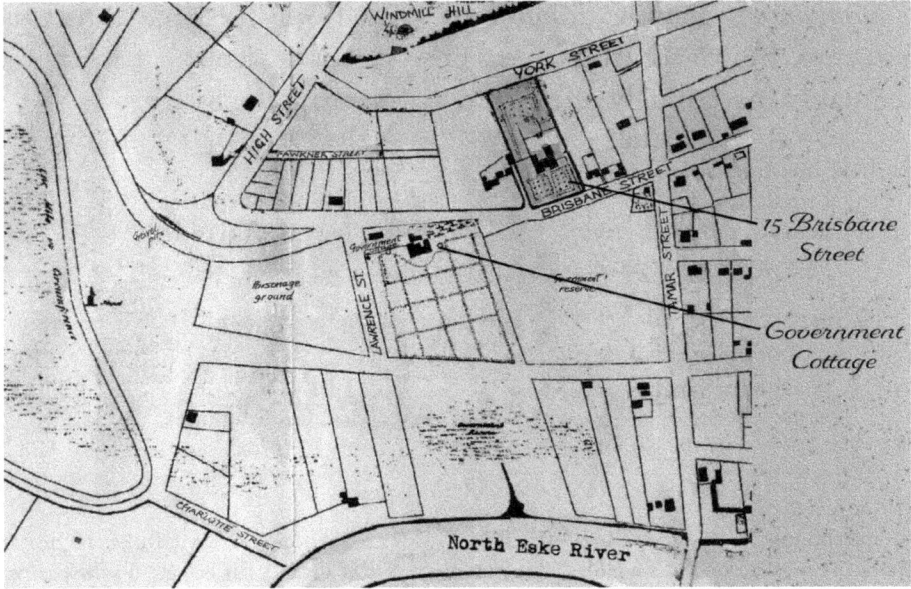

Government Cottage is seen in the centre of the picture with a rectangular grid-garden laid out below it. The alignment of Brisbane Street allowed for a gatehouse at the entrance to the drive to Government Cottage. Windmill Hill indicated on the top side of York Street. Extracted from the original - 'Plan of The Town of Launceston, VDL, from actual survey by H. W. H. Smythe, 1835.'

In the meantime, *Koorong* at 22 York Street was built at the top end of the garden, and occupied by Mr & Mrs A. M. Milligan (WEL's widow), then E. B. Lawrence (p. 143) from 1896 and sold in 1909 on a separate title to the Green family.

The current weatherboard house (now 15b Brisbane St) located behind WEL's Brisbane St home (now 15a), was built in 1930 on the site of the earlier stables built with convict labour.

WEL's house, still standing, once commanded a good view of the Tamar River and is currently owned and occupied by John and Lorraine Green. John is a great-grandson of Rose Barnard (1838-1930) (p. 275).

Sunnybanks is now difficult to view from Brisbane Street as *Somerton*, built a century later, now stands in front on it and is frequently inaccurately referred to as 15a Brisbane Street.

The 1841 inventory shows

2	carriage horses	150	100	bushels (abt) wheat		40
2	mares	100	60	bushels (abt) barley		12
1	lame entire horse	40				£52
		£290				
			household furniture, etc			671
1	chariot & harness	200	books			150
1	phaeton & harness	70				£821
2	carts	30	Plate 208oz. (avoirdupoise)			
		£300		@ 7/6 p/oz.		£78

(List of plate:
24 tablespoons, 25 desert spoons, 11 teaspoons, 2 gravy spoons, 12 table forks, 10 desert spoons, 1 soup ladle, 3 sauce ladles, 1 sugar spoon, 1 fish slice, 2 salt cellars, 6 salt spoons, 2 salvers = weight 208 oz. avoidupoise. Value £78)

TOTAL VALUE = £1541

GENERAL RECAPITULATION by Theodore Bartley, 1841

Livestock	£ 13,050		
Grain	1,007	Wool @ 1/- per advance	1,200
Hay	480	Cash	4,047
Farming implements	487	Bank shares	3,250
Household furniture	977	Bills receivable	2,151
Carriages	270	Monies due	465
Plate & books	228		

Total value of assets, excluding land properties   £27,612

ADDITIONAL NOTES
on Mrs. W. E. Lawrence

Not a great deal is known of her although a few stories have seeped down from the past and most depict her as a person of a somewhat dominating character.

On one occasion a visitor to Van Diemen's Land expressed sympathy, perhaps with a touch of condescension, at how unpleasant it must be to have convicts as servants: Mrs. Lawrence's tart reply was "Not at all, some of them are excellent; of course I have first choice after the Governor's wife." This incident probably took place when Sir John Franklin was Governor as the Lawrences were on close terms with him and Lady Franklin, quite the opposite being the case with his predecessor, Governor Arthur.

Something of her character is gleaned from a letter from Mrs. Thomas Henty to her daughter-in-law, Mary Ann (the Lawrence's eldest daughter). Mary Ann and her husband Frank Henty, had recently moved to the country, living at *Merino Downs*, in the Western District of Victoria, and away from what her mother considered the more comfortable and suitable social life of Portland (also further away from Launceston and Mrs. Lawrence). She was now a widow; was very much displeased about the move and made the fact clearly known.* We find Mrs. Henty – possibly in an attempt to pour oil on trouble waters – writing from Launceston to Mary Ann at *Merino Downs* and saying "I am not the least surprised that Mrs. Lawrence should have felt most keenly your long absence … but it would have been better if she could have restrained her feelings a little…". Such restraint does not however appear to loom large in Mrs. Lawrence's nature! A grandson (H. F. Lawrence) was once heard to remark "Oo… she's a Tartar." Nonetheless, doubtless to the family's astonishment, within three years of the death of W. E. L., she remarried (on 7th November, 1843) and gave birth to her

*Portraits of Mrs Lawrence as a widow, and her daughter Mary Ann Lawrence (later Henty), painted in 1841 by Henry Mundy (1798-1848), are in the Cowen Gallery, State Library of Victoria, Melbourne: a bequest of Elsie Hindson, 1968, through Beth Henty-Anderson, 1992 (p. 110).

last child, Eliza, on 19/9/1844. Eliza Milligan, in turn, married Charles Gaunt (6th son of Dr. M. Gaunt, from Windermere), at St. John's Anglican Church, Launceston, on 22/4/1868. There was issue from this marriage (p. 235).

Mrs. Lawrence appears to have been a remarkable woman and it is perhaps unusual that she should be remembered – almost solely – by one branch of the family (that of O.V. Lawrence) as the person who introduced them to a variety of the card game Patience. For generations, this game has been known as "Mrs. Milligan". Mrs. Lawrence died on 28th October, 1880 (aged 79 years) having borne children to two (if not all) of her three husbands. Ten of these children at least, were to William Effingham Lawrence (producing fifty-two grandchildren) and she gave the family a good start in the new land.

Genealogy

1. William Effingham Lawrence (5/3/1782-18/4/1841) was married to the widow Mary Ann George (née Smither) (bp.12/5/1799[7]-28/10/1880) 23/7/1826[8] by the Rev. John Youl at St. John's Church, Launceston. This was her second marriage as she originally married William **George** in the parish of St. Martin in the Fields, Middlesex, England on 17/7/1817[9] as an 18 year old. Mary Ann, age 43, married a third time, on 9/11/1843,[10] to Alexander Murray **Milligan** (bp.27/12/1812-15/12/1883), and had issue, Eliza Margaret Milligan (1844-1891) (p. 235).
    2. Robert William Lawrence (18/10/1807-18/10/1833) (p. 91) married Anne Emily Wedge; had one daughter.
    2. Charles Lawrence (1818 -   ) travelled to Van Diemen's Land on the *Lord Liverpool*; no further details are available except that he reached the age of ten years as recorded in

the 1828 Launceston Census,[11] "attending school, and able to read". (His exact parentage is uncertain, but he may well have been a son from Mrs. Lawrence's first marriage).

2. Mary Ann Lawrence (5/8/1821-27/11/1881) (p. 105) married Francis **Henty** (1815-1889) and had one son and three daughters. Lived in Victoria mostly after her marriage.

2. William Lawrence (16/12/1823-29/8/1898) (p. 113) married Isabella Lannon and had five sons and three daughters. Lived in New Zealand mostly.

2. Eliza Lawrence (14/12/1825-31/7/1844) (p. 127) married Dr. Joseph **Milligan** (1807-1884) reputed to be a half brother of A.M. Milligan and had a son.

2. John Effingham Lawrence (20/3/1828-13/7/1874) (p. 131) married Frances Gaunt (1827-1910) and had six sons and three daughters.

2. Edward Effingham Lawrence (12/11/1830-20/10/1890) A British Army Officer, Edward lived mainly in England as an adult. He went to England with his brother John to be educated, leaving Van Diemen's Land on the *Arab* on 2/2/1840, returning 26/5/1845. Later, on returning to London and obtaining a Commission as Cornet in the 7th Dragoon Guards (1856) he took part in the Italian War of Independence (1860-61). For a time he was a Captain in one of the London Militia regiments. He found life in London to his liking and lived there for the rest of his life. He was cited as a co-respondent in a divorce court in 1884 where the appellant was Douglas Alleyne, respondent Ada Alleyne, but there are no records for a later marriage.[12] He inherited *Danbury Park* Estate and later bequeathed it to his brother, E. B. Lawrence. Unmarried, no issue.

2. Emily Lawrence (10/6/1832-22/5/1855) unmarried.

2. Effingham Billopp Lawrence (23/2/1834-10/8/1908) Married . . .

(i) Clara Barnard (22/9/1836-24/5/1861) (p. 144) had one son and one daughter.

(ii) Grace Barnard (1840-1928) (p. 144) had eight sons and two daughters.

2. Octavius Vernon Lawrence (1/1/1836-7/2/1915) Married . . .

(i) Editha Wettenhall (1836-1872) (p. 186) had four sons and four daughters.

(ii) Jessie Barnard (1847-1939) (p. 210) had two sons and four daughters.

2. Caroline Marienne Lawrence (30/11/1837-13/2/1865) (p. 233) married William Henry **Barnard** (1831-1900) and had a son and a daughter. Lived in Victoria after her marriage.

2. Fermer Lawrence (5/6/1840-22/7/1840) – died of convulsions.

Notes

Chapter 5

ROBERT WILLIAM LAWRENCE
(1807-1833)

Robert William Lawrence (R.W.L.) was the eldest son* of W. E. Lawrence and was the first Lawrence to live at *Formosa*, Cressy, Tasmania. He did not arrive in the colony until April 1825 (travelling via the ship *Elizabeth*, to Hobart) having remained in England to complete his education. In 1830 he was introduced by a friend and Launceston merchant, Thomas Scott, to Dr. William Jackson Hooker (1785-1865), Regius Professor of Botany at Glasgow, 1820-41, and then director of the Botanical Gardens, Kew, London, until his death. Lawrence made several expeditions collecting native plants and animals, and took part in the Black Line of 1830 (a plan of Governor Arthur's to round up all Tasmanian aborigines)[1,2] which enabled him, while taking part, to develop his interest in biology. He was Tasmania's first resident botanist and while he did not make as important a contribution as Ronald Campbell Gunn, the role he did play in introducing the latter to Dr. Hooker was highly significant.[3,4]

Gunn was introduced to Dr. (later Sir) William Hooker, in 1832, and the correspondence that ensued was continued until 1849. Plants were also sent to Dr. Hooker and the contact he had with Lawrence, and more especially Gunn, enabled Dr. Hooker to produce his *Flora Tasmaniae* in 1860. The absence of colonial botanists would have delayed the production of a descriptive botanical work on Tasmania by years.

*Robert was not the son of Mary Ann George (1799-1880) (neé Smither) and his mother is unknown.

The correspondence between Hooker, Lawrence and Gunn has been published in "Van Diemen's Land Correspondents"[5] and contains extracts from Lawrence's diary, and an account he wrote of "An excursion up the western mountains". The latter was sent to Dr. Hooker who published it in his "Journal of Botany", together with a section entitled "Towards a Flora of Van Diemen's Land" with descriptions of plants sent to him by Robert Lawrence.

The following endemic plants are named for Lawrence:[6]

Genus – Lawrencia

Species

- *Correa Lawrenciana* (Mountain Correa – a variety of native fuschia).

http://anpsa.org.au/c-law.html

- *Deyeuxia Lawrencei* (Lawrence's Bent Grass)
now extinct and known only from the 1831 RWL specimen, possibly collected in the Launceston area.
No image is available.

- *Podocarpus Lawrencei* (Mountain Plum Pine)

https://www.conifers.org/po/
Podocarpus_lawrencei.php

- *Pterygopapus Lawrencei* (Sage Cushion Bush)

https://www.utas.edu.au/dicotkey/
dicotkey/AST/gnaph/gPterygopappus.htm

- *Spyridium Lawrencei* (Small leaf Dusty Miller) a rare and now endangered plant

https://www.threatenedspecieslink.
tas.gov.au/Pages/Spyridium-
lawrencei.aspx

- *Lawrencella Rosea* (formerly known as *Helichrysum lindleyi*) found in south-west WA.

http://anpsa.org.au/l-ros.html

R. C. Gunn (4/4/1808-13/3/1881) was a close friend of R. W. L. and shared his keen interest in botany. He was born in Capetown, South Africa, (being the son of a British Army Officer) educated in England and attached to the Royal Engineers in Barbados; emigrating to Tasmania when 21 years old he held various government positions, including Superintendent of convicts as well as being an amateur botanist. On the death of W. E. Lawrence in 1841 he became manager of his estates and lived at *Penquite*, a large Georgian styled double-storey brick building on the Penquite Estate, later demolished in 1957. Its location was near the southern side of the large turning circle at the top of Docking Court, Newstead. Later Gunn acquired land for himself and built a mansion *Newstead House*, 10 Newstead Crescent, Launceston in 1856. He was also very active in the early days of the Tasmanian Society (which later in 1848 became the Royal Society of Tasmania) and was elected a Fellow of the Royal Society in London in 1855 in recognition of his contributions to botany.

Robert Lawrence initially lived in *Vermont*, built for him by his father on a hill behind the North Esk river marshes near Launceston (now 48 Bill Grove, Mowbray Heights). The house now on the site is of Victorian design, built in 1872 using some of the materials from the earlier building, set on the foundations of the original house. There are still today some remnants of the original outbuildings.

In 1832 he moved to *Formosa*, Cressy, as overseer, where Gunn visited him several times. He married Anne Emily Wedge in 1832. This union was short lived however, as Emily died in October 1833 after the birth of her daughter Annie, on 3/9/1833. Her husband died just two weeks later.

We find Gunn writing to Hooker on 15th November, 1833:

> "It is with feelings of the deepest regret I have to communicate to you the death of our mutual friend Mr. R. W. Lawrence. This melancholy event took place at *Formosa* on the night of 18th October last, the day on which he had attained his 26th year, and the first anniversary day of his marriage. Twelve months ago poor Lawrence married a young and most amiable Lady, with whom he lived in the most happy state it is possible for mortals to enjoy in this world, and on 2nd Septr.

Last I left them, after a short visit, both in the enjoyment of excellent health; next day Mrs. Lawrence was safely delivered of a daughter, but from delicacy of constitution, or too sudden an exposure after her confinement, she was in a few days seized with a fever which terminated fatally within a month – fatally to Lawrence's happiness and peace."

"The Launceston Advertiser" of the time reported on the inquest held at *Formosa*, and states: "Before the coroner and a most respectable jury it was deposed that the deceased was subject to fits of apoplexy and was supposed to have expired in a fit. The verdict returned by the jury was 'died by the visitation of God'".

Anne Wedge was the daughter of Edward Davey Wedge who immigrated to Tasmania arriving on 5th April, 1824. He was a pastoralist in Tasmania, and then Victoria, and accidentally drowned in May 1852. His brother, John Helder Wedge, who immigrated at the same time, was a government surveyor, landowner and politician in Tasmania and a close friend of John Batman. J. H. Wedge's original land grant was *Leighlands* near Perth – now owned by the Youl family (p. 152). The diaries of John Helder Wedge were published in 1962 by the Royal Society of Tasmania.[7]

The only child of Robert and Anne Lawrence was brought up by her maternal grandparents, Mr. & Mrs. Edward Davey Wedge, who moved from Tasmania to Victoria in 1838. She was living with them at their property on the Werribee River at the time of the great flood on the Werribee in May, 1852. The river rose rapidly and the Wedge parents, a daughter (Lucy), Annie, Mrs. King (Annie's aunt) and two others took refuge on the roof of the house. After several hours the house collapsed and the first three were swept away and drowned (their bodies were later washed up on Williamstown Beach). Annie, and those remaining, clung to branches of a tree for 48 hours before they were rescued by among others, her future husband, Monckton

Synnot. They were married and lived successively at *Mowyong* (later known as *Bareacres*) (26,225 acres) on the Little River near Werribee, *South Brighton* (sold 1868) near Horsham, and *Terrick Terrick* (51,200 acres) near Bendigo.

In the early 1870's they moved to Melbourne and lived at *Ballyreen*, a large house on Brighton Road, St. Kilda. After Monckton's death on 23rd April 1879, Annie, and then her son Monckton Davey Synnot and his wife, lived on at *Ballyreen* for some years.

Monckton was a pioneer in selling wool to the East and expended much energy and most of his fortune in this pursuit – chartering ships, exporting wool and attempting to develop markets for wool in China and Japan. At one stage, he also owned property in the City of Melbourne in Flinders Street (opposite the Railway Station), where the Mutual Store stood for many years. His sons carried on the family interest in agriculture and operated the Melbourne firm of Synnot Bros. which, along with many other businesses associated with the pastoral industry, ran into difficulties during the Depression following the land boom of the 1890's.

Genealogy

2. Robert William Lawrence (18/10/1807-18/10/1833) lived in Northern Tasmania. Married Anne Emily Wedge (1809-2/10/1833) daughter of Edward Davey Wedge, in 18/9/1832; had issue.

    3. Anne Emily Wedge Lawrence (3/9/1833-13/7/1920) married Monckton **Synnot** (30/11/1826-23/4/1879) 25/2/1853, at St. Kilda, by special licence. Monckton was the sixth son of Captain Walter Synnot (29/11/1773-31/12/1851) (Ensign, 66th Regt. Of Foot) who had emigrated from Ireland to Van Diemen's Land with his family in 1836. He moved to

Victoria in about 1838 and took up land on Port Phillip Bay, on the Werribee and Little Rivers; had issue.

4. Monckton Davey Synnot[8] (23/8/1854-23/3/1938) owned *The Nook* and *Goonawarra* at Sunbury, Vic., and operated a Merino Stud at *Tasma*, near Deniliquin, NSW. Following the Depression in the 1890's he moved to Melbourne and worked with the AML & F.[*] *Goonawarra* is a bluestone house on the Melbourne side of Sunbury and is still standing but *The Nook*, has long since been demolished. Monckton married Emily Margaret Bostock (-29/5/1938) 22/9/1881; had issue.

5. Veara Emily Monckton Synnot (25/2/1883-13/10/1956). Died in London.

5. Monckton Synnot (4/8/1884-6/5/1954) a pastoralist who managed properties in Victoria and NSW. He later lived and worked a property near Longreach, Qld., then moved to Melbourne. He died in 1954 during a visit to England with his wife and youngest daughter. Married Mary Constance Hay (-   ); had issue.

6. Patricia Monckton Synnot (14/9/1914- 12/10/1994) married Michael Seymour **Hawker** (5/2/1903-1986) a pastoralist from Spalding SA; MA (Cambridge Univ. UK) 1/2/1941 lived at Menindie, SA; had issue.

7. Mary Elizabeth Bridget Hawker (5/4/1943-   ), BA (Flinders Univ. SA) married Dirk **van Dissel** (12/12/1947-   ) 1976; had issue.

8. Beatrix Mary Patricia van Dissel (17/12/1979-)

[*]Australian Mercantile Land & Finance Co., Ltd. incorporated in England 1863; operating in Melbourne from 1865.

8. Michael Dirk Hawker van Dissel (7/3/1982-   )
8. Dirk Charles Hawker van Dissel (15/4/1984-   )
7. Michael Charles Seymour Hawker (12/3/1948-   )
BA, B.Agr.Sc. (Adelaide Univ. SA) lived in
Adelaide SA.
6. Timothy Monckton Synnot (15/1/1916-18/5/1997)
joined the Royal Australian Navy in 1930 and
became a Commander in 1951 before retiring as
a Captain after being awarded the DSC and being
mentioned in dispatches while serving on *HMAS
Hobart* in WWII. Lived at *Naberoo*, Keith, SA.
Married Patricia Louise Storey (-   ) and had issue.
7. Jennifer Mary Synnot (11/11/1942-5/10/1992)
married Robert **Schmidt**; lived in Adelaide, SA;
no issue.
7. David Monckton Synnot (21/8/1944-   ) BAgr.
Sc. (Univ. of Sydney), married Meredith Wyn
Cooker (-   ) 28/12/1976 lived in Adelaide,
SA; had issue.
8. Annielise Jane Synnot (20/10/1978-   )
8. Myvanwy Ann Synnot (20/9/1981-   )
8. Ceridwen Emily Synnot (1/9/1985-   )
7. William Monckton Synnot (29/9/1947-   )
BAgr.Sc. (Univ. Adelaide, 1971) BEcon. (Adelaide
Univ. 1973) married Jitlada Plookpholngam (-   )
1981, lived in Adelaide SA; had issue.
8. Nathan Monckton Synnot (30/8/1990-   )
8. Andrew Monckton Synnot (22/11/1994-   )
7. Richard Monckton Synnot (3/9/1949-   )
BA (Hons.), BEcon. (Adelaide); lived in
Canberra.

7. Elizabeth Emily Synnot (16/5/1951-   )
studied law at Adelaide University.
6. Virginia Monckton Synnot (30/6/1918-12/9/1991)
married Roy Outram **Lewis** (-   ), 29/6/1940
at Longreach, Qld.; lived at *Munkora*, Tara,
Queensland; had issue.
7. Lavinia Rosalind Lewis (28/3/1941-   ) married
John David **Tritton** (-   ) 1961 in Brisbane,
and lived at Hamilton, in Brisbane. Divorced
1973; had issue.
8. Patricia Jane Tritton (13/7/1963-   ) married
Scott Leighton **Hill** (-   ) 1981; had issue.
9. Matthew James Leighton Hill (3/9/1989-   )
9. Annabel Sophie Jane Hill (2/4/1991-   )
9. Angus Alexander Leighton Hill (20/8/1994-)
8. Lucinda Sarah Tritton (15/2/1967-   )
married Michael David **Yung** (-   ) 1996,
lived in Adelaide, SA; had issue.
9. Joshua Samuel Yung (21/9/1993-)
8. Jeremy Matthew Tritton (13/9/1970-)
7. Annabel Christian Lewis (20/9/1943-)
married John Grafton **Booth** (-   ) 1968, in
Brisbane, Qld.; lived in Perth, WA; had issue.
8. Sarah McKinlay Booth (7/2/1973-   )
8. Joanna Monckton Booth (23/10/1976-   )
7. Rosemary Virginia Lewis (28/11/1951-)
married Nicholas Taggart **Robson** (-   )
1971, lived at Gordon, NSW. Divorced 1991;
had issue.
8. Susannah Clare Robson (27/9/1974-   )
8. Michael Hugh Lewis Robson (29/10/1976-   )

6. Christina (Kitty) Mary Monckton Synnot
   (4/4/1920- /6/ 2008) married Peter **Howson**
   C.M.G. businessman and politician (22/5/1919-
   1/2/2009) 4/8/1956. Lived in South Yarra, Victoria;
   had issue.
   7. George Peter Synnot Howson (26/9/1959-   )
      married Marie Louise Mhyrman (-   )
      10/9/1983; had issue.
      8. Natasha Dozon Howson (27/2/1984-   )
      8. Anna Theresa Howson (11/2/1986-   )
      8. Rebeckah Mary Howson (12/10/1988-   )
      8. Hannah Joan Mhyrman Howson (28/4/1995-)
6. Anthony Monckton Synnot AO KBE (5/1/1922-
   10/7/2001). Born in Corowa, NSW. Joined the
   Royal Australian Navy in 1939 and attended the
   Royal Naval College, Dartmouth, England, and
   subsequently had a distinguished career in the RAN.
   - Rear Admiral (1970)
   - Vice-Admiral (1976) and Chief of Naval Staff
     (1976-1979)
   - Admiral and Chief of the Defence Force Staff
     (1979-1982)
   - Chairman of the Council of the Australian War
     Memorial, Canberra, 1982-1985
   - AO (1976), KBE (1979)
   lived at Deakin, ACT; married.
(i) Mary Virginia Davenport (1930-2/7/1965)
    30/10/1959; had issue.
    7. Jane Monckton Synnot (24/9/1960-   )
       married Keith **Scoble** (-   ), of London,
       UK.

7. Amanda Mary Monckton Synnot (7/7/1964-   )
(ii) Elizabeth Anne Colvin (née Manifold)
(12/12/1925-15/12/1987) 17/5/1968, in London,
UK.
5. Reymond Synnot (5/5/1886-Oct.1965) a well known
Sydney architect in the 1920's and 30's; served in
World War I (Major, 2nd Aust. Div. Artillery and awarded
the M.C.) and World War II (Flt. Lieut. In the R.A.A.F.)
4. Jane Elizabeth Synnot (1855-22/11/1933) married David
Boswell **Reid** (1835 -   ) in 1875; had issue.
5. David Monckton Synnot Reid (1877-19/4/1961)
5. Lawrence Jasper Boswell Reid (1878-21/9/1959)
married Edith Emily Dealtrey (1877-1968)
5. Ann Emily Reid (1879-   ) married Howard Gartney
Challen (-   )
5. Harold de Boisville Boswell Reid (1881-25/10/1955)
4. Richard Walter Synnot (2/3/1857-9/11/1932) lived at
Kalamunda, W.A. (buried in Guildford cemetery) married
Marie Louise De La Greverie (1852-5/8/1939) 24/2/1853
in Melbourne, Victoria.
Marie was born at Niévre, Bourgogne, France. Died in WA;
had issue.
5. Richard Boswell Synnot (25/3/1883-21/10/1947) lived
at Esperance, WA.
5. Nathalie Lucy Synnot (1886-16/6/1973) lived in
Canning (in Perth hills) WA.
5. Annie Synnot (-   )
5. Maude Marie Synnot (-   )
4. John Patrick Synnot (25/4/1858-25/2/1891) married
Caroline Marie St. John (16/6/1861-   ) 13/12/1881.
4. Marcus Synnot (1860-1946) married Argentina Theresa

Margaret Todd (-   ) 1889; Died in Melbourne, Victoria; had issue.

5. Marcus Seton Synnot (1909-1982) lived in Melbourne, Victoria.

Married . . .

(i) Annette Mary Powell (-   ) 1937; had issue.

   6. Ronald (-   )

(ii) Ilse Simon (-   ) 1960.

4. Lucy Ann Synnot (1862-1911) married Edward William **Vaux** (-   ) 1892.

4. George Houston Synnot (23/9/1863-10/8/1932) married Ellen Teresa Deasy(-   ).

5. Ellen Lucy Synnot (1887-28/10/1967) married Francis Heron **Pitcher** (c.1892-6/11/1957) lived in WA.

5. Gladys Juliet Monckton Synnot (1892-8/1/1993) Married John George Sexton **Mayhew** (17/6/1896-31/3/1969) lived in WA.

5. Dorothy Maud Synnot (23/2/1893-12/5/1993) lived in WA.

5. George Houston Synnot (10/3/1895-10/4/1940) Enlisted for service abroad on 20th July 1915 and served in WWI achieving the rank of Sergeant (No. 3844) in the 11th Australian Field Artillery Brigade, A.I.F. Awarded the Meritorious Service Medal in 1918, for services rendered during the battle of Passchendaele, Jul-Nov. 1917, in Belgium. Married Hazel Jean Ellen Marshall (1899-12/4/1968) 1927; lived in WA.

5. Aileen Beatrice Synnot (1901-3/4/1963) married Francis (Frank) Henry **Powell** (1902-11/4/1959) lived in WA

4. Alice Maud Synnot* (1864-1951) a nursing sister, lived in Victoria.
4. Pierce Wedge Synnot (1867-1911) unmarried.
4. Mary Synnot* (1868-1946) a nursing sister, lived in Victoria.
4. Stephen Bolane (Jack) Synnot (10/1/1870-1949) married Alice Catherine Waters (c.1863-1937) 18/9/1893, lived in Victoria; had issue.
   5. Nugent Bolane Synnot (5/4/1896-7/7/1935) an engineer, BA (Cambridge, UK) lived in Victoria.
   5. Stella Maud Lawrence Synnot (-17/10/1979) married Harry **McKinley** (28/12/1890-19/12/1952) 10/6/1920, lived in Vic; had issue.
      6. Gordon Bolane McKinley (2/4/1921-   ) a dentist, married Joan Margaret Walker (-) 1949, lived at Ballarat, Victoria; had issue.
        7. Andrew Gordon McKinley (20/12/1949-   ) an international oarsman and dentist, BDSc. (Univ. of Melbourne) lived at Ballarat, Vic. Married . . .
        (i) Janet Beckingsdale (-)19/5/1972; had issue.
          8. Andrew Campbell McKinley (30/1/1975-)
          8. Kate Elizabeth McKinley (19/8/1977-)
        (ii) Linda Florence Baynam (-) 12/5/1983
        (iii) Virginia Ann Corden (-) 12/8/1989; had issue.

---

*Alice and Mary Synnot managed an army hospital in Durban (RSA) during the Boer War (1899-1902). One of their patients was fianceé of Alice. He was later killed in action during this war. They also worked in army hospitals in England and France during the Great War of 1914-18.

8. Benjamin James Corden McKinley (22/11/1990-   )
8. Stephanie Ann Corden McKinley (18/2/1993-)
7. Susan Elizabeth McKinley (21/1/1951-   )
7. Elizabeth Anne McKinley (2/9/1955-   ) A medical librarian, married Charles Richard **de Fegely** (-   ) 19/4/1980. Lived at *Quamby*, Ararat, Victoria; had issue.
  8. William Richard de Fegely (1/11/1982-   )
  8. Richard Gordon de Fegely (18/6/1985-   )
  8. Alistair Gordon Strachan de Fegely (30/1/1989-   )
6. Geoffrey Alexander McKinley (18/2/1923-   ) BAgr.Sc. (Melb. Univ.) married Joyce Lynette Lay (-   ) 27/2/1951) lived in Victoria; had issue.
7. Jane Amanda McKinley (23/1/1953-   ) married Robert Cameron **Galbraith** (-   ), BSc. Forestry (Melbourne Univ.), lived in Victoria; had issue.
  8. Penelope Jane Galbraith (29/10/1991-)
  8. Hamish Robert Ian Galbraith (9/6/1993-   )
7. James Geoffrey McKinley (20/7/1954-   ) an accountant, lived in Victoria. Married Susan Rose Wiseman (-   ) 30/10/1987; had issue.
  8. Sophie Rose McKinley (3/2/1989-   )
  8. Thomas James McKinley (22/4/1991-)
6. Noel Anne Lawrence McKinley (12/12/1932-   ) married Jeremy Barton **Marrie** (-   ) 25/11/1959; had issue
7. Jane Anna Lawrence Marrie (29/12/1967-   ) BA (Melbourne Univ.) a law librarian.

Chapter 6

MARY ANN LAWRENCE
(1821-1881)

Mary Ann was the eldest daughter of W.E.L. and the only daughter to leave a continuing line of descendants. She married Francis Henty on 15th January, 1842 at St John's Anglican Church, Launceston and then went with him to live at Portland, Victoria. Francis was the youngest of the Henty brothers who emigrated with their father, Thomas (1775-1839) from West Tarring, Sussex, England, to Australia in 1829 and 1831.[1]

Mary Ann Henty

The family first lived in Western Australia then moved to Tasmania in 1832. This did not prove to be a total success mainly because of land problems, and Francis and his elder brother Edward (1810-1878) moved to Portland Bay – Edward landing there on 19th November, 1834 and Francis a month later. They had been settled there for some months before the settlement on Port Phillip Bay by John Batman and others. The full story of the role the Henty family played in the early settlement of Australia is given in "The Hentys" by Marnie Bassett.[2] Following, is an extract quoted from an introduction to this fascinating account of a pioneer family in this country:

"Thomas Henty, a leading Merino sheep breeder in Sussex, sold his farm and emigrated to Australia with his wife, his only daughter, and his seven sons. He had been tempted by the favorable reports of the new colony to be formed at the Swan River (Western Australia) and sent three of his sons as an advance guard to take up a selection there. Disillusionment met them in the colony and they eventually moved to Van Diemen's Land (now Tasmania) where the family reunited. They arrived just too late to secure a land grant, and protracted negotiations with the Government to secure a concession were unavailing.

Thomas sent the boys ranging far and wide in search of suitable land. On one trip Edward saw Portland Bay in the Port Phillip District of New South Wales (later to become Victoria) where the boys eventually engaged in pioneering ventures like grazing, whaling and wool growing. But the family was not to be permitted to reap at once the full benefit of their efforts.

For ten years they had to fight to establish rights to the land, a struggle which meant several trips to Sydney to argue with the Governor in person, and where a brother-in-law, Richard Windeyer, a prominent New South Wales barrister, was able to assist them. Eventually they were forced to accept an unfair compromise. The brothers, who stayed in Tasmania, also achieved for themselves positions of importance: William, a solicitor and politician, Charles, a bank manager and James, a leading businessman both in Launceston and Melbourne.

A family so large and widely scattered as this, made many friends and not a few enemies. Even the only daughter married into a family which was at cross purposes with the authorities

– they boasted, in fact, that they had brought about the recall of Governor Arthur. Principally, the story is of the educated settler in a new land, whether in town or bush, of his success and failure, his days of danger and his years of steady toil, his relations with his fellow settlers and all powerful Governors, his loneliness, his love affairs, his marriage, and the work of husband and wife in creating a new home in the wilderness."

Mary Ann first lived at Francis Henty's Portland house, *Claremont* (in Julia Street), and then moved inland to be mistress at *Merino Downs* near the present-day town of Henty; nearby were the other Henty properties of *Muntham* and *Sandford*. The marriage produced four children, two of whom married and continued the line.

Caroline (1849-1914) married Alexander MacLeod, a member of Clan MacLeod from the Isle of Skye. The MacLeods lived at *Talisker*, Merino, Victoria, which consisted of a portion of *Merino Downs* plus land belonging to the MacLeod family (the house there is a fine example of early colonial architecture, and was built around 1898). *Talisker* passed out of the family in 1965 on the retirement of the grandson, Alexander Silvester (1918-2001).

The third daughter of Francis and Mary Henty, Alice (1852-1932) married John Hindson and lived at *Shrublands*, Canterbury, Melbourne and later at *Seacombe*, Sorrento. Both these properties were later bequeathed to the Anglican Church.

Descendants of the sisters Caroline and Alice live mainly in Victoria, but also other parts of Australia – many of them on properties in the original area in Western Victoria first settled by Edward and Francis Henty. These include *Merino Downs*, *Girrahween*, *Wurt Wurt Koort*, *Iona* and *Worthing* and the local towns of Henty and Merino, reflect the name of the early settlers and their occupations.

Genealogy

2. Mary Ann Lawrence (5/8/1821-27/11/1881) married Francis **Henty** (30/11/1815-15/1/1889) 5/1/1842; lived in Western Victoria; had issue.
   3. Lawrence Shum Henty (9/4/1845-10/2/1877) unmarried: studied at Cambridge University.
   3. Louisa Henty (14/8/1847-24/7/1924) unmarried.
   3. Caroline Agnes Henty (29/8/1849-1/10/1914) married Alexander Magnus **MacLeod** (7/8/1846-19/7/1910); lived at *Talisker*, Merino, Victoria; had issue.
      4. Caroline Agnes Henty MacLeod (29/10/1892-2/4/1943) married Kenneth **McWhae** (24/2/1892-2/4/1943); both died when they were passengers on the cargo ship *Melbourne Star* en route from Scotland to Australia which was torpedoed by the German submarine U-129 in the Atlantic Ocean, 480 miles southeast of Bermuda. The ship sank within minutes and there were only eleven survivors (on two *Carley* floats[*]) out of the one hundred and seventeen passengers and crew on board.[3]
      After being questioned by the crew of the U-Boat the survivors were left to their own devices. Four, set adrift on one float, were rescued after 38 days.
      The seven on the other float were never found and presumably perished. Had issue.
         5. John Henty McWhae (28/1/1917-8/2/1943); served in the Royal Navy (Fleet Air Arm) in World War II. He died while aboard an aircraft from *HMS Devonshire*

---

[*]A large emergency raft, carried on board a ship, consisting of a buoyant canvas ring with a wooden grid deck.

which crashed in the sea off the Queensland coast and was buried in the Townsville War Cemetery.

4. Alexandra Frances McLeod (31/1/1892-3/9/1943) married Grenville Archer **Silvester** (15/7/1883-20/5/1933) 12/10/1915, a solicitor at Casterton, Victoria; had issue.

5. Caroline Mary Silvester (7/10/1916-   ) married Ronald Andrew **Gilling** (27/10/1917-   ) 22/6/1944; lived at Kirribilli, Sydney; had issue.

6. Julienne Henty Gilling (10/10/1945-   )

6. Caroline Henty Gilling (7/10/1947-   ) married Ian James **Grace** (-   ), 6/9/1969; had issue.

7. Nicole Grace (-   )

5. Alexander Noel Henty Silvester (25/12/1918-31/7/2001) married Ethel Colton Gilkes (9/9/1918-5/3/1993) 29/4/1944; lived at *Talisker* 1948-1965, then in East Malvern, Melbourne and latterly at Bairnsdale in eastern Victoria; had issue.

6. Alexander Henty Silvester (10/1/1946-   ) a solicitor.

6. Ian John Henty Silvester (22/8/1948-   ) an accountant.

6. Mary Anne Henty Silvester (4/6/1954-   )

5. Francis Henty (26/2/1920-2/1/1990) married Diana Henty Smallpage (-   ) and lived at *Girrahween*, Merino; had issue.

6. Gael Henty Silvester (8/8/1946-   )

6. Robyn Henty Silvester (28/3/1948-   ) married Barry **Blake** (-   ) 7/4/1972.

6. Grenville Henty Silvester (7/4/1951-   )

3. Alice Henty (8/2/1852-16/12/1932) married John **Hindson** (9/12/1839-4/4/1919), 15/4/1875, and lived at *Wurt-Wurt-koort*, Henty; had issue.
4. William Francis Hindson (6/3/1876-25/1/1921) married Ada Butler (-), no issue.
4. Ruby Alice Hindson (2/12/1978-17/2/1945), unmarried.
4. Elsie Mary Eliza Hindson (14/3/1880-29/7/1968) unmarried.
4. John Lawrence Henty Hindson (17/6/1883-   ) married Margaret Grace Burland (18/5/   -1962); had issue.
  5. Alice Henty Hindson (31/3/1914-2/2/2005) married Norman Lithgow **Tait** (5/11/1917-7/8/1967) 24/4/1943, and lived at Creswick, Vic.; had issue.
    6. Evelyn Margaret Tait (12/4/1945-   ) married H. J. **Sheldrick** (-) 21/2/1969.
    6. Sandra Marian Tait (25/9/1946-   ) married W. O. **Trainor** (-) 28/11/1970.
  5. Beth Henty Hindson (5/3/1916-   ) married Graham Glover **Anderson** (2/10/1919-   )(assumed the name **Henty-Anderson**) 15/3/1944 and lived at *Merino Downs*, Henty; had issue.
    6. Francis Henty-Anderson (20/5/1954-   )
  5. Margaret Henty Hindson (1/1/1918-   ) married Dougald Webster **Matheson** (-) 12/1/1944, and lived at *Iona* Henty; had issue.
    6. Anne Margaret Matheson (21/1/1947-   )
    6. Judith Louise Matheson (1/5/1951-   )
  5. John Henty Hindson (25/9/1923-   ) married Norma Anne Devereux (-) 1/11/1952, and lived at *Worthing* Henty; had issue.

6. Christine Alice Hindson (18/6/1954-   )
6. Geoffrey Henty Hindson (20/9/1955-   )
6. Stephen James Henty Hindson (6/3/1957-   )
6. Jennifer Anne Henty Hindson (5/7/1960-   )
4. Louisa Charlotte Frances Hindson (24/4/1885-
28/9/1963) unmarried; lived at *Seacombe*, Sorrento,
Victoria.
4. Winnifred Caroline Henty Hindson (11/8/1887-1967);
unmarried.
4. Dora Henty Hindson (1/6/1890-28/12/1990)

Notes

Notes

112

Chapter 7

WILLIAM LAWRENCE
(1823-1898)

This branch of the family lived mainly in New Zealand (Southland) and many of the sons were engaged in the pastoral industry. William was the third son of W. E. Lawrence and, while he inherited *Formosa* from his brother Robert, after the death of the latter in 1833, he never lived there. Details of his life are rather scarce but we do know that he travelled extensively as evidenced by two of his passports, issued in London on 21/3/1851 and 12/8/1853. These contain entries concerning travel to Constantinople (Istanbul), southern Europe, Germany, France and England in the period 1851-1855. He was married to Isabella Lannon, at St. John's Parish church, Cork, Ireland, on 7th October, 1861.

William apparently settled at *Verulam*, near Invercargill, Southland, and had interests in several other properties. His sons Cornelius ("Con") (1864-1940), Samuel (1866-1913) and George (1870-1943) were educated at Kew High School, Melbourne (later Trinity Grammar School) and then worked at Makarewa (a locality 7 km from Invercargill) in partnership from 1890-1899.

Con, in particular, was obviously well thought of locally as a pastoralist and a businessman, and in the early 1900s when he and the family moved back to Australia, a silver tray was presented to "Mr and Mrs C. H. Lawrence, as a token of esteem by the residents of Hedgehope, Southland, NZ, 7/2/1903". He lived at *Formosa* from 1905, but was forced by ill-health to retire to Geelong in 1914. He eventually died in East Camberwell, Melbourne,

1/1/1949, and was buried in the Burwood Cemetery. His cousin, Leonard Lawrence (1883-1967) managed *Formosa* for much of the period 1914-1949 finally purchasing the property from his estate in 1949. Con's two sons, Cecil and Roy, both attended Longeronong Agricultural College, Vic., and both died within a few months of each other in 1926 – Cecil from tuberculosis and Roy following a tree lopping accident. Cecil managed *Formosa* for a brief period prior to his death.

Of the other sons of William Lawrence, Sam inherited *Verulam* but lived at Makarewa, NZ, as did his son Bill (1899-1967). George was a pastoralist at *Greenhead*, Hedgehope, Southland, NZ.

Genealogy

2. William Lawrence (16/12/1823-29/8/1898) inherited *Formosa* from Robert William Lawrence but never lived there; a pastoralist at *Verulam*, Invercargill, Southland, New Zealand. Married Mary Isabella Lannon (1839-22/7/1875) 7/10/1861 in Ireland. Mary died at Makarewa, NZ. In his latter years William moved to Melbourne, Victoria, where he died; had issue.*

    3. Alfred William Lawrence (26/9/1862-4/7/1900) unmarried, died in Victoria.

    3. Cornelius Henry Lawrence (7/2/1864-1/1/1940) born at Makarewa, Invercargill, NZ; married Mary Lind (1880-1954); had issue.

*There was another William Lawrence (1825-   ) who lived in the Longford area, married, and had a son Thomas (1859-   ). It is thought he was not a member of the family of W E Lawrence.

4. Iris Maude Lawrence (1899-1957) trained as a landscape gardener at Burnley Horticultural College; went to England in 1927 and joined an Anglican religious order; died in England, unmarried, in 1957.

4. Cecil Effingham Lawrence (1900-1926) attended Longeronong Agricultural College, Horsham, Vic., and managed *Formosa* 1923-1926; unmarried.

4. Daphne Victoria Lawrence (3/2/1903-1972) married Robert James **Simpson** (17/9/1902-10/5/1972) 10/3/1933 and lived at *Colleen*, Alexandra, Vic.; trained as a commercial artist; had issue.

  5. Robert Lawrence Simpson (5/3/1934-3/11/2017) a computer consultant and ex-Kings Cup oarsman (Victoria 1955/1956); BChem.Eng. (Univ. of Melb.); MEng. (Yale Univ.); lived in Melbourne; married Jean MacSporan (8/8/1940-   ) 19/1/1966; had issue.

    6. Robert Donald Euan Simpson (30/9/1967-28/2/2014)

    6. Fiona Lawrence Simpson (24/4/1969-   ) lived in Queensland; married Nicholas John Sweet (-   ) 1/2/1992; had issue.

      7. Jamie Nicholas Sweet (18/4/1993-   ); married Helen Duncan (-   ) 2/1/2015

      7. Lachlan Donald Sweet (19/4/1996-   )

      7. Asher John Sweet (24/4/2003-   )

      7. Grace Elizabeth Sweet (7/11/2005-   )

    6. Michael Stewart Simpson (28/5/1974-   ) lived in Melbourne, married Brooke Dellios (-   ) 27/6/2009; had issue.

      7. Sibylla Olive Simpson (19/4/2016-   )

  5. William Alexander Simpson (17/9/1937-   )

graduated BCom (Univ. of Melb.) and worked in Melbourne with the Department of Trade; a first class golfer. Married . . .

(i) Judith Mary Fleming (2/12/1938-17/2/1991) 12/8/1961; had issue.

6. Andrew William Simpson (20/8/1963-   ); graduate of Glenormiston Agricultural College (Vic.), BBus. (Swinburne Univ.) CPA; married Amanda Catherine Ryan (25/2/1964-   ) 8/2/1992; had issue.

7. Chloe Judith Simpson (8/12/1995-   )
7. Ella-Rose Joan Simpson (11/5/2001-   )

6. David James Simpson (15/1/1966-   ) BMech. Eng. (RMIT Melbourne) a project engineer, married Jane Melissa Noble (22/7/1964-   ) 7/4/1990; had issue.

7. Jackson Thomas Simpson (1/1/1992-   )

6. Richard Gregory Simpson (4/12/1969-   ) BBus. (Victoria Univ., Melbourne) Commercial Finance Manager; married Samantha Lisa Bradley (9/1/1969-   ) a registered nurse; 11/11/1995; had issue.

7. Georgie Patricia Simpson (26/10/1999-   )
7. Thomas Benjamin Simpson (29/1/2002-   )
7. James Richard Simpson (22/3/2004-   )
7. Alexander Brian Simpson (16/12/2006-   )

(ii) Robin Beverley Taylor-Clark (18/10/1938-   ) (second wife of William Alexander Simpson) 1/4/1999.

5. Barbara Anne Simpson (8/5/1940-   ) married Thomas Hugh **Thompson** (5/1/1935-   ) 8/5/1965 and lived at Point Lonsdale, Victoria; had issue.

6. Janice Leanne Thompson (30/4/1969-   ) a child centre director; lived at Mosman, NSW. Married Troy **Creamer** (-   )March 2016.
6. Thomas James Thompson (2/2/1967-   ) a photographer, lived at Geraldton, WA.
4. Dorothy Frances Lawrence (25/12/1904-21/4/1984), a kindergarten teacher, married Arthur Leslie **Park** (18/7/1905-6/4/1994) 1939, from Sunderland, England; BA (London Univ.) LLB (Univ. of Melbourne) and later a Principal of the Melbourne Law firm, McKean & Park, lived at Middle Brighton, Victoria; had issue.
5. Richard Lawrence Park (5/11/1940-10/7/2010) graduated LLB (Univ. of Melbourne 1963) and joined McKean & Park; lived at Albert Park, Melbourne. Married Alison May Dodds (20/5/1951-   ); no issue.
5. Geoffrey Arthur Park (26/1/1943-   ) graduated LLB (Univ. of Melbourne 1965) and also joined McKean & Park; rowed for Victoria in the Penrith Cup in 1965, married Joyce Rogan (10/1/1946-   ) 22/8/1969; had issue.
6. Dean Rogan Park (3/2/1972-   ) married Catherine Diana Farquharson (26/5/1973-   ) lived in Melbourne; had issue.
7. Skye Farquharson Park (11/12/2005-   )
7. Alexandra Catherine Park (20/8/2007-   )
7. Thomas Geoffrey Park (1/2/2010-   )
6. Sally Margery Park (28/1/1974-   ) married Timothy Jackson **Gillard** (15/5/1973-   ) lived in Melbourne; had issue.
7. Nicholas Park Gillard (18/9/2006-   )

7. Elizabeth Christine Gillard (3/10/2008-   )
7. Matthew Geoffrey Gillard (16/6/2011-   )
6. Angela Lawrence Park (17/4/1977-   ) married
Richard Hordern **Bligh** (14/12/1975-   ) lived at
Sale, Victoria; had issue.
7. Abigail Park Bligh (6/3/2008-   )
7. Georgiana Sally Bligh (14/1/2010-   )
7. Edward Michael Bligh (20/9/2012-   )
4. Roy William Lawrence (1906-1926) attended
Longeronong Agricultural College then lived at *Mt.
Mercer*, near Ballarat, Vic. until his death following a tree
lopping accident.
3. Samuel Billopp Lawrence (10/1/1866-9/12/1913) a
pastoralist; lived at Makarewa, Southland, NZ; married Jane
Hyslop (23/12/1876-28/4/1962); had issue.
4. William Lawrence (1899-1967) married Esther Victoria
Coutts (1901-27/2/1975) and lived at Makarewa; had
issue.
5. Linda Lawrence (Aug 1933-   ) married Maurice
Jones (-   ) (Production Manager for the New
Zealand Wool Board) lived in Wellington; had issue.
6. Glenda Jones (-   )
6. Shelley Jones (-   )
4. Beatrice Jane Lawrence (1901-   ) married Gordon
Gilmour (-   ) and lived in Invercargill; no issue.
4. May Isabella Lawrence (1906-   ) married Walter
Lionel **Bews** (-   ) and lived in Central Otago; had
issue (two sons and two daughters, all married; had issue.)
No other details available.
4. Louise Ellen Lawrence (1909-   ) married Ray **Martin**
and lived in Wellington, NZ; had issue.

5. Gay Martin (1/1/1933-   ) married; had issue.
  6. Mark Watson Martin (3/9/1963-   )
  6. James Lawrence Martin (15/9/1965-   )
5. Gillian Martin (13/10/1935-   ) married; had issue.
  6. Stephen Martin (22/7/1962-   )
  6. Bettina Ann Martin (9/3/1963-   )
  6. Phillip Ramon Martin (20/3/1966-   )
3. Maria Jane Lawrence (1866-17/5/1926) married Dr. Gilbert John King **Martyn** (1869-5/12/1950) 18/7/1905; lived in Paddington, London, England; no issue
3. Harriet Lawrence (8/12/1868-12/12/1943) unmarried. Lived and died in UK.
3. Robert Effingham Lawrence (31/7/1869-4/5/1939) born in New Zealand (but birth not registered until 1871), attended Launceston Church Grammar School 1885; married Myra Lillian DeVaney (1886/1892-1/1/1944) born in Ulverstone; 1906; had issue.
  4. Robert William Lawrence (18/05/1910-14/7/2004) married Signa Ho Sing (8/02/1914-26/4/2004); had issue.
    5. Peter Wayne Lawrence (22/2/1938-18/6/2011) married Kim Frances Brundle (23/8/1955-   ) 13/12/1975. Kim Brundle-Lawrence, OAM, was awarded the Order of Australia medal (OAM) June 2019 for services to the community of northern Tasmania; lived at Carrick, Tasmania.
    5. Robert Effingham Lawrence (18/11/1947-   ) Married ...
  (i) Christine Monaghan (28/4/1950-   ) 21/8/1970; had issue.
    6. Andrew Robert Lawrence (18/2/1971-   ) married Anne-Marie Musika (-   ).

(ii) Judith Lorraine Donnelly (17/1/1950-   )
14/4/1984.

4. Leo Effingham Lawrence (18/08/1925-25/01/1997)
unmarried; lived in Brisbane.

4. Dorothy Mabel Lawrence (6/3/1913-   ) married Sidney
Frederick **Evans** (-9/01/1997) 20/01/1945; had
issue.

   5. Nigel Leo Evans (14/3/1947-   ) married Susan
   Scott (-   ) 19/9/1969; had issue.
      6. David Leigh Evans (8/7/1973-   )

4. Phyllis Lillian Lawrence (12/6/1907-22/9/1983) married
Alfred Sylvester **Woolston** (7/3/1910-15/9/1974)
electrician; had issue.

   5. Beverley Myra Woolston (21/9/1929-11/7/2009)
   married Kevin Herbert **Pennicott** (15/6/1926-
   19/12/2002) a school principal, 12/5/1950; had issue.
      6. Graeme John Pennicott (27/2/1955-   )
      Married . . .
      (i) Sue Miller (-   ) 10/1/1976; no issue.
      (ii) Geraldine Kaye Ingram (17/10/1959-   )
         12/10/1981; had issue.
            7. Liam Guthrie Pennicott (17/8/1983-11/9/2017)
            partnered Clare Dunlop (-   ); had issue.
            8. Poppy Arlo Pennicott (24/4/2013-   )
            8. Hugo Jasper Pennicott (24/11/2015-   )
            7. Emma Leila Pennicott (1/9/1985-   ) married
            Ben **Galvin** (28/8/   -   ) 15/1/2012; had issue.
            8. Percival (Percy) Hobbins Galvin (4/9/2014-   )
            8. Theodore (Teddy) Galvin (29/1/2017-   )
      6. Julie Maree Pennicott (12/4/1956-8/3/2010)
      Married . . .

(i) Rod Taylor (-   ) 6/4/1979. Divorced
(ii) Donald Vaughan **Telfer** (8/5/1952-   )
    23/12/1991; had issue.
    7. Alexandra Julie Telfer (10/1/1992-   ) lived in
       Perth, WA.
6. Diane Louise Pennicott (12/4/1956-   )
Married . . .
(i) Cranston Charles **Claridge** (2/8/1954-22/4/1981)
  7/2/1981
(ii) David **Wotherspoon** (-   ), divorced.
(iii) James (Jim) Simon **Heritage** (12/4/1954-   )
    16/9/1989
6. Timothy James Pennicott (2/4/1965-   )
    married Anita Maree Nettlefold (31/3/1962-   )
    11/11/2000; had issue.
    7. Sarah Jane Pennicott (7/2/2001 -   ) an
       Australian representative at ten pin bowling.
  5. Barry Effingham Woolston (21/12/1944-27/6/2014)
    married Vicki Bornstein (30/1/1950-   ) 7/10/1972;
    had issue.
    6. Christopher James Woolston (16/10/1979-   )
      partnered Sarah Bailey; had issue.
    7. Sebastion Woolston (/ /2012-   )
    7. Mayer Woolston (14/12/2014-   )
3. George Lawrence (6/5/1870-24/10/1943) married
  Elizabeth Shaw Hyslop (17/4/1878-7/2/1928) 17/5/1904,
  lived at *Greenhead*, Hedgehope, Southland; NZ; had issue.
  4. Herman Firma Lawrence (25/6/1911-24/11/1976)
    unmarried.
  4. Dora Elsie Lawrence (13/1/1913-22/8/2004) married
    Joseph Henry **Sharp** (18/1/1906-7/2/1992); had issue.

5. Melva Elizabeth Sharp (26/11/1950-   ) married Robert John **Wilson** (9/2/1948-   ); had issue.
   6. Lisa Jane Wilson (21/12/1968-   ) married Stephen **McLauchlan** (-   ) 31/1/2002; had issue.
      7. Clark John McLauchlan (18/11/2002-   )
      7. Ella Lucia McLauchlan (24/11/2004-   )
   6. Brendan John Wilson (9/3/1973-   ) married Helen Badcock (-   ) 29/3/2008; had issue.
      7. Bonnie Wilson (26/5/2009-   )
      7. Stevie Belle Wilson (6/12/2010-   )
      7. Mae Wilson (4/10/2012-   )
   6. Aimee Nicole Wilson (30/10/1976-   ) partnered John **Kilgour** (-   ); had issue.
      7. Lucas Robert Kilgour (4/2/2010-   )
      7. Isla Paige Kilgour (26/1/2012-   )
4. Dorothy Thelma Lawrence (3/3/1915-1999) married Joseph **West** (-12/12/1977) 23/3/1942; had issue.
   5. Owen Leslie Lawrence West (14/9/1937-   ) married Relda Eileen Blondell (12/7/1940-   ); had issue.
      6. Carol Lesley West (9/10/1957-   ) married Murray Donald **Graham** (18/12/1951-   ); had issue.
         7. Hannah Kylie Graham (2/4/1982-   ) married Craig **Drummond** (-   ); had issue.
            8. Briar Honor Drummond (12/2/2013-   )
            8. Luke James Drummond (9/8/2016-   )
         7. Kirsty Alice Graham (13/4/1985-   )
      6. Lynette Ann West (1/11/1958-   )
      Married ...
      (i) Graeme Lex **Dyet** (-   ); had issue.

7. JoAnna Maree Dyet (21/6/1975-   )
(i) Married Gavin **McLay** (-   ); had issue.
   8. Chloe Ann McLay (4/2/1999-   )
   8. Taylor James McLay (8/9/2002-   )
(ii) Partnered Scott **Beal**; had issue
   8. Lily Beal (21/11/2007-   )
7. Carl Lance Dyet (18/4/1978-   ) married Kelly
   Phillips (-   ); had issue.
   8. Olivia Dyet (6/12/2002-   )
   8. Emma Dyet (11/9/2004-   )
   8. Lauren Dyet (12/2/2008-   )
(ii) Brian Raymond **Hughes** (-   ) (second
   husband of Lynette Ann West)
6. Rodney Allan West (11/1/1960-1978)
6. Joan Lea West (5/10/1962-   ) married Brent
   David **Wilson** (-   ); had issue.
   7. Terie Lea Wilson (28/9/1986-   )
   (i) partnered Graeme **Moss** (-   ); had issue.
      8. Caleb Wilson Moss (6/9/2006-   )
   (ii) married Steven Alford (-   ); had issue.
      8. Keira Lea Alford (5/2/2013-   )
   7. Christopher Lawrence Wilson (1988-   )
      partnered Katie Blakie (-   ); had issue.
      8. Ruby Lea Wilson (5/1/2017-   )
6. John Owen West (20/10/1970-   ) partnered
   Catherine Ivar (-   ); had issue.
   7. Shaun Owen West (12/11/2004-   )
5. Lois Joan West (4/9/1942-   ) married   Alastair
Hansen (-   ) 2/3/1962; had issue.
   6. Joanne Helen Hansen (6/8/1963-   ) married Paul
   Birtwhistle (9/11/1963-   ) 26/1/1989; had issue.

7. Samantha Emma Birtwhistle (30/12/1989-   )
married Kain James **Martin** (7/8/1989-   ); had
issue.
    8. Enzo James Martin (18/10/2016-   )
    8. Xander James Martin (25/10/2018-   )
7. Thomas James Birtwhistle (4/1/1994-   )
partnered Sophie Ruecker (-   ); had issue.
    8. Mia Birtwhistle (14/5/2013-   )
    8. Teo Birtwhistle (28/3/2017-   )
6. Robyn Joy Hansen (6/10/1964-   ) married Peter
Waaka (-   ) 4/2/1995; had issue.
    7. Alyssa Rangitamoe Waaka (12/2/1996-   )
    7. Jamie Te-rohu Waaka (5/7/1997-   )
6. Stuart Alastair Hansen (22/6/1969-   )
5. Kenneth James West (3/10/1943-   )
(i) married Marie Daniel (-   ); had issue.
    6. Dean West (-   )
    6. Nathan West (-   )
(ii) partnered Lil Te Puke (-   ); had issue.
    6. Joseph West (-   ); had issue.
        7. Gayvain West (-   )
5. Ronald Henry West (28/2/1945-   ) married Coleen
Jane Coster (-   ); had issue.
    6. Viki Jane West (9/11/1966-   ) married Neville
    Joseph Cory (-   ); had issue.
        7. Amy Jane Cory (3/11/1991-   )
        7. Jason Thomas Cory (26/7/1995-   ) married
        Jacki Benn (-   ).
    6. Mark Jason West (20/6/1971-   ) married Karen
    Gail Cliff (-   ) 20/10/1995; had issue.
        7. Josh Keegan West (27/9/1999-   )

7. Ben Jason West (10/2/2002-   )
7. Jodi Brooke West (17/1/2004-   )
6. Pania Anne Marie West (1976-   ); had issue.
  7. Stephen Sommerville (-   ); had issue
    8. Maurece Waetford (-   )
    8. Mania   (-   )
    8. Malcia   (-   )
    8. Mahalia   (-   )
5. Jean Dorothy West (27/7/1946-   ) married Tom
Brown (-   ); had issue.
  6. Carmen Lee Brown (1971-   ); had issue.
    7. Jason Waetford Brown (-   )
    7. Blake Stingel Brown (-   )
    7. Jade Dye Brown (-   )
  6. Jodeen Lara Brown (1972-   ); had issue.
    7. Jazim Hatherly Brown (-   )
    7. Henri Brown (-   )
5. Linda Elizabeth West (12/9/1948-4/8/1986) married
Jock **Rhind** (-   ) 1968; had issue.
  6. Brenda Rhind (20/9/1968-   ) married Rodger
  Strang (7/12/1965-   ) 14/10/1994.
  6. Mervyn John Rhind (8/6/1970-   )
  6. Clarke Raymond Rhind (18/4/1974-   ) married
  Nardine Frost (24/7/1974-   ) 18/11/2000; had
  issue.
    7. Nathan John Rhind (20/10/2003-   )
    7. Harry Earl Rhind (9/11/2006-   )
5. John Phillip West (12/9/1948-2/5/1999) married
Hilary Ann Roden Ingill (19/10/1949-   )
18/7/1969; had issue.
  6. Sharon Kimberley West (21/1/1971-   ) partnered

Michael **Rodney** (-   ); had issue.
    7. Jarrod Phillip Rodney (23/10/1993-   )
    7. Teneeka Jane Rodney (23/10/1993-   )
    7. Caleb Dane Rodney (9/3/1998-   )
  6. Kylie Marie West (15/11/1972-   ) married Michael **Donaghy**; had issue.
    7. Angus John Donaghy (8/2/2012-   )
    7. Tait Marie Donaghy (3/3/2014-   )
5. Allan Alexander West (16/10/1952-   ) married Dell Humphrey (-   ); had issue.
  6. Arron West (17/10/1979-   )
  6. Sarah West (5/11/1981-   ) married Edgar Jos Gonzaleš **Prada** (-   ); had issue.
    7. Marley Prada (-   )
    7. Haille Prada (-   )
5. Denise Ann West (24/2/1954-27/7/2014) married Terrance Michael **Dowling** (-   ) 25/4/1971; had issue.
  6. Kitina Dowling (24/10/1971-   ) married Scott **Little** (-   ) 24/2/2001; had issue.
    7. Jack Little (9/8/2006-   )
    7. Harry Little (31/10/2007-   )
    7. Tom Little (12/7/2010-   )
  6. Nardon Dowling (3/9/1973-   )
  6. Adam Dowling (8/5/1975-   )
  6. Lisa Dowling (6/12/1978-   ); had issue.
    7. Emma Dowling (8/1/2005-   )
    7. Katie Dowling (3/4/2007-   )
4. Vera Effie Lawrence (24/6/1916-1954)
4. Isabelle Gwendoline Lawrence (13/2/1918-10/2/1984)

Chapter 8

ELIZA LAWRENCE
(1825-1844)

Eliza Lawrence was the second daughter of W. E. Lawrence and died on Flinders Island at the age of eighteen from complications following childbirth. She married Dr. Joseph Milligan (16/3/1843), a brother of Alexander Murray Milligan (1812-1883, p. 235) who was the third husband of Mrs. W. E. Lawrence.

Dr. Milligan was a surgeon and had come to Van Diemen's Land in 1831. After the marriage they lived on Flinders Island where Dr. Milligan had been appointed superintendent and medical officer of Aborigines; she died there in 1844. Her grave, in a lonely cemetery near Emita, was pointed out to the author in 1956, long before this genealogy was commenced. Her restored gravestone now has a plaque which reads as follows -

"Eliza, the much loved wife of Joseph Milligan Esq.
and daughter of W. E. Lawrence Esq. M.L.C.
Van Diemens' Land
– departed this life 31st July 1844 the day after her confinement* and in the nineteenth year of her age
– she lived in the practice of every Christian and womanly virtue and died in the full assurance of a better life beyond the grave."

*The discrepancy between the date of birth of the son, Joseph, and the date of death of Eliza is noted, and it is thought that an error may have been made in the transcription from the original headstone to the more recent metal plaque.

Following is the entry on Dr. Milligan in the Australian Dictionary of Biography by W. F. Hoddinott.[1]

"**Milligan, Joseph** (1807-1884), surgeon, was born in Dumfriesshire, Scotland. He obtained the diploma of the Royal College of Surgeons of Edinburgh in January 1829 and in June 1830 was appointed surgeon to the Van Diemen's Land Co's establishment at Surrey Hills, where he arrived in February 1831. During his appointment as surgeon, and later surgeon-superintendent, he became interested in the natural history of the island, formed a close acquaintance with R. C. Gunn and collected specimens for W. J. Hooker.

In February 1842 he left the company and settled briefly in Launceston. He was invited by Lady Franklin to accompany an overland expedition to Macquarie Harbour from March to May that year as medical attendant and naturalist. After his return he held a number of important government positions.

In September he became inspector of convict discipline and a member of the Board for Distributing Convicts.

In March 1843 he married Eliza, second daughter of William Effingham Lawrence of Launceston. She died on Flinders Island on 31st July 1844, after giving birth to a son.

In December 1843 he was appointed superintendent and medical officer of the Aboriginals, a position which he occupied until 1855, except for the period April 1846 to May 1847, when he was visiting magistrate and medical officer at the short-lived second penal settlement at Macquarie Harbour. In October 1847 he supervised the transfer of the Aboriginal settlement, then totalling forty-six persons, from Wybalenna on Flinders Island to Oyster Cove on D'Entrecasteaux channel, south of Hobart, where the numbers dwindled rapidly until in 1854 only sixteen remained. During this period of duty he compiled an extensive "*Vocabulary of the Dialects of Some of the Aboriginal Tribes of Tasmania*" with observations on native languages and customs.[2]

Through his interest in natural history he became secretary of the Royal Society of Van Diemen's Land in 1848 to 1860, its members and activities increasing under his guidance. In 1848 at Lieut. Governor Denison's request, he surveyed the coal resources of the island and in April 1855 became chairman of the Douglas River Coal Mining Co.

In 1856 he explored the eastern slopes of the western mountains for the Fingal Gold Exploration Co.

He was retired from government service with a pension in April 1860, and in June sailed for England with his son, on eighteen months leave from the Royal Society. He did not return to Tasmania but at the exhibition of 1862 acted as Commissioner for Tasmania. He died in London in 1884 leaving £350, as well as land at George Town and Bicheno, Tasmania, to the Royal Society of Tasmania. (However, his estate in England was valued at £16,751 and double probate was charged to his executors.)

Milligan's thirty years in Tasmania were marked by immense industry. His official duties were carried out with conscientiousness and good sense. J. D. Hooker called him "one of the most indefatigable and able of Tasmanian botanists" and gave his name to the native lily genus *Milligania* and a number of species of other plants.[*] He was elected a fellow of the Linnean Society in 1850.

As a geologist he carried out surveys in all parts of the colony, discovering coal, copper and gold as well as numerous fossils.

---

[*]Thirteen endemic plants honour his name; Milligania, and others with suffix 'milliganii'.

But perhaps his most notable work was his study of Aboriginal languages. This permanent contribution to knowledge, although not free from error, was a remarkable achievement for a man who was said to be unacquainted with any language but English."

Genealogy

2. Eliza Lawrence (14 /12/1825-31/7/1844) married Dr. Joseph **Milligan** (3/9/1807-6/12/1884) 16/3/1843, and lived on Flinders Island in Bass Strait after the marriage; had issue.
3. Joseph Lawrence Milligan (21/7/1844-23/10/1867) entered military service and was gazetted to the 14th Hussars (British Army) in 1860. He died while still an active serviceman in England and his certificate of death states "pulmonary consumption, congestion of the lung" as the cause. However, a Launceston newspaper reported that he died at York following a fall from a horse.[3] Joseph Lawrence Milligan's estate was "under £800".

Notes

Chapter 9

JOHN EFFINGHAM LAWRENCE
(1828-1874)

John Effingham Lawrence (J.E.L.) was the fourth son of W. E. Lawrence and lived at *Point Effingham* Estate on the East Tamar, Tasmania. It was bought by his father, and included twelve miles of river frontage near where Bell Bay is today. The size of the Estate was 8800 acres and, in later years, was divided into smaller farms for purposes of leasing – these farms were *Point Effingham*, *Lauriston* and *Williams Creek*. JEL died in 1874 from diphtheria, and the estate was eventually sold to the Archer family in 1900.

John Effingham Lawrence

In 1832, W. E. Lawrence was a founder of the Tamar Steam Navigation Co., and this company, as well as being of importance to *Point Effingham*, played a significant role in developing the entire Tamar River Valley in the years 1832-1846. *Point Effingham* was used as a holiday retreat by W. E. Lawrence and his family and, in early correspondence, there is mention of sailing down-river to the "Point" to spend the summer holidays there.

After the sale of *Point Effingham* this branch of the family has scattered somewhat. Francis Horace Lawrence moved to Melbourne and a son and grandsons worked in the newspaper trade. Leslie Frank lived in New Zealand, and left a large family of descendants. Theodore Ernest also went to New Zealand and died there in the late 1950's. Arthur William had one son who joined the British Army (the Dublin Fusiliers) and was murdered in Aden, as reported in the Melbourne "*Argus*" of 16th September 1924:

"A private cable received in Melbourne from the War Office states that Captain Leonard Lawrence, son of Mrs. Lawrence, formerly of *Pasley*, Domain Road, South Yarra, Victoria was murdered a few days ago at Peerim, near Aden.

Captain Lawrence was well known in society here. He was educated at Geelong Grammar School, and Melbourne University. When the war broke out he was studying medicine at Edinburgh University, and relinquished his course to take a commission in the Imperial Army. Captain Lawrence remained in the army until his death.

Only meager details of the tragedy have been released by the war office. It appears that Captain Lawrence, who had been stationed at Aden, was shot by a sentry, who escaped, and so far as is known here the murderer is still at large.

Captain Lawrence's mother left Melbourne about 18 months ago. After having spent a few months with her son at Aden she went up the Nile. She was accompanied by Miss Gilder. At present she is staying with Dr. and Mrs. McIlwaine, in London.

At one time Mrs. Lawrence was matron at Geelong Grammar School. Later she purchased *The Oaks* and *Pasley*, two of the most fashionable boarding houses in South Yarra. She retired before she left Australia, her intention being to see as much of the world as possible.

Captain Lawrence spent a few months in Australia after the

war. He was a fine soldier, and won several decorations. During the war he was in the Dublin Fusiliers."

Genealogy

2. John Effingham Lawrence (20/3/1828-13/7/1874) lived at *Point Effingham*, East Tamar, Tasmania, married Frances Gaunt (25/9/1827-24/5/1910) 8/8/1855 (a daughter of Dr. Matthias Gaunt of Windermere). She later lived at *The Laurels*, opposite Mayne St. in Invermay, Launceston; had issue.

   3. Herbert John Effingham Lawrence (29/8/1856-17/3/1936) a farmer at Lilydale, Tasmania; married Alice Beatrice Webb (-1915), 1900; no issue known.

   3. Charles Edward Lawrence (26/12/1857-2/6/1938) unmarried; lived at Casterton, Victoria.

   3. Emily Jane Lawrence (20/3/1859-11/2/1894) married Robert Ephram **Beauchamp** (20/3/1859-10/1/1945) (grandson of Sir William Beauchamp-Proctor, 3rd Bt. Admiral, RN, 1781-1861) 18/6/1890; lived at Holwell, Tasmania; had issue.

      4. Harold (Hardy) Lewis Beauchamp (1889-1/5/1931)

      4. John Robert Beauchamp (10/7/1891-10/9/1964), born in Launceston, Tasmania. Farmed for many years at Frankford, West Tamar, then retired to Mole Creek.

      4. Fanny Elizabeth (Beth) Beauchamp (31/10/1894-4/11/1958) married John Connell **Brown** (22/10/1889-4/8/1973) and lived at St. Leonards, Tasmania; had issue.

         5. Lindsay George Brown (8/3/1923-   )

         5. Frances Mary Brown (18/2/1926-   ) married Charles Eric **Cleary** (-14/2/1985) lived in Brisbane, Qld.; had issue.

6. Judith Mary Cleary (10/6/1961-   ) lived in Brisbane.
6. Peter John Cleary (7/5/1963-   ) lived in Brisbane.
5. Phyllis Rae Brown (27/8/1927-21/11/2019) married John F. **Stewart** (-   ) lived in Launceston, Tasmania; had issue.
6. John Craig Stewart (3/10/1948-   )
6. Leighton Fraser Stewart (15/10/1952-   )
5. Veronica (Von) Mary Brown (16/5/1931-   ) married D. Murray **Columbine** (-   ) lived at Mentone, Victoria; had issue.
6. Anne Elizabeth Columbine (25/12/1953-   ) married B. S. **Wood** (-   ) lived at Edithvale, Victoria; had issue.
7. Janelle Marie Wood (12/4/1976-   )
7. Andrew Guy Wood (16/9/1978-   )
6. Helen Mary Columbine (16/8/1956-   ) married K. J. **Razga** (-   ) lived at Mt. Eliza, Victoria; had issue.
7. Kirk Andrew Razga (27/12/1980-   )
7. Troy Anthony Razga (15/5/1983-   )
7. Daniel James Razga (26/11/1988-   )
6. Wayne Peter Columbine (18/1/1958-   ) married Susan Cole (-   ) lived at Beaumaris, Victoria; had issue.
7. Wayne Peter Columbine (11/7/1989-   )
7. Victoria Jane Columbine (13/9/1993-   )
6. John Michael Columbine (16/12/1962-   ) married Leanne Hannasky (-   ) lived at Rochester, Victoria; had issue.

7. Jackson Thomas Columbine (24/6/1992-   )

7. Mitchell James Columbine (16/3/1994-   )

3. Walter Sidney Lawrence (2/6/1860-2/7/1865)

3. Leslie Frank Lawrence (5/7/1861-18/7/1947), lived at Kaponga, Taranaki, NZ, married Lelia Eileen Latham (15/6/1867-8/8/1952), in Christchurch NZ, 25/11/1891; had issue.

4. Walter Leslie Nicholas Lawrence (13/6/1892-27/11/1931) m. Marjorie Hope Barton (1896-13/6/1970) 1919; no issue.

4. Lelia Francis Lawrence (1/11/1894-1/10/1984) married George Grigg **Lowe** (-15/1/1956) 12/5/1918; had issue.

5. Lelia Elizabeth Lowe (16/3/1919-26/3/2013) married Harry **Drummond** (-   ); lived on Waikeke Island, Auckland, NZ; no issue.

5. Audrey Joy Lowe (26/10/1921-   ) married Bruce **Hunter** (-   ); lived at Manakau, near Levin, Wellington, NZ; had issue.

6. Gillian Hunter (10/4/1945-   ) married Russell **Mathers** (-   ) lived at Cambridge, NZ; had issue.

7. Nicola Mathers (17/12/1969-   ) married Scott **Lucock** (-   ); had issue.

8. Renée Lucock (-   )

7. Joanna Mathers (23/5/1972-   ) married Mark **Podjursky** (-   ); had issue.

8. Daniel Podjursky (-   )

8. Ashleigh Podjursky (-   )

7. Jonathon Mathers (11/4/1974-   )

6. Dennis Hunter (15/1/1947-   ) married Ileen Glifton (-   ); had issue.

7. Paul Hunter (23/11/1972-   )

7. Christopher Hunter (3/7/1975-   )

6. Kay Hunter (25/3/1949-   ) lived at Palmerston North, NZ.
Married . . .
(i) Richard **Skow** (-   ); had issue.
  7. Karl Skow (25/10/   -   )
  7. Sonia Skow (-   )
(ii) Neil **Bolland** (-   ); had issue.
  7. Graeme Bolland (-   )
  7. Shanna Bolland (-   )
6. Stephanie Hunter (3/5/1951-   ) married Peter **Welham** (-   ) lived at Stowmarket, England; had issue.
  7. Gayleen Welham (-   )
  7. Andrew Welham (-   )
  7. Sylvia Welham (-   )
6. Mary Beth Hunter (28/5/1953-   )
Married . . .
(i) Dirk **Vreede** (-   ) lived at North Auckland, NZ; had issue.
  7. Pieter Vreede (13/4/1976-   )
  7. Jeannie Vreede (27/7/1977-   )
  7. Martin Vreede (26/8/1980-   )
(ii) Howard **Dixon** (-   )
  7. Michelle Dixon (-   )
6. Nicholas Hunter (10/7/1955-   ) married Beryl Beer (-   ) lived at Levin, near Wellington, NZ; had issue.
  7. Beverley Hunter (8/9/1977-   )
  7. Michael Hunter (9/2/1980-   )
  7. Ernest Hunter (-   )
5. Mary Jocelyn Lowe (16/11/1927-10/5/1995) married

Arnold **Allan** (19/12/1919-19/10/1976); had issue.

    6. Mary Heather Allan (26/3/1963-   )

    6. Barbara Rosemary Allan (17/4/1964-   ) married William **Mathieson** (20/9/1959-   ); had issue.

        7. Tobias William Murdoch Mathieson (30/5/1987-)

        7. Coco Mathieson (-   )

4. Marjory Jean Lawrence (1897-18/3/1945) married Harry William **Barnes** (1899-16/1/1945) 1918, lived in Auckland, NZ; had issue.

    5. Lawrence Barnes (-   ) married; had issue.

        6. _____ (-   )

        6. _____ (-   )

    5. Basil Barnes (-   )

4. Sheila Kathleen Lawrence (9/9/1899-2/10/1980) married Claude **Hope** (4/8/1887-5/8/1959) 4/6/1919; had issue.

    5. Trevor Claude Hope (17/9/1920-14/9/1923)

    5. Marjory Gweneth Hope (11/9/1921-   ) married Robert Francis **Wright** (-   ) 8/9/1943, lived at Opotiki, NZ; had issue.

        6. Diane Mary Wright (18/3/1944-   ) married Anthony David Roderick **Wooten** (-), lived at Whakatane, NZ; had issue.

            7. Benjamin Charles Wooten (28/3/1969-); had issue.

                8. Miko Wooten (1992-   )

            7. Nathan James Wooten (27/10/1972-   )

            7. Amos John Wooten (22/5/1974-   )

        6. Sheila Frances Wright (27/3/1945-   ) Married...

    (i) John **Greaves** (-   ) lived at Tauranga, NZ; had issue.

        7. Jacqueline Ann Greaves (2/4/1963-   ) married

David **Burgess** (-   ) 1995.

7. Andrew John Greaves (6/3/1967-   ) married Karen _____ (-) 1991; had issue.

   8. Joshua Michael Greaves (1996-   )

7. David William Greaves (28/5/1971-   ) married Corrina _____ (-) 1992; had issue.

   8. Hailey Rose Greaves (1995-   )

   8. Reilley Liam Greaves (1997-   )

(ii) Bruce **Lee** (-   ) -/7/1989; no issue.

6. Helen Elizabeth Wright (18/1/1947-   ) married Neil **Bishop** (-   ) lived at Wellington, NZ; had issue.

7. Nicholas Robert Bishop (5/1/1966-   ) married Monie _____ (-) 1990; had issue.

   8. Victoria Bishop (1995-   )

6. Juliet Susan Wright (30/1/1974-   )

6. Heather Marjory Wright (19/10/1953-   ) Married...

(i) Rodney Dereck **Hawken** (-   ) lived at Tauranga, NZ; had issue.

7. Jason Dereck Hawken (1972-   ); had issue.

   8. Stacey Hawken (1995-   )

(ii) Donald Ernest **Moir** (-   ) had issue.

7. Joanne Moir (14/10/1974-   )

7. Donald James Moir (10/3/1976-   )

5. Dorothy Patricia Hope (8/9/1923-   ) married Robert Kitchener **Oxenham** (10/8/1915-20/8/1982) 1963, lived at Whakatane, NZ.

5. Gary Lindsay Hope (23/6/1931-   ) married Dorothy Jones (-   ) 19/2/1984.

5. Cushla Morea Hope (-   ) married Alexander Bruce **Fraser** (-   ) lived at Omaru, NZ; had issue.

    6. Cushla Joy Fraser (26/8/1957-   ) married Malcolm James **Garvan** (13/4/ -) 22/5/1982; had issue.

        7. Timothy Garvan (15/12/1983-   )

        7. Claire Helene Garvan (11/11/1985-   )

    6. Christine Mary Fraser (10/6/1961-   ) married Bruce Albert **Tonion** (-   ) 15/12/1984; had issue.

        7. Jenna Tonion (5/7/1985-   )

    6. Deborah Kaye Fraser (2/6/1965-   )

    6. Jeremy Alexander Bruce Fraser (18/5/1968-   )

    6. Annabelle Jane Fraser (11/4/1974-   )

3. Arthur William Lawrence (22/7/1864-11/3/1890) married Dorothy Simpson (-), 22/12/1888; had issue.

    4. Leonard Arthur Lawrence (1890-1924) unmarried; a captain in the Dublin Fusiliers (British Army); murdered in Aden, Yemen in 1924.

3. Oswald Vernon Lawrence (3/8/1865-22/5/1896) unmarried.

3. Fanny (born Frances) Marianne Lawrence ("Aunt Minnie") (10/12/1866-6/12/1944) unmarried.

3. Caroline Maude Lawrence (14/6/1868-14/4/1869)

3. Francis Horace Lawrence (1/3/1870-5/1/1939) trained as an accountant and initially worked in Launceston with Dunning and Brown; farmed at Ulverstone, Tasmania from 1907-1911 then moved to Melbourne and worked with the Liverpool and London and Globe Insurance Co.; married Kate Therese Adams (1868-1938); had issue.

    4. Stanley Effingham Lawrence (19/8/1898-14/1/1972),

worked for the "*Herald*" Newspapers Ltd., Melbourne, 1921-1950 (as Staff Superintendent, 1934-50) married Fiona May Hevingham Root (23/10/1899-3/9/1982) 25/2/1922; had issue.

5. Blake Effingham Lawrence (20/9/1923-25/7/1992) a process engraver with the "*Herald*", lived at Boronia, Vic.; married Monica Genevieve Keating (30/11/1926-16/3/2016), 29/1/1955; had issue.

    6. Francis John Lawrence (4/1/1957-   ) lived at Eltham, Victoria.

    6. Elizabeth Mary Lawrence (9/10/1958-   ) a librarian, lived at Eltham, Vic. Married Craig Alan **Price** (3/11/1958-   ) 29/3/1992 but retained the name Lawrence; had issue.

        7. Greyden Blake Price (30/9/1992-   )

        7. Kaine Ross Price (29/1/1998-   )

    6. Therese Bernadette Lawrence (24/6/1961-   ) a nurse, lived at Werribee, Vic., married Colin John **Holloway** (31/1/1953-   ) 8/9/1982; had issue.

        7. Katherine Anne Holloway (16/7/1987-   )

        7. Matthew John Holloway (14/10/1990-   )

    6. Bernard Jerome Effingham Lawrence (1/12/1962-) lived at Narre Warren, Vic.

    6. Matthew Philip Lawrence (7/1 0/1964-   ) lived at Templestowe, Vic; had issue.

        7. Jimi Danaan Lawrence (6/6/2001-   )

5. Donald Hevingham Lawrence (14/8/1925-12/8/1994), a golf and tennis writer for the "*Age*" newspaper in Melbourne, and later News Editor. In 1973 he became the golf writer for the "*Herald*" newspaper. Don was a highly respected sports journalist in Melbourne (1946-

1986) and was inducted into the Sport Australia Hall of Fame in November 1991[1] and was the author of two books.

In his career he covered more than twenty Davis Cup ties and a similar number of Wimbledon and British Open events, as well as many other international events. Don Lawrence was famous internationally for dubbing Jack Nicklaus "The Golden Bear" and assisted with autobiographies of tennis player Margaret Smith[2] and golfer Greg Norman.[3] He also wrote a history of the Victoria Golf Club,[4] Melbourne. During his career he was considered to be the "doyen" of his profession. Lived at Beaumaris, Vic. and on 23/12/1950 married Muriel Therese Dickinson (5/12/1925-17/2/2020); had issue

6. William Hevingham Lawrence (30/10/1953-13/12/2011) an insurance consultant; lived at Toowoomba, Queensland.

6. Suzanne Bernadette Lawrence (16/7/1955-　) lived at Brisbane; married Terence Henry Charles **Timms** (17/9/1952-　) 28/3/1985; had issue.
    7. Jonathon Donald Timms (24/10/1987-　)
    7. Olivia Grace Timms (23/10/1991-　)

6. Fiona Anne Lawrence (7/3/1962-　) married Timothy John **Doyle** (26/3/1960-　) 4/2/1989 (retained the surname Lawrence) lived at Prospect, South Australia; had issue.
    7. Georgia Kate Lawrence Doyle (13/2/1990-　) a graduate Univ. of Adelaide, SA, PhD (History) (Univ. of Sydney) married Nicholas **Skeer** (24/10/1987-　) 1/12/2019

7. Matilda Montana Lawrence Doyle (10/12/1996-)
a nursing student (in 2018)

7. Thomas Finn Lawrence Doyle (12/2/2002-   )

5. Fiona Judith Lawrence (13/1/1927-   ) married Charles
Raymond **Scherman** (6/6/1920-22/1/2015) 24/4/1948;
lived at Seaholme, Melbourne, Vic.; had issue.

6. Eric William Scherman (12/1/1952-   ); had
issue.

7. Laura Gene Scherman (9/5/1988-   ) married
David **Rowan** (23/12/1981-   ) 30/6/1918.

7. Kirby Rae Scherman (29/1/1990-   ) married
Mitchell **Lawrence** (21/9/1989-   ); had issue.

8. Eli Eric Lawrence (28/3/2018-   )

6. Raymond Stanley Scherman (19/11/1954-   )
Married . . .

(i) Martha Plazier (-   ) had issue.

7. Jacinta Anne Scherman (10/10/1985-   )
married Kain **Williams** (12/4/1983-   )
27/2/2015; had issue.

8. Eviarna Williams (8/2/2014-   )

8. Kayden Williams (4/1/2017-   )

(ii) Jill Schultz (-   )

4. Brian Lawrence (10/1/1903-July1972) an officer in the
Australian merchant navy, lived in Brisbane, Qld.; married
Gladys Rene Ottrim (-   ) 25/7/1942; no issue, but
she had issue from a previous marriage.

3. William Effingham Lawrence (1/2/1872-4/7/1874)

3. Theodore Ernest Lawrence (1/2/1872-   ) lived near
Hastings NZ, died in the 1950's; married Fanny Pinkerton
(-   ) (issue uncertain.)

Chapter 10

EFFINGHAM BILLOPP LAWRENCE
(1834-1908)

Effingham Billopp Lawrence (E.B.L) was the sixth son of W.E. Lawrence and was the first Lawrence to live at *Billopp*, moving there in 1865 after his second marriage, to Grace Barnard, on 19/8/1865. Prior to this, the property had been operated on an 'absentee' basis, and for a period, had been leased to G.H.G. Fletcher. E.B.L. married twice – his first wife, Clara Barnard, was the elder sister of Grace and Jessie Barnard. The latter married Octavius Vernon Lawrence.

Effingham Billopp Lawrence

In those times it was considered impolite for an elder sister to be left unmarried, hence, according to family "legend", marriage to both sisters. His son by the first marriage, Frank Effingham (F.E.L.) (1858-90) lived at *Billopp* but died at an early age. His eldest son from the second marriage, Effingham Dryburgh (E.D.L.) (1866-1949), lived at *Billopp* from 1896 to 1948, having trained as a surveyor as a young man. The eldest son of E.D.L., Effingham Lambert (E.L.L.) (1898-1967), worked at *Billopp* during the Depression years of the early 1930's, and eventually succeeded his father in the ownership of *Billopp* in 1948.

E.L.L. was followed by son Ian Martin Lawrence (1944-   ),
1967 to 1998 and then his son, Samuel Ian Effingham Lawrence
(1974-   ) from 1998 to 2014. Both were residing at *Billopp* until
its sale in February 2014.

Two other sons of E.B.L., Archie (1868-1945) and Vernon
(1875-1949), followed careers with the Union Bank of Australasia;
Owen (1881-1956) served with the Imperial Forces in South Africa
during the Boer War and then became a pastoralist in the Transvaal
and the youngest son, Leonard (1883-1967), also a pastoralist,
managed, then eventually purchased *Formosa* from the estate of
Cornelius Henry (Con) Lawrence in 1949.

Flora Gwendoline Lawrence (1878-1962) married Kenneth
Loane and two of their sons entered the Anglican Church; the
eldest, Marcus, becoming Archbishop of Sydney Diocese in 1966.
Descendants of this branch of the family are most numerous and
scattered widely in most Australian states, New Zealand and South
Africa.

Genealogy

2. Effingham Billopp Lawrence (23/2/1834-10/8/1908) a
   pastoralist at *Billopp*, Cressy from 1865-1896, and had 12
   children. Lived in retirement at *Koorong*, 22 York Street,
   Launceston and died there in 1908.
   Married . . .
   (i) Clara Barnard (22/9/1836-24/05/1861) 2/4/1857; died of
   consumption; had issue.
      3. Frank Effingham Lawrence (19/1/1858-31/08/1890)
        unmarried; lived at *Billopp*.
      3. Annie Lawrence (10/7/1859-01/04/1938) unmarried.
   (ii) Grace Barnard (1840-10/4/1928) 19/8/1865; had issue.

3. Effingham Dryburgh Lawrence (24/5/1866-20/01/1949) pastoralist and an authorized surveyor; lived at *Billopp* from 1896 to 1948 and extensively developed the garden there; married Eleanor Kate Lambert (1/12/1874-20/12/1958) 11/3/1897 (daughter of Rev. Henry John Lambert, 20/3/1836-14/7/1924, of Norwood, SA); had issue.

4. Effingham Lambert Lawrence (4/7/1898-14/11/1967) a pastoralist, managed *Connorville* Estate near Cressy for the O'Connor family from 1934-1948, then as a 50 year old moved to and owned *Billopp* from 1948-1967; married Elizabeth Muriel Martin (4/7/1906-29/5/1993) 15/1/1934; had issue.

5. Anne Martin Lawrence (13/7/1937-   ) a mothercraft nurse, lived near Campbelltown, Swan Bay and Longford in northern Tasmania;
Married . . .

(i) Robert Alexander **Liebmann** (19/6/1933-   ) 7/4/1959, divorced, had issue.

6. Stuart Alexander Liebmann (15/1/1960-   ) married Divina Ayadi (20/12/1982-   ); lived in Brisbane, Qld.; no issue.

6. Colin Lawrence Liebmann (13/8/1961-   ) BEng. (Civil) (Univ. of Sydney, 1987) MBA (Cranfield University, UK 1997), a civil engineer who worked in wind and solar energy, married Julia Batchelor (née Sherman) (-), 28/9/1996, lived in Sydney; had issue.

7. Alexander James Liebmann (23/9/1998-   ) BBus. (Univ. of Technology, Sydney, 2021)

6. Rowan Bruce Liebmann (29/1/1963-   ) BBus. (Accounting) (TSIT, 1986), Grad. Dipl. in Applied Finance (1998); Master of Science Mineral

Economics (Curtin Univ. Perth, WA 2001), Dipl. of Financial Planning (1994) Chartered Accountant (1990-2019), lived in WA and latterly northern NSW.

Married . . .

(i) Sally Morgan (9/12/1962 -   ) 1/12/1992, divorced, no issue.

(ii) Miranda Duncan (28/1/1963-   ) 1/4/2000; had issue.

    7. Grace Agnes Elizabeth Liebmann (25/9/2002-   )

6. David Benjamin Liebmann (1/1/1968-   ) BSc. (App.Sc. Metallurgy) (Ballarat Univ., 1991), Diploma of Project Management (Swinburne Univ., 2019) lived in Vic. Married Kylie Smith (19/10/1969-   ) 29/7/1994, divorced; had issue.

    7. Benjamin Thomas Liebmann (28/3/1999-   ) BComm. (Deakin Univ., 2021)

    7. Jesse James Liebmann (6/12/2002-   )

(ii) David Christian Angus **Wilson** (6/1/1931-7/2/1998) January 1979; divorced; no issue.

(iii) Charles William **Burman** (16/1/1937-   ) (third husband of Anne Martin Lawrence, p. 145) 11/5/2002; a logistics and marketing manager and later a landscape photographer; no issue.

5. Katherine Elizabeth Lawrence (13/5/1939-   ) a paediatric nurse, married Peter Hamilton **Houghton** (29/11/1935-11/6/2010) 17/2/1962, lived in Melbourne, later near Benalla and then at Point Lonsdale, Victoria; had issue.

    6. Elizabeth Thackray Houghton (29/1/1963-   ) business woman, lived in Vic. Married William

Billopp House, c. J L Lawrence 2013.

Gorman (-   ) 1988; divorced; had issue.

7. William Toby Gorman (12/4/1990-   ) BCom. (Univ. of Melb.), MEng. (Univ. of Melb.)

7. Marjie Kate Gorman (23/12/1991-   ) BCom. (HR) (Swinburne Univ.).

7. Frederick John Gorman (14/6/1994-   ) BSc. (Monash Univ.).

6. John Lawrence Houghton (27/9/1964-   ) BEd., pastoralist and later a teacher, lived in Qld. then Vic. Married . . .

(i) Natalie Hammer (26/2/1967 -   ) 1990; had issue.

7. Sophie Elizabeth Houghton (24/6/1994-   ) married Jack Andrew **Nugent** (17/1/1994-   ); had issue.

8. Bernie John Nugent (16/10/2016-   )

8. Oscar Roy Nugent (9/6/2018-   )

8. Jim Clancy Nugent (19/8/2020-   )

7. Eliza Victoria Houghton (13/2/1996-   )

7. Zara Alexandra Houghton (15/1/1999-   )

(ii) Johanna Aurelia Shäfer (25/7/1973-   ) (second wife to John Lawrence Houghton); 7/12/2018.

6. Sarah Katherine Houghton (27/8/1968-   ) BEd., a teacher, married James Francis **Tehan** (16/4/1965-   ) 17/2/1996; lived at *Wappan*, Mansfield, Victoria; had issue.

7. Lily Katherine Tehan (3/3/1998-   )

7. Isabel Marie Tehan (10/9/1999-   )

7. Alice Elizabeth Tehan (27/1/2002-   )

7. Joseph James John Tehan (15/11/2004-   )

5. Effingham Frank Lawrence (1/8/1941-   ) a medical practitioner MB, BS (Univ. of Adelaide 1966), lived in Hobart, Tasmania, married Beatrice Mary Bennison OAM (15/10/1944-   ) 9/6/1967, Dipl. of Early Childhood Education (Kindergarten Training College, Melbourne 1964). Awarded the medal of the Order of Australia (OAM, 2000) for "service to youth through guiding in the Community (Girl Guides Australia)"; had issue.

6. William Effingham Lawrence (10/6/1970-   ) manager with the ANZ Bank mostly in Tasmania, but NT and South Australia as well; lived in Tasmania; married Melanie Lee Ross (28/5/1973-   ) 27/2/2010; had issue.

7. Jack Malcolm Effingham Lawrence (11/7/2013-   )

6. Emma Jane Lawrence (27/10/1972-   ) BPharm. (Univ. of Tasmania, 1993) Grad Dipl. Pharm.

(Univ. of Tasmania, 1994) clinical pharmacist, lived in Tasmania; married Richard Simon **Hooper** (25/7/1972-   ) BAgr.Sc. (Univ. of Tasmania), MEnv.Man. (Univ. of NSW); had issue.

7. Grace Elizabeth Lawrence Hooper (14/11/2005-)

7. Samuel Richard Hooper (11/6/2008-   )

7. Olive Jane Lawrence Hooper (16/5/2010-   )

6. Timothy James Bennison Lawrence (9/4/1974-   ) a pastoralist, and farming contractor, married Kate Jillian Donaghue (26/2/1975-   ) 5/3/2001, lived in northern NSW; had issue.

7. Archi Jack Lawrence (20/1/2004-   )

7. Banjo Effingham Lawrence (1/2/2007-   )

5. Ian Martin Lawrence (4/9/1944-   ) married Gwendoline Augusta Mary Greenhill (21/2/1944-   ) 31/12/1969; a pastoralist, lived at *Billopp,* Cressy until 2014, then Launceston, Tasmania; had issue.

6. Madeleine Jane Lawrence (14/10/1971-   ) BA, LLB (Hons.) (Univ. of Tas. 1995) lawyer; married David Palser (10/6/1970-   ) BCom., LLB (Univ. of Melbourne 1995), 11/11/2000; had issue.

7. Zachary Lawrence Palser (19/6/2002-   )

7. Siena Rose Lawrence Palser (18/2/2004-   )

7. Jed Lawrence Palser (1/11/2006-   )

7. Samuel James Lawrence Palser (16/12/2010-   )

6. Samuel Ian Effingham Lawrence (29/4/1974-   ) Dipl. Farm Man. (Marcus Oldham College, 1997) a pastoralist living at *Billopp* until sold in February 2014, then an insurance consultant and lived in southern Tasmania; married Cilla Armstrong (10/5/1977-) BA (Univ. of Tas. 2017) 27/3/2005;

had issue.

    7. Frederick Effingham Armstrong Lawrence
       (29/4/2007-   )

    7. Wesley Armstrong Lambert Lawrence
       (28/2/2009-)

5. John Lambert Lawrence (20/2/1947-   ) farm
   manager, lived near Hamilton in Western Victoria
   and then WA, before being employed for twenty seven
   years in an alumina refinery near Pinjarra, WA, owned
   and operated by Alcoa World Alumina; awarded the
   City of Mandurah's "Community Citizen of the Year"
   (2020) in the annual Australia Day awards, for charity
   work in the community. Married Suzan Lynette King
   (15/5/1949-   ) 13/11/1971, from Martinborough,
   New Zealand; had issue.

    6. Cameron Martin Effingham Lawrence (13/9/1973-)
       a contractor in the wine and associated industries,
       lived at Margaret River, WA; unmarried.

    6. Matthew James Lawrence (5/11/1975-   ) BSc.
       (Geophysics) (Curtin Univ. 1995) and Grad.Dipl.
       in Applied Geology (Curtin, 2010) a geophysicist
       and geologist, lived in Perth, WA; married Cassandra
       (Cas) Sprague (27/3/1973-   ) Bachelor of
       Nursing (Deakin Univ. 1993) 5/12/2009; had issue.

       7. Archie James Effingham Lawrence (9/9/2007-   )
       7. Bonnie May Lawrence (5/12/2010-   )

    6. Samantha Jane Lawrence (10/8/1979-   )
       Customer Service and Sales Coordinator with Capral
       Aluminium, Perth WA, lived in Mandurah, WA;
       unmarried.

4. Spencer Billopp Lawrence (15/3/1900-12/1/1984) a

pastoralist, lived at *Fermer*, Westbury, Tasmania; married Tui Lillian Evelyn Fryer (8/6/1904-28/3/1972) from New Zealand, 5/3/1929; had issue.

5. James Lindsay Effingham Lawrence (18/2/1940-15/3/2007) a pastoralist, lived at *Fermer*. Married Lynda Joan Boyes (17/8/1941-1/11/2007) 20/4/1963; had issue.

  6. Kenneth Gordon Effingham Lawrence (17/5/1965-) a pastoralist, lived at *Fermer*, had issue.
Married...

(i) Celia Josephine Leverton (30/10/1962-) 15/5/1993; had issue.

    7. Henry Herbert Effingham Lawrence (23/11/1994-)

    7. Meg Lillian Leverton Lawrence (11/7/1996-)

    7. Jemma Alice Leverton Lawrence (11/7/1996-)

    7. Fergus James Leverton Lawrence (25/10/2001-)

(ii) Jill Mary Alice Kershaw (9/5/1964-) 8/7/2006; had issue.

    7. Sam Douglas Lawrence (29/4/2008-)

  6. Brian William Lawrence (29/11/1966-) a pastoralist, lived near Meander, Tas., married Michelle Tasker (25/1/1969-) 3/1/1998; had issue.

    7. Sophie Lawrence (29/1/1999-10/12/2019)

    7. Bradley Lister Lawrence (19/3/2001-)

    7. Joseph William Lawrence (16/6/2003-)

  6. Brenda Lynne Lawrence (7/5/1969-) Dipl. Appl. Sc. (TSIT, 1989), BHealth Sc. in Midwifery (Univ. of Tasmania, 1992) married Glenn Alexander **Stubbs** (2/6/1970-) 25/1/1997, lived in

northern Tasmania; had issue.

7. Abigail Lily Stubbs (4/9/1998-   )

7. Naomi Rose Stubbs (6/9/2000-   )

4. Helen Grace Isabelle Lawrence, MBE (18/7/1901-23/1/1986) awarded the Membership of the British Empire (MBE, 1942) for service as Assistant Controller of the Voluntary Aid Detachment (VAD) in Northern Tasmania. Married Geoffrey Arthur Douglas **Youl**, MC (6/2/1892-25/1/1971), 23/12/1922, who originally trained as a midshipman on *HMS Worcester* in the UK. Despite topping his final class in 1910, he was not offered a position in the Royal Navy. He served with the British East India Company until 1914 then joined the Royal Field Artillery, British Army, as a Second Lieutenant. By the end of the war he had been promoted to rank of Major and was awarded the Military Cross (MC), the Belgian Croix de Guerre, and he was twice mentioned in dispatches. During the 1930's he was promoted to the rank of Lieutenant-Colonel.

Colonel Youl was C.O. of the 12th/50th Battalion in Tasmania from 30/6/1938 to 30/6/1940 and then was C.O. of the 2/40th Btn., an infantry battalion being formed and trained for service overseas.

In November 1941 he was controversially removed[1] from this position several weeks before the unit was sent to Dutch West Timor as part of "Sparrow" force to defend the Penfui airfield on that island.

In February 1942, facing overwhelming odds and great numbers of battle-hardened Japanese troops, valiant efforts by the battalion failed and surrender took place followed by long years in captivity as prisoners-of-war.[2]

Following his dismissal Col. Youl did not serve in West Timor but was appointed C.O. of a training battalion in Tasmania.

Geoff Youl later became a pastoralist, and lived at *Leighlands* near Perth, Tasmania, and for many years, was involved in Longford (Tas.) municipal affairs (he was Warden from 1955 to 1960). Geoff was a very keen trout fisherman and a man of exceptional energy. It is worth noting that his grandfather, Rev. John Youl, officiated at the marriage of W. E. Lawrence and Mary Ann George at St. John's Anglican Church, Launceston on 23rd July 1826 (p. 88).

Had issue.

5. Alfred Geoffrey Lawrence Youl (4/9/1923-25/7/1926)
5. Beatrice Helen Isabelle Youl (11/2/1925-5/11/2009) married Major George William Cecil **Harding** (12/7/1916 -30/1/2015) born in Belfast, Ireland, joined the Royal Artillery, British Army, (2nd Lieut. 1936, Major 1949-1955), she lived in England and, latterly, Tasmania; had issue.
   6. Virginia Hope Isabelle Harding (10/3/1948-   ) married Robert John **Maunder-Taylor** (30/10/1941-7/9/2010), a chartered surveyor, 9/8/1969, lived in Hertingfordbury (p. 12), England; had issue.
      7. James William Maunder-Taylor (3/3/1972-   ) a chartered surveyor, lived in Hong Kong and England. Married Sally Anne Stead (12/2/1971-) 22/12/2007; had issue.
         8. Poppy Aurelia Maunder-Taylor (22/7/2008-   )
         8. Tilly Eliza Maunder-Taylor (1/8/2011-   )
      7. Timothy John Maunder-Taylor (24/1/1974-   )

lived in England; married Marie-Claire Hazelden (28/3/1976-   ) 18/9/2004; had issue.

      8. Archie James Maunder-Taylor (1/2/2005-   )

      8. Madeleine Alice Maunder-Taylor (9/3/2006-)

      8. Hope Isabelle Francesca Maunder-Taylor (23/8/2007-   )

      8. Bertie William Quartus Maunder-Taylor (20/10/2010-   )

   7. Tanya Hope Maunder-Taylor (27/11/1975-3/12/2009) a secretary, lived in England.

   7. William Robert Maunder-Taylor (27/4/1982-   ) lived in England.

  6. Rosalind Beatrice Harding (1/9/1949-   ) lived in England, Tasmania and Ireland.

  6. Karin Elizabeth Harding (3/12/1954-   ) lived in England and Ireland.

5. James Arndell Youl (September 1928-30/5/1953). A lieutenant in the British army, he served in the Suez Canal zone in Egypt during part of the occupation by British forces from 1945-1956. This was not a popular posting for service personnel because of the weather, disease and resentful local nationalists. He contracted poliomyelitis and died at a British army hospital on 30th May 1953; buried at the Moascar cemetery in Egypt.

5. Annette Margaret Youl (3/3/1930-   ) married John Douglas **Goble** (12/4/1923-31/5/2016) 13/6/1953; lived in Sydney.

John Goble was one of three sons of Stanley Goble, a WWI air force fighter ace and pioneering aviator - later Air Vice-Marshal and in command of the Royal

Australian Air Force in 1939.

John had a distinguished career in the Royal Australian Navy from 1937-1976, serving in many roles, including on landing craft as part of the D-Day landings in Normandy, France, on 6th June 1944. At retirement in 1976 he held the rank of Commodore and later, had a second career as a lawyer in Sydney, retiring for a second time, in 1992. Annette and John lived in Sydney and had issue.

6. James Wodehouse Goble (13/7/1957-30/6/1972)

6. Margaret Kate Goble (11/9/1959-   )

5. Gwendolyn Isabelle Irene Youl, AM (13 /12/1941-31/10/2020). A successful pastoralist and a passionate educator about agriculture and women in agriculture, and involved in Landcare for several decades receiving a Life Membership of Landcare Tasmania in 2019. Lived at *Leighlands*, Perth, Tasmania and awarded membership of the Order of Australia (AM) in 2006, for services to the agricultural sector in Tasmania. Married . . .

(i) Dieter **Grant-Frost** (-   ) 1962, divorced; no issue

(ii) Peter William **Reynolds** (9/9/1942-   ) 13/7/1974, divorced; no issue

(iii) Vivian **Adams** (-   ); no issue

4. Margaret Kate Lawrence (19/4/1904-15/1/2003) married Roberts John Leake **Foster** (18/2/1900-21/1/1978) in 1929, lived at *Pleasant Banks*, Evandale, Tas.; had issue.

5. Pauline Elizabeth Leake Foster (9/3/1930-28/5/2018) married James **Morrison** (1927-1971) in 1958 and lived in New Guinea and latterly Melbourne; had issue.

6. James Andrew Morrison (2/3/1959-   ) an artist,

lived in Melbourne, married Traude Helene Beilharz (25/11/1961-   ) 4/1/1992; had issue.

7. Elizabeth Beatrice Gertrude Morrison (4/9/2006-)

6. Juliet Morrison (1960-   ) lived in Melbourne.

5. Valerest Margaret Foster (14/7/1931-   ) married Charles Claridge **Yencken** (27/11/1927-25/5/1989) in 1953; a pastoralist. Lived near Kojonup, WA before moving to Albany, WA; had issue.

6. Phillippa Josephine Yencken (5/10/1955-   ) lived at Kuranda, north Qld.
Married . . .

(i) Nigel **Bennett** (23/5/1943-7/6/2011) 1981; had issue.

7. Amalie Claire Bennett (17/4/1984-   )

(ii) partnered Paul Graeme **Fisk**; had issue.

7. Summer Breeze Ellen Fisk (15/11/1994-   )

6. Charles Ronald Foster Yencken (14/11/1957-   ) BBus. Accounting (Churchlands College, Perth, 1981) and practiced at Kojonup then Fremantle, WA; married Pui Ling (Laura) Law (22/12/1966 -) 16/5/2009; had issue.

7. Johanes Ferdinand Yencken (22/3/2013-   )

6. Alistair John Duncan Yencken (18/11/1959-   ) a pastoralist, lived at Tamworth in northern NSW, married Robyn (Robbie) Sefton (10/4/1962-   ) managing director of *Seftons* at Tamworth, 14/7/1990.

6. Maryellen Margaret Yencken (25/9/1965-   ) MB, BS (Univ. of WA, 1989), FRACGP, a medical practitioner. Worked in private practice at Palmyra, WA. Lived at Cottesloe, WA. Married Edward

Simon **McGrath** (10/5/1959-   ) a businessman in real estate, 8/5/1999; had issue.

7. Charles Edward Effingham McGrath (4/9/2000-)

7. Montague (Monte) John Lloyd McGrath (14/10/2003-   )

5. Angela Lawrence Foster (26/1/1933-5/10/2007) lived at *Pleasant Banks*, Evandale, Tasmania; had issue.

6. Richard James Sargeant (22/6/1964-   ) lived in Melbourne. An investment advisor, married Carolyn McKellar (4/10/1964-   ) of Vernon, British Columbia, and project manager; 8/12/2011, had issue.

7. Catherine Frances Foster Sargeant (26/10/2012-   )

5. Henry John Lawrence Foster (1935-27/6/2012) lived at *Pleasant Banks*, Evandale, then Green's Beach, Tasmania.

Married . . .

(i) Frances Patricia Barton (24/5/1947-   ) 30/1/1971; had issue.

6. Robert John Foster (12/1/1972-   )

Married   . . .

(i) Ella Lida Hardosz (-   ) 15/4/1995; had issue.

7. Fiona Amy Foster (20/12/1996-   ) married Joshua **Dunne** (-   )

(ii) Fiona _____ (-   ) 5/6/2020

6. William Henry Foster (26/5/1973-   ) lived at Colac, Vic.

6. James Carmichael Foster (8/10/1976-   ) lived at Kyneton, Vic., married Melanie Carrol (-   ); had issue

7. Lucy Maree Foster (3/7/2007-   )

7. Kate Edith Foster (27/4/2009-   )

(ii) Gwen Bishop (-   ) (second wife of Henry John Lawrence Foster)

4. Barbara Effingham Lawrence (6/6/1910-26/4/2000) married Edward Stephen **Gibson** (-   ), 10/4/1935, lived at *Woodhall*, near Perth, Tasmania; divorced; had issue.

5. Helen Lawrence Gibson (30/7/1936-   ) married Christopher (Kit) James Safford **Morris** (30/1/1930-30/5/2020) 28/10/1961; he trained as a naval officer and latterly worked with the Australian National Shipping Line (ANL) in Melbourne and Tasmania (Commercial Manager, 1972); lived in Melbourne, then latterly at Castlemaine, Victoria; had issue.

6. Susan Valentia Morris (30/8/1963-   ) married Nigel Banks **Borthwick** (29/5/1962-   ) 8/1/1994; had issue.

7. Claire Sarah Borthwick (25/4/1995-   )

7. Samuel Thomas Christopher Borthwick (13/5/1999-   )

6. Celia Kate Morris (12/8/1965-   ) married Kristan **Krawinkel** (-   ) 3/3/1995; had issue.

7. Thomas Lawrence Krawinkel (2/3/1996-   )

7. Guy Peter Krawinkel (5/4/1999-   )

6. Megan Elizabeth Morris (8/3/1970-   ) married Jason **Edwards** (-   ) 17/3/2001; had issue.

7. William Morris Edwards (1/10/2006-   )

5. Frances Eleanor Gibson (16/3/1944-   ) BEd, MEdSt (Monash Univ., Melb. 1989) (masters degree on Ada a'Beckett,[3] p. 161-162) married Bruce Gordon **Douglas**

(13/9/1938-16/11/2005) 30/11/1968, an architect. Lived in Melbourne and then Tasmania; had issue.

6. Tanis Aletta Douglas (1/5/1970-   ) lived in Melbourne.

(i) married Greg **Muller** (20/11/1971-   ) 6/8/2004; had issue.

7. Mia Hazel Douglas-Muller (16/8/2004-   )
7. Alice Jenna Douglas-Muller (18/1/2006-   )

(ii) partnered Neil Philip **Wines** (17/5/1969-   ); had issue.

7. Chester Bruce Douglas-Wines (15/4/2011-   )
7. Frederick Jack Douglas-Wines (15/4/2011-   )

6. Kate Minette Douglas (30/7/1972-   ) lived in Melbourne; partnered Martin **Reeves** (-   ); had issue.

7. Oliver Angus Reeves (14/3/2004-   )
7. Hugo Alexander Reeves (13/10/2006-   )
7. Lily May Reeves (4/4/2009-   )

6. Angus Alexander Gordon Douglas (29/4/1975-   ) BAgr.Sc. (Univ. of Tasmania) an artist,[4] lived at *Woodhall*, Perth in northern Tasmania. Married Vanessa Brenda Holmes (29/12/1982-   ) 8/5/2004; had issue.

7. Rory Alexander Gordon Douglas (5/1/2007-   )
7. Archie James Bruce Douglas (21/7/2009-   )
7. Ada Gwyneth Eleanor Douglas (13/12/2013-   )

3. Archie Barnard Lawrence (17/8/1867-17/7/1945) a Bank Manager with the Union Bank of Australia; lived in Masterton, NZ (1905-1930) then Auckland; married Nora Islay Kathleen Carr (17/11/1877-25/7/1949), 15/4/1903; had issue.

4. John Effingham Lawrence (26/3/1906-3/3/1977) a pastoralist at *Puruatanga*, Martinborough, NZ; married Nancy Collyns Martin (31/10/1916-5/7/2004) in 1938; had issue.

  5. David Effingham Lawrence (10/5/1939-   ) BSc. (Canterbury, NZ) a pastoralist at Martinborough, married Frances (Francie) Mary Debrelle Morrah (26/11/1940-) 26/11/1971; had issue

    6. Lucy Jane Lawrence (15/2/1973-   ) married Duncan William **Forbes** (-) 8/11/2008; had issue.

      7. Madeline Frances Forbes (17/6/2010-   )

      7. Angus George Lawrence Forbes (4/12/2011-   )

    6. Robert Effingham Lawrence (3/7/1974-   ) married Cynthia Lee Winkworth (-) 15/5/2010; had issue.

      7. Aston Effingham Lawrence (4/6/2012-   )

      7. Fraser Lee Lawrence (28/12/2016-   )

    6. Olivia May Lawrence (6/7/1979-   )

  5. John Martin Lawrence (18/12/1946-   ) married Katherine Thea Block (26/2/1953-); had issue.

    6. Harriet Isobel Block Lawrence (23/2/1991-   )

    6. Henry Martin Block Lawrence (23/2/1993-   )

  5. Henrietta Mary Lawrence (12/3/1950-   ) Married …

(i) John Leo **Hannah** (27/10/1948-9/12/2011) lived at Nelson, NZ; had issue.

    6. Rachael Freda Hannah (16/9/1979-   ) a music therapist, lives in London, UK, married Ben Maitland **Leith** (15/11/1979-); had issue.

      7. Harrison John Leith (4/8/2013-   )

7. Stella Ruby Leith (18/11/2015-　　)
　6. Fiona Henrietta Hannah (27/12/1981-　　) a business person, lives in London, UK.
　6. Richard John Hannah (14/4/1985-　　) a public servant, lives in Wellington, NZ.
　(ii) John **Davison** (　-　) March 2020, a retired ophthalmologist of Nelson, NZ.
4. Kathleen Jean Lawrence (11/11/1907-30/9/1982) unmarried, lived in Remeura, Auckland, NZ.
3. Norman Billopp Lawrence (2/11/1869-11/2/1873) third child of E.B.L and Grace Lawrence (p. 144) died after receiving a fractured skull following a fall from a pony.
3. Cyril Marcus Lawrence (21/6/1871-29/7/1874) died of diphtheria.
3. Clara Nellie Lawrence (20/1/1874-4/5/1959) unmarried; lived in northern Tasmania.
3. Vernon Elliot Lawrence (22/7/1875-7/2/1949) born at *Billopp*. Joined the Union Bank in Launceston, managed various branches in Victoria and NSW; retired from Wagga Wagga, NSW branch in 1938. Active in church and community affairs; was an alderman on the Wagga Wagga municipal council, and served one term as deputy mayor; married Edith Emily Hook (1882- 1967) in 1906; had issue.
　4. Hilary Elliott Lawrence (21/5/1909-10/6/1994) graduated B. Architecture (Univ. of Sydney, 1931) and practiced intermittently; married Thomas Lambert **a'Beckett** (1905-1991) in 1937. Tom's mother Ada Mary a'Beckett (née Lambert) (1872-1948) was the sister of Eleanor Kate Lambert (1874-1958) wife of Effingham Dryburgh Lawrence (1866-1949) (p. 145) in 1897.

Ada was an educationist, prominent in the development of early childhood education in Victoria in the early 1900's and was awarded the C.B.E. in 1935.[4]

Tom's brother Ted (1907-1989) was a Melbourne lawyer and an Australian test cricketer. He played four tests from 1929 to 1931 at the same period as Don (later Sir Donald) Bradman was becoming established as a test cricketer. Ted is No. 28 on the Cricket Australia Roll of Test Players, and retired prematurely due to injury problems (Sir Donald Bradman is No. 24 on the Roll). Hilary and Tom lived at *Karbarook*, near Wagga Wagga, NSW; had one daughter, by adoption.

5. Elizabeth Vernon a'Beckett (1946-   ) married Russell McLarty **Simpson** (-   ) pastoralist, company director and shareholders (Dart Mining 2017) 14/4/1967. Lived at *Boongara*, Jerilderie, and latterly Albury, NSW; had issue

4. Maxwell Elliott Lawrence (10/5/1911-25/9/1997) graduated BE Civil Engineering (Univ. of Sydney 1932); served nine years as an Alderman on Woollahra Council, including three mayoral terms and nine years councillor Sydney County Council to 1971; consulting engineer specializing in arbitration, in construction disputes; Chairman Group Engineering Ltd., Council Member of the N.R.M.A. and Director of the N.R.M.A. Insurance Ltd.; member Glebe Administration Board and Cranbrook School Council. Married Lorraine Cecile Hunter (2/10/1915-16/5/2019) 1938, MB, BS (Univ. of Sydney, 1942) retired in 1970 from position as Senior Medical Officer NSW. Public Health Dept.; had issue.

5. James Elliot Lawrence (21/5/1939- -/2/1991)

graduated MB, BS (Univ. of Sydney, 1963); in general medical practice at Glebe, NSW.

5. Michael John Lawrence (13/2/1941-   ) graduated BE, BSc. (Univ. of Sydney, 1963) PhD, (Univ. of California, Berkeley, 1967). Worked in industry (Corning Glass works, CIBA-Geigy USA, and in Switzerland).

He returned to Sydney in 1972 and joined the University of NSW in 1975 in the School of Information Systems. He became a Fellow of the Australian Computer Society (FACS).

He was made a Professor in 1991; Head of School (1996-1998); Emeritus Professor 2001; President of the International Institute of Forecasting (1997-1999). He was active in church and community affairs; on Cranbrook School Council (1987-1999); an alderman on the Woollahra Municipal Council (Independent) from 1991-1995; married Sarah Elizabeth Coombe of Sydney (25/4/1943-   ) 11/11/1963. Sarah graduated Dip. Teach. SKTC (Waverley, 1963), B. Teaching (Early Childhood) (Macquarie Univ. 1993), daughter of Hastings George Coombe and Pamela Mary Coombe; had issue.

6. Stuart Elliot Lawrence (19/5/1969-   ) BA (Univ. of New England, 1993). Grad. Dipl. in Museum Studies (Flinders Univ., 1996).

6. Emily Jane Lawrence (17/10/1971-   ) BA (Univ. of Sydney, 1993), MA (Theatre Arts) (Goldsmiths College, Univ. of London, 1995); married Christian Jonathan **Gazal** (28/9/1968-   ) 18/2/2002; had issue.

       7. Xander Elliot Lawrence Gazal (8/7/2004-   )

       7. Tresi Mary Maude Gazal (20/1/2007-   )

       7. Milo Samuel Lawrence Gazal (8/12/2008-   )

3. Sydney Jesse Lawrence (31/10/1877-3/9/1881) died because of measles.

3. Flora Gwendoline Lawrence (19/12/1878-13/2/1962) married Kenneth Owen Archibald **Loane** (1883-1962) 11/10/1910 (son of Marcus Walpole Loane, 1835-1927, of *Northdown*, Wesley Vale, Tasmania, and Anna Mary Thomas, 1843-1904).[5] Kenneth Loane was a first cousin of Muriel Annie Beecraft, mother of Elizabeth Muriel Martin wife of E.L. Lawrence (p. 145).

Kenneth was an accountant who worked with mining companies in Tasmania and Queensland, and later lived at Chatswood NSW.; had issue.

   4. Marcus Lawrence Loane, KBE [6,7] (14/10/1911-14/4/2009) Th.L. (Moore Theological College, Sydney 1933); ordained (1935); MA (Univ. of Sydney 1937), DD (Hons.) (Wycliffe College, Toronto, Canada, 1958); Vice-Principal of Moore Theological College (1938-1953); Principal (1954-1959); Canon of St Andrew's Cathedral (Sydney), then Bishop (1958-1966); Archbishop of Sydney and Metropolitan of NSW (1966-1982); Anglican Primate of Australia (1978-1981), KBE (1976).

Sir Marcus was the first Australian-born Archbishop of any Anglican diocese in Australia and the first Australian-born Primate, also a prolific author on religious topics. Married Patricia Evelyn Jane Simpson Knox (2/1/1914 -20/3/2013), daughter of Canon D. J. Knox, 31/12/1937; had issue.

     5. Mary Eleanor Loane (16/10/1938-   ) a qualified

nursing sister (triple certificate); married William Leslie **Milford** (28/9/1934-   ), an engineer with the Postmaster General's Department (now Australia Post) in Melbourne; 11/4/1964; lived at Chadstone, Victoria; had issue.

6. David James William Knox Milford (4/9/1965-   ) married Julia Ellen Sweeney (26/2/1979-   ); had issue.

   7. Andrew James Milford (16/7/1988-   )
   7. Justin Luke Milford (30/8/1990-   )
   7. Samantha Ellen Milford (12/6/1992-   )
   7. David Geoffrey William Milford (18/7/1995-   )

6. Peter Marcus Leslie Milford (25/4/1967-   ) B. Theol., accountant, lived in Melbourne; married Susan Elisabeth Bell (21/2/1964-   )   1/1/1993; had issue.

   7. Jonathan Amos Leslie Milford (17/12/1996-   )
   7. Sarah Jean Eleanor Milford (31/7/1998-   )
   7. Daniel Marcus Leslie Milford   (5/10/2000-   )
   7. Laura Elisabeth Lillian Milford (20/9/2003-   )

6. Catherine Mary Ethel Milford (20/9/1968-   ) typist, lived in Melbourne; married Andrew Phillip Wedgwood **Bond** (22/10/1966-   ) 28/11/98, divorced; had issue.

   7. Phillip Aaron Leslie Loane Bond (24/8/2001-   )

6. Stephen John Whitburn Milford (28/8/1971-   ) overseas aid worker; married Cindy Siu Ngy Te, (19/11/1971-   ) BA, BSc.; 29/6/1997; had issue.

   7. Lachlan Emanuel William Whitburn Milford (22/9/2000-   )

7. Bethany Grace Te Whitburn Milford (12/9/2003-   )
7. Rebekah Amalia Mary Whitburn Milford (17/9/2009-   )

5. Robert Marcus Loane (29/4/1943-   ) BA (Cambridge 1964), MA (Cambridge 1966) and MB, BS (Univ. of Sydney 1969), D. Obst. RCOG. (1973), FRACS (1982); married Joan Lillian Thornton (2/2/1944-   ) MB, BS (Sydney 1969); 15/2/1969; lived at Keiraville, NSW; had issue.

6. Annabel Lorna Lawrence Loane (9/3/1971-   ) B. Pharm. (Sydney 1992); married Christopher James **Mills** (25/8/1970-   ), B. Pharm. (Sydney 1991) 28/2/1998; had issue.
7. Lachlan Lloyd Mills (14/3/2002-   )
7. Lucy Caitlin Mills (7/9/2003-   )
7. Molly Lara Mills (18/4/2005-   )

6. Rosalind Patricia Loane (5/10/1972-   ) BSc. (Sydney 1993), Dip. Ed. (Wollongong 1999), Master Public Health [MPH] (Univ. of NSW 2009). Married Andrew Richard **Dickson** (5/4/1973-   ) BE (Civil) (Sydney 1999), M. Mgt. (2008) 21/1/2012; had issue.
7. Jake Richard Dickson (19/12/2012-   )
7. Charles Arthur Dickson (2/9/2014-   )

6. Marcus Charles Loane (9/1/1977-   ) BSc. (BIT) (Univ. of NSW 1998) married Cerin Louise McMillan (10/12/1980-   ) BSc. LLB (Wollongong 2003) 9/4/2011; had issue.
7. Jasmin Emma Loane (19/4/2017-   )

6. Edward Alexander Loane (1/1/1979-   ) BSc.

(Sydney 1999), BD (Moore College 2007), PhD (Cambridge, 2015). Ordained Deacon (Sydney 2008), Priest (Ely, UK, 2013). Married Jocelyn Louise Mitchel (20/1/1979-) B.Dental Surgery [BDS] (Sydney 2001); had issue.

7. Jemima Kate Loane (18/2/2006-   )
7. Sophie Lilian Loane (16/4/2008-   )
7. Benjamin Marcus Loane (18/6/2010-   )
7. Samuel James Loane (18/6/2010-   )
7. Abigail Patricia Loane (23/2/2016-   )

5. David Lawrence Loane (27/12/1945-   ) BSc.For. (Hons.) (ANU, 1970), M. App. Sc. (Remote Sensing) (Univ. of NSW, 1994); lived in Sydney, married Susan Brain (11/5/1949-   ) BA (Deakin Univ., 2006) 2/2/1971; had issue.

6. Timothy David Loane (1/12/1972-   ) BSc. (Hons.) (Univ. of NSW, 1994), married Brooke May Thurgate (13/1/1976-   ) BBus., B.Comm. (Bond Univ., 1997) 16/10/2004; lived in Sydney, had issue
7. Joshua William Loane (8/1/2007-   )

6. Elizabeth Jane Loane (27/11/1974-   ) B.Teaching (General Primary) (Univ. West. Syd, 1997)

6. Richard Marcus Loane (4/2/1978-   ) BSc, BA (Univ. of NSW, 2002) Grad.Dip. Ed. (Univ. New England, 2008). Married Susan Jee Yeon Oh (23/2/1979-   ) BSc, B.Commerce (Univ. of NSW, 2004), M.Fin. (Griffith Univ. 2016) 7/12/2002, lived in Sydney; had issue.

7. Adelaide Rebekah Dahn-Bi Loane (11/3/2006-)
7. Violet Abigail Bohm-Bi Loane (31/3/2008-   )
7. Juliet Elizabeth Eugn-Bi Loane (8/12/2010-   )

5. Winsome Margaret Loane (20/6/1948-   ), a teacher
   graduated Balmain Teachers' College; BA (Univ. of
   Sydney); married Dr. Robert **Tong** AM (2/7/1943-   )
   LLB (Sydney), LLM (King's College, London,
   England); SJD. (QUT); Member of the Order of
   Australia (AM); 8/9/1973; had issue.
   6. Robert Andrew Tong (31/3/1977-   ) BSc.
      (Hons), PhD (Sydney); married Lisa Marie Murray
      (2/10/1976-   ) BEd; BTeach. (Univ. of Tech.
      Syd.) 21/4/2001; had issue.
      7. Ryan James Tong (2/7/2004-   )
      7. Hamish Nathan Tong (27/6/2006-   )
      7. Hugo Charlie Tong (8/9/2009-   )
   6. Peter Marcus Tong (22/2/1979-   ) BA (Hons.),
      M.Phil. Ed. (Sydney); BD (Hons.) (Moore
      Theological College). Married Katelyn Florence
      Tasker (4/8/1978-) BA (Hons.) (Sydney); M.
      Clinical Psychology (Macquarie Univ. Sydney)
      21/9/2002; had issue.
      7. Chloe Diana Tong (5/11/2005-   )
      7. Lily Kate Tong (12/11/2008-   )
      7. Samuel Peter Tong (18/11/2010-   )
   6. James David William Tong (3/12/1980-   ) BSc.
      (Adv.), MBBS (Sydney); graduate in Dip. Paediatric
      Medicine; M. Public Int. Health (Univ. of NSW);
      FRACP; married Amanda Lee Paine (19/5/1982-   )
      B.Teach. Special Ed. (Univ. of Tech. Syd.)
      3/10/2009; had issue.
      7. Clementine Abigail Tong (28/10/2016-   )
      7. Joshua Sampson David Tong (8/6/2019-   )
   6. Michael Lawrence Tong (12/2/1982-   ) BSc.

(Hons.) (Sydney); Dip. in Bible and Mission (Moore Theological College); BMed. Sc. (Hons.) B.Med. (Newcastle Univ.); Dip. Child Health (Sydney); Professional Dip. in Tropical Medicine and Hygiene with merit, (Liverpool School of Tropical Medicine UK); FRACGP. Married Margot Anne Moore (15/1/1980-   ) BVSc. (Hons.) (Univ. of Queensland) 20/7/2013; had issue.

7. Alexander Thomas Tong (26/7/2016-   )
7. William Douglas Tong (3/2/2019-3/2/2019)

6. Stephen Nicholas Tong (28/8/1984-   ) BA (Hons. 1) (Sydney Univ.); graduate Dip.Ed. (Univ. of New England, NSW); MPhil., PhD (Corpus Christie College, Cambridge, England). Married Bettina Joy Cook (24/4/2005-   ) BSoc.Sc., M. Dev. Cult. (Macquarie Univ., NSW); 24/11/2007; had issue.

7. Sophie Grace Tong (22/12/2011-   )
7. Benjamin Henry Tong (1/2/2014-   )
7. Edward Stephen Tong (31/3/2016-   )

6. Sylvia Winsome Lucy Patricia Tong (10/10/1986-   ) BSc, MTeach., MB, BS, Dip. Child Health (Univ. of Sydney), FRACGP. Married David Ross **Steel** (16/5/1986-   ) BApp.Sc., MTeach. (Univ. of Sydney) 6/1/2012; had issue.

7. Isabel Grace Steel (26/7/2017-   )

4. Linley Lawrence Loane (22/6/1913-27/5/1977) a qualified nursing sister, worked with the Bush Church Society in South Australia for twenty years, and later with the Home Missions Society in Sydney; unmarried and lived at Chatswood, NSW.

4. Gwendoline Lawrence Loane (17/1/1916-9/7/2005), kindergarten teacher;
   Married …
(i) Bayard Edgell **Barnard** (29/9/1911-20/10/1980) in 1938; lived at Warwick and later Buderim, Qld
   5. Peter Bayard Barnard (9/4/1939-5/5/2016) a mechanic and businessman. Lived in Brisbane; married Susan Megan McCartie (9/2/1943-   ) 25/4/1972; had issue.
      6. Rachel Gwendolyn Barnard (25/3/1979-   )
      6. Prudence Margaret Barnard (30/4/1981-   )
      6. Lucy Louise Frances Barnard (3/8/1982-   )
   5. Kathleen June Barnard (1942-   ) BSc. (Univ. of Qld.); married Neil William **Heather** (1932-   ) BSc. (Univ. of Qld.). Kathleen and Neil worked as Entomologists with the Department of Primary Industry, Brisbane, Qld.; 17/1/1967; had issue.
      6. Owen William Heather (25/6/1968-   )
      6. Ian Neil Heather (3/8/1971-   )
      6. Malcolm Charles Heather (3/8/1971-   ) BA (Hons) LLB; lived in Brisbane.
(ii) John Westgarth **Heussler** (9/8/1900-22/8/2002) 22/9/1983
4. Kenneth ("Peter") Lawrence Loane, MBE (6/8/1917-12/8/1983) graduated Th.L. (Moore College, Sydney), worked in several parishes in NSW and latterly as Canon of St. John's Provisional Cathedral, Parramatta. Awarded the Membership of the British Empire (MBE) for services to religion and the community. Married Vera Emily Jackson (17/12/1917-11/10/2001) 5/2/1944; had issue.
   5. Ian David Loane (22/11/1944-   )

Married . . .

(i) Judith Ann Wangmann (2/5/1949-   ), a trained kindergarten teacher, 2/1/1970, divorced.

(ii) Juliet Eileen Meads (5/6/1958-   ) 31/7/1985; had issue.

    6. Samantha Prudence Loane (22/8/1996-   )

    5. Alison Vera Loane (4/9/1947-   ) an office assistant.

4. Owen Lawrence Loane (14/1/1922-9/9/1942) served with the RAAF in World War II; unmarried.

Flt. Lieut. Loane (known as "Yoppy") was a pilot in Blenheim V6507 in a raid with RAAF Squadron 66 on Japanese shipping in Akyab (now Sittwe) a deep-sea port in Burma (now Myanmar) on 9/9/1942. His plane was shot down and Flt. Lieut. Loane and two crew members, including his cousin Robin Barnard were killed in action. Three other airmen in this raid were also shot down and became prisoners-of-war.

Loane's crew was one of the original eighteen crews that had previously served in the Middle East but were then withdrawn to serve in the Indian theatre of the war.

The above raid was part of an effort by the allies to slow the progression of the Japanese army during its advance through Burma towards India.[8]

3. Owen Effingham Lawrence (12/6/1881-18/6/1956) grew up at *Billopp*, went to school at Launceston Church Grammar School, Launceston, and then developed an interest in South Africa

- Served as a Trooper with the 1st Imperial Bushmen in the Boer War (Oct. 1899-May 1902) in South Africa.

- In WWI supported General Botha's expeditionary force to German held South West Africa (now Namibia) in 1914.

- Undertook an officer's training course at Duntroon, Australia, in 1915.
- Served in France with the Australian Army from 1916-1918.
- Eventually became a permanent resident of South Africa establishing himself as a pastoralist and living at *Lawreston*, Greylingstad, Mpumulanga, from 1909.
Married Erica Caroline Gatenby (13/6/1884-18/6/1956) (daughter of Herbert and Elizabeth Mary Gatenby of Longford, Tasmania) 16/4/1916; had issue.

4. Norman Owen Lawrence (5/3/1917-6/11/1994) a pastoralist, lived at *Lawreston*. Served in North Africa as a Lieutenant in the Eastern Cape Midde-landse 42nd Regiment, South African Army, in WWII. Captured at Tobruk, Libya in 1942, he became a POW at Modena, Italy, and then at Munich, in Germany (1942-45). Later a pastoralist and lived at *Lawreston*.
Married Helen Mary Ostler (16/1/1930-30/9/2021) from White River, Mpumulanga, 29/4/1950. Helen lived at *Lawreston* until 2010, when she moved to Howick, KwaZulu-Natal; had issue.

5. Anthony Norman Lawrence (19/11/1951-   ) BSc.Ag.Econ. (Natal Univ.) a pastoralist, married Susan Fane Moubray (30/5/1954-   ) 5/1/1980, BSc. Physiotherapy (Univ. of the Witwatersrand, Johannesburg, RSA) 5/1/1980. Lived at *Lawreston* until 2015 and then at Howick, KwaZulu-Natal after the sale of the property; had issue.

6. Jennifer Anne Lawrence (15/7/1981-   ) BVet.Sc. (Univ. of Pretoria).

6. Richard Anthony Lawrence (23/3/1983-   ) B.Com.

Accs. (Stellenbosch Univ.) a chartered accountant, married Sandra Ann Morrera (28/3/1986-   ) BA (Ed.); 31/12/2007. Lived at Pietermaritzburg, KwaZulu-Natal; had issue.

    7. Olivia Ann Lawrence (10/8/2010-   )

    7. Rebecca Grace Lawrence (23/11/2012-   )

    7. Adam Richard Lawrence (14/1/2015-   )

    7. Hannah Elizabeth Lawrence (18/7/2017-   )

    7. Catherine Abigail Lawrence (25/11/2019-   )

6. Sandra Mary Lawrence (21/8/1985-   ) BCom. Marketing (Stellenbosch Univ.); married Graham **Ransom** (17/3/1983-   ) BCom. Marketing, a chartered accountant, 18/2/2012; had issue.

    7. Joshua Robert Ransom (25/5/2015-   )

    7. Gabriella Rose Ransom (15/5/2017-   )

    7. Tessa Mary Ransom (15/9/2020-   )

5. Mary Catherine Lawrence (10/3/1953-   ) BSc. Physio. (Wits. University) married Michael Alexander Vincent **Graham** (26/8/1947-   ) BCom. (Univ. of Port Elizabeth) and MBA (Univ. of Capetown) 3/11/1979; lived at Umhlali, KwaZulu-Natal; had issue.

6. Stuart Lawrence Vincent Graham (18/6/1985-   ) BCom.Bus.Management (Stellenbosch Univ.). Lived at Umhlali, KwaZulu-Natal, to marry Chantal Louise Tomlin (26/6/1989-   ) 6/11/2021.

6. Catherine (Katie) Deborah Graham (25/11/1988-   ) married Devon David **de Lange** (26/1/1985-   ) 16/5/2015; had issue.

    7. Daniel Michael de Lange (17/3/2017-   )

    7. Abigail Catherine de Lange (16/8/2018-   )

7. Annabelle Catherine de Lange (6/5/2021-   )
5. Owen Edward Lawrence (31/1/1956-   ) Dip.Ag.
(Cedara College, Pietermaritzburg, 1978) a pastoralist
in South Africa, later lived in Brisbane, Australia
from July 2002. Married Melanie Fleur Remmington
(18/8/1959-   ) Dip. Higher Ed., 1/9/1990; had
issue.
>   6. Owen Gordon Lawrence (14/5/1993-   ) studied
>   Urban Development (Quantity Surveying) (Qld.
>   Univ. of Tech.), lived in Brisbane.
>   6. Douglas Norman Robert Lawrence (18/9/1995-   )
>   studying Applied Science (Construction Management)
>   at RMIT (in 2020), lived in Brisbane, latterly
>   Melbourne.
4. Edward Effingham Lawrence (6/4/1925-26/5/1943)
4. Jean Winifred Erica Lawrence (23/2/1929-   ) married
Michael Powis **Estill** (16/8/1925-11/8/2015) 7/4/1956, a
mechanical engineer; had issue.
>   5. Susan Margret Estill (12/1/1958-   ) a teacher in
>   Johannesburg, RSA.
>   5. Judith Mary Estill (13/8/1959-   ) a trained nurse;
>   married Ross Guy **Johnston** (14/12/1955-   )
>   9/1/1982, a pastoralist at Kokstad, KwaZulu-Natal,
>   RSA; had issue.
>>   6. Stuart Guy Johnston (24/7/1983-   ) Dip.Ag.
>>   (Cedara College, PMB.) a pastoralist, married
>>   Odette Olivier (8/9/1986-   ) BSc.Physio.
>>   (Masters) (Univ. of Cape Town), 14/4/2012. Lived
>>   at Kokstad, KwaZulu-Natal; had issue.
>>   7. Siena Beryl Johnston (1/7/2014-   )
>>   7. Annabelle Mary Johnston (10/3/2016-   )

7. Nicola Janet Johnston (19/1/2018-   )
6. Jessica Mary Johnston (-   ) BA, PPE
(Stellenbosch Univ.) married Garrick Wayne **Jones**
(14/6/1985-   ) 19/6/2021, lived in Cape Town.
6. Laura Jean Johnston (21/10/1988-   ) BCom.
(Hons.) Bus. Management (Stellenbosch Univ.)
CFP. Married Thomas Simon Howard **Brukman**
(30/10/1986-   ) BCom. (Hons.) Economics
(Rhodes Univ. Grahamstown, Eastern Cape) CFP;
16/12/2018; lived in Cape Town; had issue.
7. Simon Ross Brukman (17/4/2020-   )
5. Edward David Estill (6/9/1964-   ) Nat.Bus.Man.
(Univ. of Johannesburg) FSP, married Samantha Leigh
Glassock (9/11/1969-   ) LLB (Univ. of Natal,
PMB), 9/1/1997; had issue.
6. Bridget Jamie Estill (13/10/1999-   )
6. James Michael Estill (25/6/2003-   )
6. Kate Nicole Estill (13/9/2006-   )
5. Andrew Michael Estill (2/4/1976-   ) BTech.
Elec. Eng. (Wits. Tech.) Married James Rautenbach
(17/7/1987-   ); lived in Johannesburg.
3. Leonard Linley Lawrence (22/3/1883-11/10/1967) a
pastoralist and major Polwarth sheep breeder, lived at and
managed *Formosa*, Cressy, for his cousin Cornelius Henry
"Con" Lawrence (p. 113-114) from 1908 until he bought
the property, with his sons, in 1945. Married Eveline Cooze
Rice (1882-6/8/1965) 15/4/1914 in Sydney; had issue.
4. Geoffrey Linley Lawrence (27/10/1915-16/6/1984) a
pastoralist, lived at *Formosa* and for many years was a top
breeder and exhibitor of Polwarth sheep; President of the
Tasmanian branch of the Australian Polwarth Breeder's

Association, 1956-1958, and President of the national body 1961-1964; President of the Campbell Town Show Association, 1978-1980. Geoff is remembered through the "G. L. Lawrence Award for the top Tasmanian Commercial Sheep Flock of the Year", awarded by the Campbell Town Show Association in the years 1988-1997. Married Ardyn Carington Smith (15/8/1916-29/7/2015) 15/10/1949; had issue.

5. Philippa Ann Lawrence (3/1/1954-   ) married Leigh **Heard** (25/9/1954-   ) 10/3/1984, a veterinary surgeon and pastoralist; lived in Victoria, divorced; had issue.

> 6. Geoffrey Bromwell Heard (4/11/1986-   ) a financial analyst, BComm. (Finance Major); BSc (Maths & Statistics Major) (Univ. of Melb. 2010), lived in Victoria. Partnered Joe Romo (19/5/1992-) of Maine, USA.

> 6. John Douglas Lawrence Heard (15/8/1988-   ) an agronomist and pastoralist; BAgr.Sc. (Univ. of Melb. 2009) managed *Formosa* (May 2016-   ); married Margot Shirley Lowther   (6/6/1987-   ) physiotherapist, 19/5/2018; had issue.

>> 7. William Douglas Heard (5/8/2019-   )
>> 7. Olive Esme Heard (10/9/2021-   )

5. Roslyn Linley Lawrence (14/1/1956-   ) married Michael **Propsting** (25/5/1954-   ) a pastoralist, 19/10/1985; lived in Launceston, divorced; had issue.

> 6. Sarah Louise Lawrence Propsting (13/3/1987-   ) a pelvic floor physiotherapist BPhysio. (Hons.), (Univ. of South Australia 2010); M.Physio. (Univ. of SA 2015); PG Cert. Physio. (Univ. of SA

2018). Married Patrick **Walsh** (26/10/1984-   )
9/2/1919 a barrister and solicitor. BSc
(Jurisprudence) (Univ. of Adelaide 2006), LLB
(Univ. of Adelaide 2008). Lived in Adelaide, had
issue.

7. Sophie Elizabeth Walsh (2/8/2020-   )

4. Richard Effingham Lawrence (27/7/1920-29/6/1995) a
pastoralist and entrepreneur, lived at *Rockthorpe*, Cressy,
Tasmania. Richard (Dick) enlisted in the Australian army
in 1940 and was sent to Timor as part of the 2/40th
Battalion debacle in 1941 (p. 152). Facing overwhelming
odds, "Sparrow" force surrendered to the Japanese in Feb.
1942 and Dick became a prisoner-of-war for the next
three-and-a half long years serving on the construction of

Dick Lawrence with tiger snake 'livestock' on his snake farm
and abbatoir near Cressy, Tasmania, courtesy of
The Examiner newspaper, photo taken 3/4/1991.

Formosa homestead. Photo c. J. D. L. Heard, 2021

the Burma Railway and in coal mines in Japan.

In later years he was a top Polwarth sheepbreeder, exhibitor and exporter, a period that included the sale of a *Rockthorpe* ram in Uruguay in 1983 for the then world record $A150,000. Dick was active in the Polwarth Assoc., both statewide and nationally, also the Campbell Town Show Association. After attending the World Sheep & Wool Congress in Calgary, Canada, he organized the next World Sheep & Wool Congress, held 1st to 3rd March 1989 in Launceston.

In his 70s, Dick built and established a game meat abattoir, and an independent tiger snake farm, both located on Burlington Road, Cressy.

He had an intense involvement in politics and the organizational side of the Liberal Party of Australia receiving a Life Membership on his retirement from this activity. Married Patricia Nellie Viney (27/10/1928-5/1/2013) 14/12/1949; had issue.

5. Diana Elizabeth Lawrence (17/5/1951-   ) a library technician, lived in Launceston, Tas. Married Kenneth Hugh **Targett** (19/1/1947-   ) barrister and solicitor of the Supreme Court of Tasmania, 16/2/1974; had issue.

  6. Claire Zoë Linley Targett (30/12/1979-   ) compounding pharmacist and fashion designer, BPharm. (Univ. of Tasmania, 2004), Adv. Dip. Fashion Design (Ultimo TAFE, 2010), lived in Canberra.

  6. Olivia Thea Dora Targett (13/7/1981-) a naturopath, BHealth Science (Complimentary Medicine) (Charles Sturt Univ.); married Jock Robert **Nivison** (27/10/1982-   ) 10/12/2010, lived at *Yalgoo*, Walcha, NSW; very progressive Hereford cattle and Merino sheep breeders; winners of the "Weekly Times Coles Farmer of the Year Award, 2017"; had issue.
    7. Francesca Isla Nivison (20/5/2012-   )
    7. Eliza Grace Nivison (6/10/2014-   )
    7. Edie Rose Nivison (18/7/2018-   )

  6. Nicholas Alexander Hugh Targett (27/8/1984-   ) a truck driver and plant operator; married Rebecca Kate Sullivan (5/8/1983-   ) 2/3/2016, lived in northern Tasmania; had issue
    7. Cassidy Grace Dotty Targett (18/1/2021-   )

5. Graeme Richard Lawrence (27/11/1952-   ) a pastoralist in Tasmania in his early years.
Married . . .
(i) Joanna Elizabeth Parkes (5/9/1953-   ) 24/11/1973, divorced; had issue.

6. Sarah Rachael Lawrence (19/2/1975-19/9/1975)
6. Melanie Tamsyn Lawrence (15/7/1977-   )
married Timothy Robert **Paddison** (16/4/1974-   )
15/1/2000, BCom. (Property Economics) (UWSH),
hotel owner; lived in Windermere, Tas.; had issue.
7. Alexis Victoria Paddison (30/11/2007-   )
7. Angus Jack Paddison (19/3/2009-   )
6. Angus James Effingham Lawrence (8/9/1979-
10/11/2004) an Australian Army Serviceman,
including service in Iraq, died of heat exhaustion
while on military exercises in northern Australia near
Darwin.[9]
(ii) Janet Irene Tabler (21/7/1951-   ) partner.
5. Owen Leonard Lawrence (19/4/1956-12/3/1987)
a pastoralist and inventor, died from pneumonia
in Perth, WA. Lived in Tasmania and WA; married
Virginia Eileen Florance (1/6/1953-   ) 20/11/1976
in Kojunup, WA, divorced; had issue.
6. Veronica Jane Lawrence (31/8/1979-   ) a
financial advisor; married Robert Edward Clifford
Terry (23/10/1981-   ) 7/4/2007, lived in NW
Tasmania; had issue.
7. Edward Lawrence Terry (23/11/2009-   )
7. Zara Florance Terry (5/8/2012-   )
6. Prudence Evelyn Elizabeth Lawrence (20/7/1981-)
an architect, lived in Melbourne, Victoria

Chapter 11

OCTAVIUS VERNON LAWRENCE
(1836-1915)

Octavius Vernon Lawrence (O. V. L.) was the seventh son of W. E. Lawrence, and the only one to enter the medical profession. He was born and educated in Launceston, Tasmania, initially lived at *Penquite*, near Launceston and then studied medicine at Cambridge University in the UK. Ill health forced him to return to Launceston during the course and he later completed his medical degree at the University of Melbourne.

Octavius Vernon Lawrence

O.V.L. was among the very early graduates from this medical school (awarded the MB, 2/12/1868), the first intake of medical students being in 1862; he was awarded the Bachelor of Surgery degree, Univ. of Melb., in 1880.

This was the second year in which the BS was conferred on Melbourne graduates – prior to this the medical degree was an MB only and Melbourne graduates had difficulty in obtaining positions at the Melbourne Hospital (opened in 1848) because of alleged deficiencies in their surgical training. The fact that the hospital medical staff were graduates of English medical schools and looked down on "colonial" degrees may also have been relevant. O.V.L. was admitted "ad eundum" to an English degree, as well, after completing his training. On 18/4/1871 he was awarded the first MD degree conferred by the new Melbourne medical school (by examination, not thesis).

He was appointed Resident Physician at the Melbourne Hospital in 1868 (one of two) and Senior Resident Medical Officer (a salaried position, equivalent to the present superintendent) in 1869. In the years 1870-73 he was an Honorary Assistant Physician; he was then absent for a year, but returned in 1875 as Honorary Physician and held this position until 1878. He continued in busy medical practice at Fitzroy until his retirement in 1890.

In retirement he lived at *Invermay*, in Grandview Grove, Hawthorn, Victoria where he died in 1915. He was interested, as a hobby, in horse racing, and bought a property in Gippsland where he kept horses. He married twice – firstly, Editha Wettenhall in 1856 (she was daughter of Commander Robert Wettenhall R.N., who arrived in Tasmania in 1835, from Cheshire, England) and secondly, Jessie Barnard (sister of Clara and Grace Barnard) in 1878 and has numerous descendants from both marriages.

Three children from the first marriage have a continuing line of descendants. Percy Vernon (1858-1918) was a pastoralist, lived in Victoria, and his family now live mainly in Tasmania.

Ada Caroline (1861-1892) married Richard Vinicombe Dennis (1842-1912) whose father, Alexander Dennis (1811-1892) and two brothers had come to Australia on the "*John Bull*" from Penzance, Cornwall, arriving in Port Phillip Bay in 1840. They moved west to unsettled land in the present day Western District of Victoria and became established as pastoralists. At one stage in the late 1800s, family holdings were 84,000 acres. *Tarndwarncoort* near Birregurra has been the main Dennis property over the years and various family members have lived on properties originally part of this land -

- *Bleak House* – sold in 1842 because of difficult

182

seasons, and re-purchased by W. J. Dennis (1887-1941) (p. 189) in 1926

- *Uondo* – detached from *Tarndwarncoort* in 1871
- *Korongee*, 1920
- *Coorameet*, 1940 - sold 2009
- *Lariggan*, 1925
- *Brolga*, 1950 – sold 1996

Eeyeuk (north of Terang, Vic.) is another Dennis property, purchased 1867.

The Dennis family has had a major role in the establishment, and the development, of the Polwarth breed of sheep (p. 265) over many years.

Herman Fermor Lawrence (1862-1936) (p. 202) was the third son from the first marriage and followed his father into the medical profession. To quote his obituary:[1]

"In his youth, Herman Lawrence had a magnificent physique and was a splendid athlete, a good footballer and one of the best pair oarsmen of his day on the river. Although for a time he attended Wesley College, Melbourne, and the Geelong Grammar School, the major portion of his education was given to him at Scotch College, Melbourne.

He entered the medical school in the University o Melbourne in 1881, and before graduating went to the Edinburgh Medical School. On June 7, 1889, he was registered by the Medical Board of Victoria as Licentiate and Licentiate in Midwifery of the Royal College of Physicians and Royal College of Surgeons of Edinburgh, 1888; Licentiate of the Faculty of Physicians and Surgeons of Glasgow, 1888; Member of the Royal College of Physicians, Edinburgh, 1889.

When Saint Vincent's Hospital was founded in Melbourne in 1893, Lawrence was a member of the original staff, the remaining survivors of which are A.L. Kenny and J. H. Nelly.[2]

Lawrence was appointed as honorary specialist for diseases of the skin. Soon after the announcement of the discovery of Rontgen rays he became deeply interested in them, and from that time onward was in frequent consultation with Professor (now Sir) Thomas Ranken Lyle, Physicist at the University of Melbourne. Lawrence procured the earliest tubes available and equipped a room for their use in his practice. He had as many as six of these early tubes in action at one time with patients in his consulting room, without any protection for himself, no one being at that time aware of the dangerous ill-effects of these early tubes. He suffered much illness in later years as a result, and lost much of the robustness and apparent vigor of his earlier days. On the discovery of radium and its properties by Madam Curie, he was even more deeply interest in radium than he had been in x-rays; he devoted himself for the rest of his life to their intensive study and carried out continuous series of exhaustive experiments as to the properties and correct use of radium.[3] For many years Dr. Lawrence was physician to outpatients at the Melbourne Hospital. When the Department of Dermatology was founded, he was appointed dermatologist.[4] He was also consulting dermatologist at the Queen Victoria Hospital.

He founded a school of radiotherapy in Melbourne, through his assistants, which has been most successful and of incalculable benefit to the people.[5]

He was president of the British Association of Dermatology and Syphilology (Victorian Branch) since its inauguration.

He gained a world-wide reputation as a result of his studies and experiments. He wrote two books, published numerous papers on radium, and received repeated queries and requests for papers from radiological journals throughout the world. Few of his colleagues knew how great his reputation was abroad."

A Melbourne University professor once wrote: 'Lawrence was a good man, the right breed, and one who could be trusted implicitly, both within his profession and outside of it.'"

The second marriage of OVL with Jessie Barnard produced six children, four of whom married. Bruce Effingham (1897-1948) was a pastoralist near Trafalgar, in Victoria, living on the property that originally belonged to his father.

George Douglas (1880-1960) graduated Bachelor of Laws, Melbourne University, and practiced law in Melbourne, being associated with the law firm, Akehurst, initially, then having his own firm, G. D. Lawrence. During service in World War I he reached the rank of Captain in the 3rd Field Artillery. He was associated with the establishment and building of St. Mark's Church, Camberwell (completed 1927) and also the early development of Camberwell Girls' Grammar School (opened in 1920 and, in 2021, a major girls school in Melbourne with over 700 pupils). The "G. D. Lawrence Memorial Prize" is, to this day, one of the major academic prizes awarded at the school annually, and one of the four houses at the school is "Lawrence House". He was a member of the School Council for many years, as well. His interest in the Anglican Church of Australia extended to membership of the Council of the Melbourne Diocese (1920-1960) the church of England Men's Society and the Diocesan Book Society. For the last twenty-five years of his life (approximately) he lived at 31 Maysia Street, Camberwell and died suddenly on 21st April 1960, his eightieth birthday. The author has pleasant memories of visits by Douglas Lawrence to *Billopp* in Tasmania during the early 1950s and being instructed in the art of catching rabbits!

Two daughters from the second marriage of O. V. L, who married, were Jessie Katherine (to Rev. C. T. Rodda) and Helen Ruth (to E. D. Cobb); both have descendants at the present time.

Genealogy

2. Octavius Vernon Lawrence (1/1/1836-7/2/1915) studied medicine at Cambridge and Melbourne Universities; senior Resident Medical Officer at the Melbourne Hospital (equivalent to Superintendent) in 1869, Senior Honorary Physician, 1875-1878;
Married...
(i) Editha Caroline Wettenhall (1836-26/12/1872) in 1856; had issue.

   3. Percy Vernon Lawrence (21/1/1858-29/11/1918) a pastoralist, lived at *Vernondale*, near Shean's Creek, Euroa, Victoria; died as a result of injuries received following a fall from a horse at his property (Shepparton Advertiser, 9 Dec 1918). Buried at the Brighton General Cemetery, Melbourne. Married Mary Kate Bateman (1864-1959) 1888; had issue.

      4. Lawrence Howard Lawrence (8/2/1891-4/8/1976) a pastoralist, sold *Vernondale* and lived at *Yallock,* near Holbrook, NSW, and then at *Woodbury House*, Antill Ponds, Tasmania (1950-1967). Served with the allied forces in France in WWI and was invalided out because of injuries in 1918; married Dorothy Jessie Maude Fisher (1903-11/2/1965) in 1929 in Melbourne; had issue.

         5. Lynette Lawrence (11/8/1934-1994) married George Henry Alistair **Keach** in 1955; had issue.

            6. Sally Ann Keach (1956-   ) married Lindsay **Chugg** (-   ) 6/9/1971, lived in Tasmania and then NSW; had issue.

               7. Katrina Chugg (14/1/1984-   ) married; had issue.

                  8. Skylar House (1/12/2006-   )

8. Jonty House (14/3/2009-   )
8. Elody House (10/8/2011-   )
7. Alistair Chugg (9/6/1987-   ) lived in NSW.
7. Nicolas Chugg (16/2/1991-   ) lived in Dubbo, NSW.
6. George William (Bill) Keach (10/8/1960-   ) lived in Tasmania.
5. John Howard Lawrence (13/11/1935-28/5/2001) a businessperson and pastoralist; lived in Tasmania; married Margaret Anne Allison (4/10/1938-   ) 12/9/1959; had issue.
6. Amanda Margaret Lawrence (28/11/1961-   ) a businessperson, lived in Canberra, ACT; married Jerry **Tonon** (20/12/1960-   ) 6/9/1986; had issue.
7. Kylie Marie Tonon (2/3/1988-   ) married Craig **Whitehead** (-   ) 26/9/2020; had issue.
8. Sophie Annie Whitehead (20/3/2020-   )
7. Daniel Tonon (12/10/1990-   )
6. Michael John Lawrence (3/10/1964-   ) a businessperson, lived in Geelong, Vic.; married Harriet Florence Gunn (15/5/1966-   ) 17/7/1993; had issue.
7. Walter John William Lawrence (15/5/1994-   )
7. Maxwell Richard Lawrence (6/10/1996-   )
7. Wilbur Harry Lawrence (17/12/1998-   )
7. Tabitha Grace Lawrence (2/8/2001-   )
7. Archibald Charles Lawrence (24/9/2003-   )
7. Digby Michael Lawrence (7/9/2006-   )
7. Frederick Basil Lawrence (6/2/2009-   )
6. Merrilyn Ann Lawrence (13/10/1969-   ) lawyer,

lived in Hobart, Tas., married John Nicholas Dryll **Williams** (25/12/1965-   ) 12/2/1994; had issue.

    7. Lillian Olivia Williams (12/9/1999-   )

    7. Montgomery John Dryll Williams (26/11/2004-)

5. Flora Marcia Lawrence (7/10/1941-   ) a property developer, married Serge **de Kantzow** (-   ) 1971, lived in Sydney, NSW, and then Tasmania; had issue.

    6. Lars de Kantzow (21/5/1973-   )

    6. Signe (Poppy) de Kantzow (1/12/1975-   )

5. Dennis Patrick Lawrence (7/9/1943-   ) a pastoralist and property developer.
   Married . . .

(i) Katherine Elizabeth Gunn (15/6/1944-   ) 14/6/1966, lived at *Moana* near Low Head, Tasmania; divorced, had issue.

    6. Timothy Patrick Lawrence (3/5/1968-   ) a businessperson, lived in northern Tasmania, married Belinda May Hooper (21/12/1967-   ) 13/3/1995; had issue.

        7. Josephine Isabel Lawrence (14/12/1995-   )

        7. Sally Annabelle Lawrence (18/2/1998-   )

    6. Sally Elizabeth Lawrence (17/6/1970-   ) a businessperson and teacher, married Matthew David **Lowe** (30/9/1969-   ) 4/1/1995; had issue.

        7. Ruby Elizabeth Lowe (10/6/1999-   )

        7. Alice Emily Lowe (13/7/2004-   )

    6. Edward (Eddie) Thomas Lawrence (14/3/1973-   ) a businessperson, lived in Hobart, Tasmania; married Kristin Sarah Percy (2/10/1971-   ) from Ottawa, Canada, 31/1/2003; had issue.

        7. Tobias (Toby) James Lawrence (9/2/2005-   )

7. Sienna Rose Lawrence (11/11/2007-   )

(ii) Roslyn Grace Weeding (née Strong) (31/12/1946-   ) 9/2/1990; no issue.

3. Harold Holford Lawrence (5/9/1859-1876) drowned in the Yarra River, Melbourne, as a schoolboy.

3. Ada Caroline Lawrence (31/7/1861-24/1/1892) married Richard Vinicombe **Dennis** (12/2/1842-13/11/1912)[6] lived at *Uondo* and later, Richard and family lived at *Tarndwarncoort*, Warncoort, Victoria, following the death of Ada from tuberculosis. *Tarndwarncoort* remains in family ownership, the original property of this Dennis family in Western Victoria; had issue.

4. Catherine Vernona Dennis (26/3/1885-1/2/1969) married William James **Dennis** (25/4/1877-21/8/1941) in 1910 and lived at *Uondo*, Warncoort, Vic.; had issue.

5. Richard Charles Dennis (5/1/1911-24/1/1977) married Katherine Lena Parsons (5/2/1915-2005) in 8/1/1942, and lived at *Bleak House*, Birregurra, Victoria; had issue.

6. Hilare Mary Dennis (22/4/1944-23/3/2000) married Hugh Donald **McIntyre** (22/1/1940-   ) 3/4/1965 and lived at *Wanderriby*, Inverleigh; had issue.

7. Michael Donald McIntyre (17/5/1967-   ) married Johanna Kate Carnegie (30/8/1968-   ); had issue.

8. Hamish James McIntyre (1999-   )

8. Hannah Rose Hilare McIntyre (2001-   )

7. Charles Hugh McIntyre (30/8/1969-   )

(i) married Fiona Samantha Bogle (4/8/1973-   ) 30/1/1998, divorced; no issue.

(ii) partnered Michelle Ballis (-); no issue.
6. Diana Katherine Dennis (26/9/1946-   ) MSc.
(Univ. of Melb.); married Hew Gardiner **Richards**
(5/5/1946-   ) 21/2/1970; had issue.
7. James Christian Richards (2/5/1971-   )
married Deborah Carol Hodge (4/1/1972-   )
13/9/1997; had issue.
8. Lachlan James Richards (12/3/2001-   )
8. Kyle Matthew Richards (21/2/2004-   )
8. Jasmine May Richards (6/11/2007-   )
7. Rosemary Jane Richards (17/3/1974-   )
married William Edwin Peter **Kenwick** (1973-   )
1999; had issue.
8. Nicholas Edwin Peter Kenwick (16/6/2003-   )
8. Jeremy Hew Gardner Kenwick (12/2/2006-   )
8. Charles Richard Dennis Kenwick (13/7/2009-   )
7. Matthew Charles Richards (29/4/1978-   )
(i) married Heather Jewell (-) divorced.
(ii) partnered Catherine Harrison (1975-   ); had
issue.
8. Henry Lawrence Richards (21/6/2008-   )
8. Olive Josephine Richards (15/3/2012-   )
6. James Edgar Richard Dennis (29/10/1948-   )
BAgr.Sc. (Univ. of Melb.), married Claire Farnbach
(9/9/1948-   ) 9/2/1971. Lived at *Bleak House*;
had issue.
7. Scott Conrad Dennis (6/4/1975-   ) married
Melissa Claire DeVeith (1975-   ) 2001. Lived at
Bleak House; had issue.
8. Stirling Angus James Dennis (18/3/2004-   )
8. Rory Austin Charles Dennis (25/1/2006-   )

8. Genevieve Petra Katherine Dennis (2009-   )
7. Kim Catherine Dennis (1/9/1977-   ) married Mark John **Clatworthy** (23/6/1977-   ); had issue.
    8. Sienna Claire Clatworthy (2009-   )
    8. Eva Johanna Clatworthy (2013-   )
    8. Maya Elizabeth Clatworthy (2014-   )
7. Ross James Dennis (7/3/1986-   ) married Madeline Mitchell (-   ) 2012.
6. Susan Vernona Dennis (9/7/1951-   ) married Dennis **Hamilton** (1948-   ) from California, USA, 1975; had issue.
    7. George Charles Dennis (1978-   ) married Paige Simpson (1969-   ) 2005; had issue.
        8. Chloe Lena Dennis (2006-   )
        8. Jack Dennis (26/6/2010-   )
    7. Jessica Helen Dennis (1981-   ) married Bradley Ian **Burchell** (1978-   ) in 2007; had issue.
        8. Freya Susan Burchell (2009-   )
        8. Nathan Bradley Burchell (2011-   )
    7. Elizabeth Katherine Dennis (1984-   ) married Steven Daryl **Winter** (1984-   ) in 2009; had issue.
        8. Olivia Susan Winter (2011-   )
        8. William Percy Winter (2014-   )
        8. Rowan Dennis Winter (2016-   )
6. Wendy Margaret Dennis (31/3/1957-   ) a teacher, lived at Ocean Grove, Victoria. In 2017 Wendy printed privately a 120 page[7] pictorial account of the Dennis family, 1633-2017.
(i) married Franz Josef **Tuechler** (28/8/1960-   )

30/6/1984; divorced 2000, had issue.
7. Anna Katherine Tuechler (30/8/1987-   )
partnered Arnaud **Charlier** (5/1/1984-   )
7. Alexandra Claire Tuechler (11/12/1990-   )
partnered Benjamin **Evans** (10/9/1989-   ); had issue
8. Charles Dennis Evans (5/9/2020-   )
(ii) partnered Colin **Burrett** (9/1/1953-   ) 2005.
5. Donald James Alexander Dennis (8/1/1920-2/8/1997) married Rhonda Violet Shaw (14/4/1927-18/6/1974) 29/10/1947 lived at *Eeyeuk*, Kolora, Victoria; had issue.
6. Alice Jane Dennis (5/9/1949-   ) married John Damian **Kenna** (9/1/1948-   ) 27/9/1969; had issue.
7. James William Kenna (12/4/1970-   ) married Linda Jayne Wilson (14/9/1971-   ) 25/3/1995; had issue.
8. Meg Isobel Kenna (2000-   )
8. Samuel James Kenna (2003-   )
8. Alexander Mitchell Kenna (2005-   )
8. William John Kenna (2007-   )
7. Fiona Jane Kenna (5/4/1971-   ) married Angelo **Pagano** (25/9/1963-   ) 12/1/1997; had issue.
8. Ella-Rose Jane Pagano (1999-   )
8. Matteo Pasquale Pagano (2002-   )
8. Louis John Pagano (2004-   )
6. Alexander Thomas Dennis (25/2/1951-   ) married Susan Baulch (27/6/1955-   ) 27/8/1977; had issue.

7. Sophie Helen Dennis (12/11/1980-   )
married Mark **Grace** (1978-   ) 2010; had
issue.
   8. Olivia Susan Grace (2013-   )
   8. Charley Owen Grace (2015-   )
7. Phoebe Rhonda Dennis (8/10/1983-   )
married Paul **Malseed** (1978-   ) 2008; had
issue.
   8. James Alexander Malseed (2010-   )
   8. Jack Christopher Malseed (2012-   )
   8. Eleanor Paula Malseed (2016-   )
7. William Joseph Alexander Dennis (26/11/1985-   )
married Stephanie K. Rendell (1986-   ) 2015;
had issue.
   8. Patrick Alexander Dennis (19/11/2016-   )
6. Pepita Dennis (10/1/1955-   ) married John Alan
Hay **Marshall** (5/5/1953-   ) 27/12/1978; had
issue.
7. Clare Elizabeth Hay Marshall (12/91984-   )
married Paul Anthony **Dunn** (1980-   ) 2008;
had issue.
   8. Crawford John Dunn (2013-   )
   8. Phillippa Dunn (2017-   )
7. Alanna Jane Le Messurier Marshall (12/11/1986-)
married Daniel Joel **Finn** (-   ) 2014; had
issue.
   8. Phoebe Ivy Finn (2015-   )
7. Nicholas Thomas Shaw Marshall (17/2/1992-   )
5. Jessie Caroline Dennis (24/9/1924-2013) lived at
Uondo.
4. Francis Caroline Dennis (1886-1962) unmarried.

4. Alexander William Dennis (19/10/1887-14/9/1969) lived at *Tarndwarncoort*.[8] Married Nita Renee James (27/8/1885-9/8/1969) 1913; had issue.
5. Norman Alexander Dennis (25/11/1915-17/4/2009) married Sheila Currie (1919-2019) 1941; had issue.
   6. David Alexander John Dennis (1944-   ) married Wendy Scott Greenfield (1941-   ) 1971; David and Wendy operated *Tarndwarncoort* from the mid-1980s and took a diversified approach to Polwarth wool growing with direct wool sales, craft work shops and public accommodation in farm workers' cottages; had issue.
      7. Michael Richard Currie Dennis (29/10/1972-   ) married Annelies Johanna van Beest (1969-   ); divorced; had issue.
         8. Olivia Johanna Scott Dennis (9/12/2003-   )
         8. Finley Alexander Dennis 1/12/2006-   )
      7. Georgina Scott Dennis (15/10/1974-   ) Married . . .
      (i) Gregory Michael **Lenehan** (-   ) 2000, divorced; had issue.
         8. Phoebe Kathleen Lenehan (22/10/2001-   )
         8. Lachlan Alexander Dennis Lenehan (24/9/2004-)
      (ii) Paul **McMillan** (-   ) 2020; had issue
      7. Alastair James Dennis (11/11/1978-   ) married Jemma Grace Lewis (6/4/1985-   ) 2018; Alastair has returned after thirteen years in construction in Tanzania, and runs the farming side of the business at *Tarndwarncoort* in 2020; had issue.

8. Pippa Jane Dennis (9/1/2019-   )
8. Myles Hartley Dennis (30/4/2021-   )
7. Thomas Mackay Dennis (17/10/1981-   )
partnered Jason Mark Arnell (22/8/1985-   ).
Tom lives at *Tarndwarncoort* and continues to
operate the agri-tourism business (in 2020).
6. Celia Mary Dennis (4/12/1947-   ) married
Andrew Robert **Gubbins** (18/1/1948-   ) 1976;
had issue.
   7. Timothy Andrew Gubbins (11/11/1981-   ) married
   Julia Claire Ogdin (27/1/1981-   ); had issue.
      8. Alexander Timothy Gubbins (12/12/2014-   )
      8. Georgina Claire Gubbins (14/10/2016-   )
      8. Philippa Jean Gubbins (21/5/2021-   )
   7. Simon Hugh Gubbins (14/11/1983-   )
6. Thomas Currie Dennis (20/9/1950-   )
married Monica Mary Lightfoot (18/8/1949-   )
1/12/1973; had issue.
   7. Samuel John Dennis (16/10/1976-   ) married
   Sarah Jennings Prowse (16/7/1977-   )
   5/3/2002; had issue
      8. Annabel Cullross Dennis (5/9/2007-   )
      8. Elizabeth Donaldson Dennis (7/10/2009-   )
      8. Alice Hefferman Dennis (2/3/2013-   )
   7. Jane Caroline Dennis (30/9/1979-   ) married
   Matthew Adam **Whitehead** (28/1/1976-   )
   10/11/2007; had issue
      8. Harriet Sarah Whitehead (28/1/2009-   )
      8. Tess Trixie Whitehead (5/3/2011-   )
   7. Sarah Currie Dennis (26/9/1983-   ) married
   Dorothy Baker **Ellington** (5/6/1984-   )

2/4/2010; had issue

8. Magnolia Shar Ellington (2/11/2020-   )

6. Edward Richard Dennis (1954-   ) married
Frith Campbell Penny (1954-   ) 1975; had issue.

7. Joshua Alexie Dennis (1979-   ) married Sarah
Gibbins (1982-   )

7. Zoe Emily Dennis (1982-   ) married Mathew
Wisdom (1982-   )

7. Mathew James Jarvis Dennis (1987-   ) married
Merrin Jones (1988-   ); had issue.

8. Milo Alexander Moncrieff Dennis (2016-   )

8. Maple Della Rose Dennis (11/9/2020-   )

6. Rowena Dennis (1960-   ) married Paul **Church**
(6/2/1959-   ) 9/4/1983.

5. Mary Nita Dennis (Oct. 1919-15/7/1920)

5. Robert James Lawrence Dennis (6/1/1922 -13/6/2002),
lived at *Lariggan* and later Philip Is. Vic., died at
Cowes, Philip Is.

Married . . .

(i) Dorothy Mavis Gay (née Carter) (25/6/1920-
15/3/2018) 1946, divorced; lived at *Lariggan*,
Warncoort; had issue.

6. William Lawrence Dennis (1947-   ) married
Wendy Alison Austin (1950-   ) 1975; had issue.

7. Peter Alexander William Dennis (18/7/1985-   )
married Yi (Annie) Xin (1984-   ) 15/11/2015;
had issue.

8. Harriet Jane Dennis (18/3/2019-   )

7. Sarah Catherine Dennis (12/1/1989-   )

6. Elizabeth Ann Dennis (5/8/1949-   ), studied at
Deakin Univ. Lived at Birregurra.

Married...

(i) Geoffrey Alistair **Grant** (1945-   ) 1970; had issue.

   7. Sophie Louise Grant (20/12/1970-   ) married Richard **Wilson** (1967-   )

(ii) David **Tucker** (1948-   ) 1980; had issue.

   7. Charles David Tucker (30/11/1980-   ) married Jennifer Batchelor (1983-   ) 23/12/2007; had issue.

      8. Hugo Henry Tucker (17/5/2009-   )

      8. Vivienne Daisy Tucker (25/7/2010-   )

(iii) Ron **Menz** (1941-   ) 1995.

(ii) Helen Marion Wilson (1943-   ) 15/9/1973; (second wife of Robert James Lawrence Dennis, p. 196); had issue.

   6. Emily Jane Dennis (1975-   ) married Peter Richard **van Beveren** (1973-   ) 4/7/1998; had issue.

      7. James Robert van Beveren (13/1/2003-   )

      7. Ruby Albertha van Beveren (14/4/2005-   )

5. Noel Charles Richard Dennis (18/12/1926-23/6/2010) a highly regarded and successful Polwarth sheep breeder, exhibitor and stud sheep exporter over many years. Noel was also the author of two books,[9] one being on the history of the Polwarth breed.[10] Married Kathlyn Joan Christian (18/2/1925-2007) 31/1/1948; lived at *Brolga*, Warncoort, Vic.; had issue.

   6. Carolyn (Cal) Noel Dennis (8/11/1948-   ) BAg.Sc. (Univ. of Melb.) agricultural scientist; married Stanley John **Menzies** (known as Bob) (11/2/1948-   ) MB, BS (Univ. of Melb. 1972) M.Med (Univ. of Melb.

Noel Dennis with three prized Polwarth rams at
Brolga in 1968.
Ian M. Lawrence (p. 149), followed by his brother
John L. Lawrence (p. 150), from *Billopp*, jackerooed
at *Brolga* in 1966 to 1969.
Brolga was sold out of the family in 1996.

1988) DRCOG, FRACGP, general practitioner;
2/12/1972, lived at Camperdown, Vic.; had issue.
7. Robert Alexander Menzies (11/10/1974-   )
   BVet.Sc. (Univ. of Qld. 2000), Dip. AVDC, Dip.
   ECVAA, veterinary dental specialist, married
   Maria Paula **Larenza** (9/3/1971-   ) from
   Argentina, BVet.Sc. (La Plata Univ., Argentina
   1993) PhD (Univ. of Berne, Switzerland
   2012), Dr.Med.Vet., Dip.ECVAA, Professor
   of Veterinary Anaesthesia; 3/11/2012, lived at
   Camperdown, Vic; had issue

8. Ruaraidh John Carlos Menzies (18/8/2015-)
8. Emily Stella Carolyn Menzies (18/8/2015-)
7. Nisha Carolyn Menzies (2/5/1976-   ) BOT
(Latrobe Univ. 1997) PhD. (Univ. of Melb.
2005), paediatric occupational therapist, married
Liam Tamas **Brown** (28/4/1975-   ) BPhysio.
(Univ. of Melb. 1997) LLB (Hons) and LLM
(Latrobe Univ. 2003 and Univ. of Melb. 2015)
barrister, 15/2/2003; had issue.
8. Eloise Bonnie Menzies Brown (10/5/2007-   )
8. Auley Stanley Menzies Brown (2/11/2009-   )
8. Arnoud Tamas Menzies Brown (9/3/2011-   )
7. Karensa Kathlyn Menzies (6/11/1978-   ) BSc.
(Hons) (Univ. of Melb. 2002) PhD (Univ. of
Melb. 2008) agrifood specialist married Liam
Delany (10/5/1976-   ) 27/3/2010; divorced;
no issue.
7. Bindi Jennifer Menzies (12/3/1981-   ) BA
(Hons) (Univ. of Melb. 2002) LLB (Latrobe
Univ./ Univ. of Melb. 2005) communications
specialist, married Oliver **Dupouy** (8/8/1981-)
from Bordeaux, France, an engineer; 20/5/2007,
lived in France; had issue.
8. Louis George Alexandre Dupouy (24/1/2010-)
8. Gabriel Henri Dennis Dupouy (2/1/2013-   )
6. Jill Louise Dennis (1949-   ) married Ian William
Urquhart (1945-   ) 1976; lived at Camperdown,
Vic.; had issue.
7. Angus Charles Urquhart (1977-   ) married
Annabel Forbes (24/3/1978-   ) 2006; had issue.
8. Edward Hamish Forbes Urquhart (2009-   )

8. Thomas Ian Dowling Urquhart (2011-   )
8. Henrietta Jane Dennis Urquhart (2015-   )
7. Lachlan Ian Urquhart (1979-   ) married Erin Roche (24/4/1981-   ) 2007; had issue.
8. William Patrick Urquhart (2010-   )
8. Nicholas James Urquhart (2012-   )
8. Henrietta Maria Urquhart (2015-   )
7. Jennifer Nita Urquhart (1982-   ) married William **Sangster** (11/10/1978-) 2010; had issue.
8. Annabelle Louise Sangster (2013-   )
8. Edwina Sophie Sangster (2016-   )
8. Charlotte Elizabeth Sangster (2018-   )
6. Timothy Richard Dennis (1951-   ) a pastoralist, lived at Brolga, and latterly Hamilton, Vic., married Lesley Malpas (1952-   ) 1975; had issue.
7. Sally Louise Dennis (1977-   ) BSc. (Hons) (Univ. of Melb.) a geneticist, lived at Anglesey, Vic., married Daniel Robert **Lester** (-   ) 28/3/2009; had issue
8. Nita Isobel Lester (29/6/2011-   )
8. Jock Robert Lester (10/7/2013-   )
7. Jacqueline Fiona Dennis (1979-   ) a primary school teacher, married Peter **Duxson** (-   ) 11/1/2008; had issue
8. Clara Frances Duxson (8/7/2010-   )
8. Matilda Rose Duxson (12/8/2013-   )
8. Oliver William Duxson (9/2/2015-   )
7. Charles William Dennis (1981-   ) a construction manager, married Michelle Atkins (-   ) 11/11/2006, and lived at Ceres, Vic., divorced; had issue

8. Harrison William Dennis (19/4/2010-   )
8. Alexander Richard Dennis (19/12/2011-   )
7. Katrina Alison Dennis (27/6/1983-   ) a nurse,
married Hamish Benedict **Crittenden** (-   )
19/11/2011, and lived at Anglesey, Vic.; had issue
8. Mabel Joan Crittenden (16/5/2013-   )
8. Bea Francesca Crittenden (28/7/2015-   )
4. Richard Lawrence Dennis (27/11/1888-6/2/1972)
married Isobel Lewis Kininmonth (1889-1960) 1930;
lived at *Lariggan*, Warncoort, Victoria.
4. John Vernon Dennis (26/11/1891-5/3/1970) born at
Uondo, later lived at *Korongee,* Warncoort. Served in the
Australian Army as a Lance Sergeant in World War I at
Gallipoli and in France; married Lucy Ethel Valentine
Smith (30/3/1893-2/6/1964) 1920; had issue.
5. Richard Vernon Dennis (9/7/1921-8/7/2007)
Married . . .
(i) Faye Cameron McDougall (23/3/1923-25/6/1982)
1949; lived at *Korongee*, Warncoort; had issue.
6. Barbara Jean Dennis (7/11/1950-   ) married
Malcolm John **Little** (2/12/1948-   ) 1978; had
issue.
7. Mark William Little (10/11/1981-   ) married
Sarah Frauenfelder (28/1/1985-   ) 2011.
7. David James Little (25/2/1984-   ) married
Jessica Taylor (26/10/1983-   )
7. Steven John Little (11/7/1986-   ) married Eilis
Lenaghan (31/5/1986-   ); had issue.
8. Nina Little (1/9/2016-   )
6. Linda Valentine Dennis (29/10/1952-   ) married
Kenneth Ian **McDonald** (24/3/1955-) 1975; had

issue.
      7. Amanda Jane McDonald (27/3/1978-   )
      married Shaun **Hobson** (-   ); had issue.
        8. Ella Hobson (7/2/2017-   )
      7. Sally Louise McDonald (29/10/1981-   )
      married Patrick **Esplin** (-   ); had issue.
        8. Liam Esplin (15/8/2014-   )
        8. Molly Esplin (13/4/2017-   )
   (ii) Audrey Roberts (née Wilson) (-   ) 1988
3. Herman Fermor Lawrence (5/8/1862-20/10/1936)
(p. 183) studied medicine at Melbourne and Edinburgh
Universities, M.R.C.P. (Edinburgh), Honorary Physician
and Dermatologist at various Melbourne hospitals. He
also studied the uses of x-rays and radium and gained
worldwide repute for this (p. 157); married Thirza Leach
Aitken (11/6/1870-20/2/1963) 1891 (a daughter of
Thomas Aitken, a pioneer of the brewing industry in
Victoria); had issue
   4. Dennis George Herman Lawrence (8/6/1892-8/8/1976)
   married Beatrice May Maidment (Maisie) Parbury
   (4/12/1894-15/3/1971) in 1927 and lived at *Brantwood*,
   Avenel, Victoria and latterly WA. Served in the armed
   forces during World War I at Gallipoli and in France (2nd
   King Edward Horse and later a tank regiment), and was
   decorated for bravery; had issue.
      5. Margaret Elizabeth Lawrence (14/8/1928-2/11/2010)
      married Edward William Derek **Jeffares** (24/5/1918-
      14/10/1994) 1949, in Madras, India and lived latterly
      at *The Mill House*, Levitstown, Athy, County Kildare,
      Ireland (and more recently in Perth, WA); had issue.
        6. Michael Derek Jeffares (9/9/1950-6/6/2020) married

Elizabeth (Lys) Tobin (31/5/1958-   ) 1984, lived at *Brantwood*, Geraldine, Athy, County Kildare, Ireland; had issue.

7. Alan Derek Jeffares (24/7/1994-   )
7. David Lawrence Jeffares (17/2/1999-   )

6. Jacqueline (Jacquie) Anne Jeffares (20/11/1952-   ) married David Leslie **Weaver** (-   ) 1977; lived at *Willina*, Gidgegannup, WA; had issue.

7. Claire Anne Weaver (19/11/1979-   ) partnered Ross **Bilton**; had issue.

8. Monty Richard Bilton (28/3/2009-   )
8. Rocky David Bilton (3/4/2012-   )

7. Simon David Weaver (3/12/1981-   ) married Miranda Marie Halikas (-   ) 2009; had issue.

8. Noah David Weaver (19/4/2010-   )
8. Amelia Emmanuella Weaver (28/11/2011-   )

7. Mark Alastair Weaver (27/11/1988-   )

6. Nicola (Nikki) Carolyn Jeffares (5/6/1959-   ) married James Anthony **Carslaw** (-   ) 1984; lived in Nedlands, Perth, WA; had issue.

7. Timothy (Tim) Carslaw (28/3/1988-   ) married Katie Ellen Macliver (-   ) 15/12/2019.

7. Rosannagh Louise Carslaw (18/7/1990-   ) partnered Jayden Lindsay **Williamson** (-   ); had issue.

8. Hadley May Williamson (30/8/2019-   )
8. Maeve Rose Williamson (21/2/2021-   )

5. Michael Dennis Effingham Lawrence (28/5/1930-11/9/2010) a pastoralist, extensively developed the

family property *Brantwood. Brantwood* was one of
the very early herds when Murray Grey cattle became
established as a viable breed in Australia in the 1960s,[11]
and later Michael, and his sons, developed family
pastoral interests in western NSW.[12]
Married . . .
(i) Judith Stewart Launder (2/10/1934-   ) 1957; had
issue.

> 6. David Parbury Lawrence (31/5/1958-   ) married
> Deborah Jane Purvis (-   ) 18/11/1989; lived
> at *Mittagong* and then *Brantwood*; had issue.
> 7. Jock Purvis Lawrence (11/1/1993-   )
> 7. Max Purvis Lawrence (3/12/1997-   )
> 7. Todd Purvis Lawrence (24/6/1999-   )
> 6. Susan Stewart Parbury Lawrence (7/8/1959-   )
> BHealth Sc. Married Brendan Patrick **Finnigan**
> (23/3/1955-   ) 18/5/1982, lived at *Kia Ora*,
> Winslow, Vic.; had issue.
> 7. Laura Patricia Stewart Finnigan (30/11/1982-   )
> a solicitor, married Michael Bruno **Carrocci**
> (-   ), a builder; had issue.
> 8. Serafina Grace Carrocci (7/11/2012-   )
> 8. Florence Maeve Carrocci (6/10/2014-   )
> 7. Emily Kathleen Stewart Finnigan (28/5/1984-   )
> a valuer, married Craig Daniel **Ruffin** (-   )
> 17/3/2012; had issue.
> 8. Grace Katherine Theresa Ruffin (2/1/2013-   )
> 8. Thomas Jack Ronald Ruffin (6/9/2014-   )
> 7. James Patrick Finnigan (7/12/1985-   ) a
> banker, married Nicole Straus (-   ) 6/3/2011;
> had issue.

8. Madison Joan Finnigan (16/8/2012-   )
8. Olivia Judith Finnigan (22/4/2014-   )
8. James Frederick Finnigan (19/6/2018-   )
7. Claire Ellen Stewart Finnigan (4/3/1988-   )
MB, BS (Monash Univ., Vic.)
6. Peter Michael Parbury Lawrence (8/7/1964-   )
Married . . .
(i) Julie McKinnon Paton (27/9/1963-   )
22/10/1988 and lived at *Formosa* Station, Hay,
NSW (formerly *Amoilla*); had issue.
7. Peter George Michael Parbury Lawrence
(23/10/1991-   ) married Alanna Obst
(29/11/1991-   ) 31/12/2016; had issue.
8. Henry Michael Parbury Lawrence (16/4/2018-)
8. Maisie Kaye Lawrence (27/7/2020-   )
7. Kate McKinnon Parbury Lawrence (3/1/1994-)
married Charles **Vallance** (-   ) 22/2/2020.
7. Jack Wahtee Parbury Lawrence (26/6/1996-   )
(ii) Nicola Jane Smith (née Barrie) (-   ) 4/7/2014.
6. Andrew John Parbury Lawrence (27/3/1966-   )
lived at *Burtundy* Station, Ivanhoe, NSW, married
Vivienne Jean Smith (-   ) 1/4/2000; had issue.
7. Thomas James Parbury Lawrence (5/8/2001-   )
7. Charlie Andrew Parbury Lawrence (30/1/2003-)
(ii) Rosalind Elder (-   ) (second wife of Michael
Dennis Effingham Lawrence, p. 203); no issue.
(iii) Estelle Elizabeth Coate (-   ) 17/10/1992;
(third wife of Michael Dennis Effingham Lawrence);
no issue.
4. Norman Francis Lawrence (1895-1895)
4. Beryl Effingham Lawrence (20/4/1896-1986) married

Major Philip **Russell** (20/11/1883-13/7/1969) M.C. and bar, in 1925 and lived at Carngham, a locality west of Ballarat, Vic; had issue.

5. James Russell (14/1/1926-12/12/2010) Married...

(i) Susan Patricia King (11/6/1931-   ) Oct. 1953 (a great-great granddaughter of John McArthur, *Cambden Park*, NSW) 1953, lived at Carngham, Victoria; had issue.

   6. Philip Michael Russell (27/11/1956-   ) Married . . .

   (i) Fiona Catherine Rankine, BFin.Admin. (Univ. of New England, NSW, 1995) lived in Melbourne, Vic; no issue.

   (ii) Vibeke Anna (28/1/1965-   ) 14/11/2009, a veterinary surgeon.

   6. Katrina Louise Russell (8/7/1958-   ) married Graeme John **Davidson** (26/5/1957-   ) 8/3/1990, lived at Ballarat, Vic.; had issue.

      7. Lachlan James Davidson (15/9/1990-   )

      7. Georgina Kate Davidson (18/5/1993-   )

(ii) married Eleanor King (-Jan 2011); no issue.

5. Rosemary Elizabeth Russell (6/4/1927-19/4/2021) married Lionel Griffith **Weatherly** (6/5/1917-31/8/2007) in 1947 and lived at *Blythvale*, Streatham, and then Geelong, Vic; had issue.

   6. William Lionel Weatherly (3/2/1948-   ) BSc. Hons. (Monash University, 1971), lived at *Blythvale*, then Dunkeld, Vic.; married Katrina Constance Kelly (16/2/1953 -   ) 14/12/73; had issue.

      7. Emma Katherine Weatherly (4/3/1975-   )

a teacher. Lived at Tarrington, near Hamilton, Victoria; had issue.

8. Samuel Thomas Uebergang (2017-   )
8. Sophie Isabella ____ (1/3/2021-   )

7. Georgina Sophie Weatherly (12/9/1977-   ) married William John Furneaux **Mann** (3/4/1969-   ) 24/2/2001, lived at Caramut, Victoria; had issue.

8. Dougal James Furneaux Mann (3/6/2004-   )
8. Olivia Katrina Janet Mann (21/7/2006-   )
8. Jack William Rutherford Mann (24/11/2009-)

7. Clare Elizabeth Weatherly (18/3/1980-   ) lived at Caramut, Victoria.

7. Edward Kelly Philip Weatherly (30/8/1982-   ) married Rosemary Catherine Christenson (-   ) 24/3/2012. Lived at *Blythvale*; had issue.

8. Audrey Weatherly (2012-2012)
8. Frederick William Weatherly (2013-   )
8. Isabella Rosemary Weatherly (2016-   )
8. Maggie Catherine Weatherly (21/6/2019-   )

6. Margaret Anne Weatherly (22/5/1950-   ) a trained nurse, lived at Portland, Victoria; Married . . .

(i) Ronald **Roberts** (-   ) 20/3/1976; had issue.

7. Benjamin Chester Roberts (29/10/1977-   ) married Briony Lee Cornes (20/10/1979-   ) 1/3/2008; had issue.

8. Remy William Roberts (29/7/2006-   )
8. Tully Lionel Roberts (8/12/2008-   )

7. Lincoln Howard Roberts (16/9/1979-   )

(ii) Henry Allan **Mewett** (-   ) 31/5/2009; no issue.

6. Elizabeth Jane Weatherly (24/7/1952-   ) married Michael Francis **Loughnan** (20/4/1952-   ), mechanical engineer (Univ. of Melbourne) and medical practitioner MB, BS (Univ. of Tas.), 10/1/1976. Lived at Ceres and latterly Connewarre, Victoria; had issue.

    7. Anna Sarah Loughnan (27/8/1980-   ) an occupational therapist, married Christopher **Jenkins** (11/7/1977-   ) 2017; had issue.

        8. Saskia Elizabeth Jenkins (15/3/2019-   )

    7. Elizabeth Clementine Loughnan (10/5/1982-   ) married Daniel Leo Horn **Phathanothai**, 10/1/2009, divorced.

    7. Griffith Francis Loughnan (14/10/1985-   ) a commercial engineer, married Louise Mary van den Broek (13/10/1986-   ) 2016; had issue.

        8. Digby Francis Loughnan (23/9/2019-   )

    7. Thomas William Loughnan (8/9/1987-   ) a veterinary scientist, married Camilla Aurel Smith (29/9/1988-   ) 27/9/2019.

6. Philippa Kate Weatherly (21/8/1953-17/5/1954)

6. Charles Russell Weatherly (7/11/1956-   ) Married . . .

(i) Kathryn Green (17/8/1960-   ) 15/8/1982, lived at Skipton, Victoria; had issue.

    7. David Griffith Weatherly (25/5/1983-   )

    7. Alison Kathryn Weatherly (5/3/1985-   )

    7. Faerlie Rosemary Weatherly (15/7/1988-   ) married Matthew Ross **Fidge** (3/8/1983-   ) 22/10/1914; had issue.

        8. Ruby Elizabeth Fidge (19/5/2019-   )

7. Madeline Julia Weatherly (6/1/1990-   )
married Thomas **Wormald** (-   ) in
December 2019.
(ii) Dianne Jean Matthews (1/7/1952-   )
28/11/2009.
5. Margaret Patricia Russell (20/10/1928-2/9/2009)
married Alan David **Hobbs** (20/1/1928-8/5/2018) in
1953 and lived at *Bullengarook Park*, Gisborne, Vic.;
had issue.
6. Peter Russell Hobbs (15/9/1954-   )
Married . . .
(i) Jania Charlotte Watson (1/6/1959-   ) 1983,
lived at *Pindari*, Gisborne, Vic.; had issue.
7. Alexandra Charlotte Hobbs (10/2/1985-   )
7. Virginia Sarah Hobbs (6/11/1986-   )
7. Georgina Jania Hobbs (21/3/1989-   ) married
Matthew **Nield** (-   )
7. Samantha Margaret Hobbs (8/11/1990-   )
(ii) Jenet Martinez (30/8/1958-   )
6. Robert Geoffrey Hobbs (16/9/1957-   ) married
Robyn Lesley Allitt (24/6/1963-   ) 1991, lived at
Horsham, Victoria; had issue.
7. William Russell Hobbs (28/2/1992-   ) married
Shellyn Dierdre Baldwin (-   ); had issue.
8. Cooper Russell Hobbs (5/2/2020-   )
7. Celia Lesley Hobbs (23/10/1994-   ); had issue.
8. Lewis Maxwell Hobbs (-   )
4. Jean Fermor Lawrence (22/5/1904- 20/7/1993) lived at
South Yarra, Victoria.
3. Arthur Hugh Lawrence (1866-9/3/1947) lived Sandringham,
Victoria; married Ida Kleeberger (-   ) in 1913.

3. Alice Mary Ann Lawrence* (1867-1896)

3. Edith Vernona Lawrence (1869-1887)

3. Mabel Bertha Lawrence* (1871-1929) lived in Melbourne and trained as a nurse at Launceston General Hospital.

(ii) Jessie Barnard (12/12/1847-26/6/1939) in 1878 (second wife of Octavious Vernon Lawrence) (p. 186); had issue.

3. Bruce Effingham Lawrence (1879-18/9/1948), a pastoralist who lived at *Banksia*, Narracan, Gippsland. This holding started out as a bush block which had to be cleared. Bruce was a keen horseman and he enlisted in the Victorian Mounted Rifles in 1897.

He continued on in the 10th Australian Light Horse after Federation and was commissioned an officer in 1908.

He served in the 4th Light Horse (A.I.F) at Gallipoli and then in Palestine. He also participated in the historic cavalry charge at Beersheba on 31/10/1917.[13]

Following the Great War he served in the 13th Light Horse, finally retiring after thirty years of military service with the rank of Major; married Alice Kirkham (1892-16/6/1972) 1919; had issue.

4. Percy Rupert Lawrence (2/2/1920-30/11/2011) married Norman Thomas (-   ) in 1950; lived at *Banksia*; no issue.

4. Jean Annie Lawrence (7/10/1921-20/5/2007) married

---

* Alice and Bertha Lawrence both assisted in the care of their sister Ada (1861-1892) while she was ill with tuberculosis (p.189). Alice contracted the disease as well and died in 1896. Bertha spent some time assisting her brother-in-law Richard, with his young family. Subsequently, she was a missionary nurse for a few years in China.

John Julian **Allen** (30/8/1923-30/5/2006) in 1945 and lived at Kallangur, Brisbane, Queensland; had issue.

5. Glyneth Julienne Allen (3/3/1948-   ) married Gregory Allan **Blake** (-   ) 22/5/1967; had issue.
   6. Terry Allen Blake (22/8/1967-   ) married Victoria Harrington (-   ); had issue.
      7. Jayde Maree Blake (9/11/1988-   )
      7. Jasmin Lee Blake (7/1/1993-   )
      7. Zakaree Allen Blake (21/4/1997-   )
5. Beverley Kae Allen (23/2/1950-   ) married John **Klibbe** (7/3/1948-   ) 23/12/1969; had issue.
   6. Stephen John Klibbe (15/9/1972-   )
   6. Matthew Brett Klibbe (21/4/1976-   )
   6. Kelly Deanne Klibbe (31/10/1978-   )
5. John Bruce Allen (12/8/1952-10/3/1971)
5. Ethne Alice Allen (1/1/1956-   ) married Neville **Johns** (6/5/1951-   ) 3/5/1986; had issue.
   6. Daniel Jeffrey Johns (12/6/1991-   )
   6. Michael Douglas Johns (13/8/1993-   )
   6. Patrick Julian Johns (27/11/1995-   )
5. Colin Gwyther Allen (30/1/1959-   ) married Therese Mangan (30/9/1957-   ) 11/4/1987; had issue.
   6. Justine Michelle Allen (29/3/1989-   )
   6. Meg Winifred Allen (25/1/1992-   )
   6. Declan Peter Allen (20/11/1994-   )
5. Roslyn Jan Allen (12/9/1960-   ) married Mark **Fitzgerald** (22/11/1952-   ) 28/9/1985; had issue.
   6. Brianna Louise Fitzgerald (16/7/1990-   )
   6. Alyce Morgan Fitzgerald (27/7/1993-   )
5. Kristina Dorothy Allen (13/6/1964-   ) married

Mark **Cone** (21/1/1963-   ) 2/10/1993.

4. Vernona Helen Lawrence (7/10/1921-1/9/1993) lived at *Banksia*.

4. Irene Grace Lawrence (5/10/1924-6/8/2011) married John Gerard **Mackay** (3/1/1916-8/8/2007) 14/11/1949; pastoralists; lived in Gippsland, Vic.; had issue.

   5. Peter Robert Mackay (11/8/1950-   ) married Wilma Lesley Scott (25/2/1952-   ) 5/1/1974, dairy farmers at Poowong East, Vic; had issue.

      6. Geoffrey John Mackay (25/1/1981-   ) a civil engineer, lived in London, UK.

      6. Yvonne Mackay (17/5/1982-   ) a teacher and later a manager with Special Olympics Australia. Married Luke Alan **Snell** (29/6/1978-   ) 28/12/2011, a business manager; had issue.

         7. Mitchell David Snell (14/7/2013-   )

         7. Tara Rose Snell (13/5/2016-   )

         7. Anna Grace Snell (13/5/2016-   )

      6. Janis Mackay (28/4/1987-   ) a chartered accountant, lived in London, UK, married Max **John** (14/4/1985-   ) 21/10/2018, a   software engineer.

   5. Susan Mackay (31/10/1952-   ) a physical education teacher and later an office manager. Married Ian Broughton **Watson** (7/6/1949-24/7/1981) 7/12/1974, a mathematics teacher and Australian Olympic basketballer in 1972 and again in 1976, when he was captain; had issue.

      6. Juli Watson (27/1/1981-   )

4. Eva Marie Lawrence (12/4/1927-25/9/2010) married Gordon Harris **Beck** (5/5/1927-27/2/1997) 20/8/1949, a

police officer, and lived at Warragul, Gippsland, Victoria; had issue.

5. Trevor Gordon Beck (24/7/1950-   );
(i) _____; had issue.
    6. Wayne Trevor Beck (17/6/1971-   ) married Chelsea Gail Edwards (3/3/1973-   ) 21/3/1993; had issue.
    7. Taylor Janet Beck (1/1/1995-   )
    7. Todd Wayne Beck (26/2/1997-   )
    7. Bailey Cooper Beck (10/1/2000-   )
    7. Kobe Logan Beck (15/5/2003-   )
(ii) Married Susan Margaret Irene Wilson (née Wiltshire) (17/8/1951-   ) 31/7/1982; had issue.
    6. Rowena Elizabeth Beck (9/10/1983-   ) married Christopher Alan **Wood-Davies** (18/1/1983-   ) 10/11/2012; had issue.
    7. Kenzie Beck Wood-Davies (21/5/2014-   )
    7. Stella Rae Wood-Davies (30/7/2016-   )
    7. Hayden Jed Wood-Davies (11/10/2018-   )
    6. Penelope Louise Beck (26/6/1986-   ) married Christopher Jack **Millidonis** (13/3/1986-   ) 10/10/2020; had issue.
    7. Ayce Tyler Millidonis (30/10/2015-   )
    7. Joey Bex Millidonis (15/8/2018-   )
5. Judith Lorraine Beck (24/7/1950-   ) married Kevin **Whiteoak** (12/9/1942-   ) 16/1/1971, lived at Hamilton, Victoria; had issue.
    6. Jody Beck Whiteoak (27/12/1973-   )
    6. Rebecca Jane Whiteoak (31/3/1976-   )
    6. Natasha Victoria Whiteoak (15/4/1981-   )
5. David Lawrence Beck (12/8/1951-   ) married Pam

Dawn Danks (16/9/1951-   ) 4/5/1974; had issue.
6. Brett Lawrence Beck (19/11/1980-   )
6. Tanya Maree Beck (25/8/1983-   )
5. Paul Richard Beck (14/4/1954-   ) married Margaret
Lyn Handley (28/2/1957-   ) 13/3/1976; had issue.
6. Daniel Paul Beck (30/8/1980-   )
6. Jared Leslie Beck (10/8/1982-   )
6. Prue Elise Beck (10/5/1985-   )

3. George Douglas Lawrence (22/4/1880-21/4/1960) LLB
(Melb. Univ.) lived at Camberwell, Vic.;
Married . . .

(i) Johanne Bertha Gunnersen (1882-15/6/1938) (daughter of
Captain Gunner Gunnersen), in 1906.

4. Gunner Vernon Lawrence, AM (29/12/1906-14/12/1994)
associated with his father and brothers, Harold and
Keith, in the firm, Murray Valley Coaches, in the
1940s. Since then he was a prime mover in the Murray
Valley Development League and organizing Secretary
for this organization for a number of years. Awarded a
Membership of the Order of Australia (AM) June 1979,
for community service, particularly in the development of
the Murray Darling region. Married Ilma Louisa Hooper
(31/8/1910-27/9/2004) 2/2/1933, and lived in Lisson
Grove, Hawthorn, Victoria; had issue.

5. John Vernon Lawrence (7/4/1934-   ) had a
distinguished career as a journalist and teacher of
journalism both in Australia and overseas. He was
deported from Kenya in 1994 for writing about
government and civic corruption and neglect.[14]
Married . . .

(i) Jean Alice Hay (9/10/1930-28/8/2009); had issue.

6. Gregory John Lawrence (7/12/1956-   ) partnered
   Alison Jane Cran (15/6/1955-   ); had issue.
   7. Felix James Lawrence (12/1/1985-   )
   7. Oliver John Cran-Lawrence (6/11/1987-   )
      married Vanessa Viridiana Martinez Martinez
      (13/4/1987-   ); had issue.
      8. Elilah Emily Lawrence Martinez (14/2/2010-)
   7. Luis Gregory Cran-Lawrence (12/6/1990-   )
6. Anthony Melville Lawrence (31/1/1958-   )
   partnered Marion Francis Stoney (12/12/1954-   );
   had issue.
   7. Harris Neil Lawrence (18/06/1987-   ) married
      Karia Krisel Martinez Martinez (6/3/1985-   )
      sister of Vanessa Viridiana Martinez Martinez.
   7. Lachlan Gordon Stoney Lawrence (26/7/1990-   )
   7. Susannah May Lawrence (28/4/1995-   )
6. Wendy Jean Lawrence (18/3/1959-   ) married
   Peter Rodney **Henshaw** (18/5/1944-28/3/2003);
   had issue.
   7. Tessa Louise Henshaw (15/5/1994-   )
6. Sally Elizabeth Lawrence (6/12/1961-   )
6. Kerrina Louise Lawrence (25/10/1962-   ) married
   Paul George Talbot **Edwards** (30/11/1960-   ); had
   issue.
   7. Jeremy Hunter Edwards (17/11/1989-   )
6. Fiona Margaret Lawrence (16/7/1968-   )
(ii) Diana Margaret Roberts (27/4/1950-   ) (second
   wife of John Vernon Lawrence, p. 214); had issue.
   6. Imogen Helene Roberts Lawrence (3/12/1979-   )
      married James Beale **Griffiths** (28/7/1981-   ); had
      issue.

7. Charles Beale Lawrence Griffiths (10/2 /2014-   )
7. Finn James Lawrence Griffiths (9/12/2016-   )
5. Barbara Anne Lawrence (28/1/1937-   ) born
Kew, Victoria; married Jouke (Joe) **van der Meer**
(30/8/1935-13/7/2012) 7/1/1961. Managed a citrus
orchard at Sunlands, via Waikerie, SA; retired to
Adelaide in 1993; had issue.
6. Deborah Ruth van der Meer (14/5/1964-   ) lived
at Waikerie, SA, a registered nurse.
(i) married Maurice John **Jones** (31/10/1959-   )
7/9/1985; had issue.
7. Emma Louise Jones (3/11/1990-   ) born at
The Vales, Morphett Vale, SA partnered Kristopher
Adam **Hall** (12/6/1987-   -); had issue.
8. Gabriella Ayesha Thomas Jones (29/9/2004-   )
8. Kaelyn Elizabeth Hall (6/6/2015-   )
8. Lucas David Hall (4/4/2019-   )
7. Shannon Lawrence Jones (27/11/1992-   )
7. Aaron Lachlan Jones (31/8/1995-   )
7. Natasha Lauren Jones (31/8/1995-   ).
(ii) partnered Brenton Colin **Cook** (1/5/1961-   )
6. Katrina Marie van der Meer (3/9/1965-   )
Married ...
(i) Wayne **Sadler-Wharemate** (4/61995-   )
14/7/1990. Lived at Adelaide, SA; had issue.
7. Matthew Curtis Ngawati Sadler-Wharemate
(29/10/1991-   )
7. Jasmine Marie Sadler-Wharemate (6/7/1993-   )
7. Kristi Anne Sadler-Wharemate (17/10/1995-   )
(ii) Richard Adam **Spark** (15/5/1968-) 5/07/2003.
6. Honiesha Julie Dianne van der Meer (29/7/1970-)

lived at Canberra, ACT; had issue.

    7. Riley Mitchell Perrot van der Meer (30/9/2007-) born at Canberra, ACT.

  6. Pamela Jane van der Meer (1/12/1972-   ) a disability vocational training officer. Married Steven Michael **Steffensen** (23 /9/1968-   ) 8/5/1993 in Coburg, Victoria. Divorced in 2016; had issue.

    7. Joshua Michael Steffensen (5/3/1994-)

    7. Daniel James Steffensen (13/8/1995-) partnered Naomi-Violet Liberis (4/3/1995-   ); had issue.

      8. Arabella Rose Steffensen (14/2/2016-)

    7. Brieanna Laura Jane Steffensen (18/12/1997-)

    7. Caitlin Elise Steffensen (14/11/1999-   )

    7. Andrew Jacob Steffensen (16/2/2002-   )

4. Keith Douglas Lawrence (29/1/1910-25/9/1988) married Margaret Mary Jones (29/4/1912-16/2/2001) in July 1933; lived at Albury, Wagga Wagga, NSW, then Melbourne, Vic; had issue.

  5. Ronald Keith Lawrence (2/1/1936-18/11/2018) married Gwenda Dawn Sullivan (7/2/1937-16/1/2018) in 1957 and lived at Noble Park, Victoria; a Sales Manager; had issue.

    6. Ronald Frederick Lawrence (16/8/1957-) married Roslyn Ruth Swales (18/4/1956-) lived in Brisbane; had issue.

      7. Bradley Charles Lawrence (5/10/1984-) married Esther Maree Hall (15/12/1981-); had issue.

        8. Cooper Charles Lawrence (7/4/2012-)

        8. Madison Jae Lawrence (5/6/2014-)

7. Jane Charlotte Lawrence (21/5/1987-   )
married Luke Michael **Muir** (22/1/1984-   );
had issue.
    8. Liam Riley Muir (12/8/2014-   )
    8. Sophie Ruth Muir (17/3/2016-   )
6. David Paul Lawrence (12/6/1959-   ) married
Janeen Joy Fairbanks (7/10/1962-   ) lived in Qld;
had issue.
    7. Katie Ann Lawrence (16/12/1985-   ) married
    Luke David **Kalms** (13/7/1988-); had issue.
    8. Scarlet Rose Kalms (9/1/2018-   )
    7. Jessica Joy Lawrence (15/6/1987-   )
    7. Benjamin David Lawrence (16/1/1990-   )
    married Rachel Elise Bridgman (3/12/1991-   );
    had issue.
    8. Adeline Elise Lawrence (22/7/2018-   )
    7. Zachary John Lawrence (4/8/1992-   ) married
    Meg Elizabeth Bray (14/3/1995-   )
6. Gary Keith Lawrence (8/5/1961-   ) married
Roslyn Joy Hargreaves (1/5/1963-   ); had
issue.
    7. Scott Gary Lawrence (10/6/1987-   ) married
    Sarah Elizabeth Gherardi (28/6/1992-   ); had
    issue.
    8. Abigail Renee Lawrence (30/3/2020-   )
    7. Rodney Philip Lawrence (16/9/1989-   )
    7. Kelly Joy Lawrence (27/5/1993-   ) married
    Jarryd Peter Thomas **Fell** (31/12/1992-   )
5. Ian Douglas Lawrence (19/12/1938-2/10/2005)
married Audrey Byrne (3/7/1940-   ) in 1963 and
lived at Wagga Wagga, then Towradgi, NSW; had issue.

6. Stephen Scott Lawrence (18/3/1962-   ) married Joy Schuberg (26/1/1967-   ) a police officer; had issue.
   7. Kurt Lawrence (7/5/1995-   )
   7. Renay Lawrence (23/4/1999-   )
6. Darren William Lawrence (4/4/1968-   ) married Lynette Lees (12/7/1968-   ); divorced; had issue
   7. Emma Kayla Lawrence (6/9/2000-   )
   7. Wyatt Douglas Lawrence (18/11/2007-   )
5. Carol Margaret Lawrence (1945-1980s), unmarried.
5. Peter John Lawrence (30/12/1948-   ) graduated MB, BS (Univ. of Sydney 1971), an Intensive Care Specialist and anaesthetist in Sydney. Married Mary Eileen Dean (11/3/1949-   ) a registered nurse. Lived in Sydney then Port Macquarie, NSW; had issue.
   6. James Nicholas Lawrence (1/3/1979-   ) graduated in science/law, practiced intellectual property law in Sydney. Lived in Bowral, NSW. Married Amanda Jane Raggett (28/3/1982-   ); had issue.
      7. Joshua Blake Lawrence (10/8/2014-   )
   6. Chad Martin Lawrence (12/2/1981-   ) graduated in Aeronautical engineering. Worked as a commercial pilot. Married Hayley Brooke O'Connor (19/2/1982-   ) a law graduate and author. Lived in Port Macquarie NSW; had issue.
      7. Mia Felicity Lawrence (24/5/2007-   )
      7. Zara Emily Lawrence (31/1/2009-   )
      7. Sophie Anna Lawrence (23/8/2011-   )
      7. Heidi Lea Lawrence (8/7/2013-   )
      7. Lacey Grace Lawrence (7/8/2015-   )
4. Jessie Marie Lawrence (17/9/1911-   ) married Ivan

George **Southwood** (23/1/1911-   ) 1939, lived at Watsonia, Victoria; had issue.

5. Gwenda Joy Southwood (12/6/1940-   ) married William Harold **Luke** (24/5/1937-   ) in 1962; had issue.

   6. William Peter Luke (19/8/1964-   ) married Heather Leary (-   ); had issue.

      7. Mathew Caleb Luke (27/6/2004-   )

   6. Robert Kenneth Luke (7/6/1966-   ) married Carol Bonnet (-   ), later divorced; had issue.

      7. Nathan Robert Luke (10/4/1994-   )

      7. Natalie Joy Luke (19/12/1995-   )

      7. Liam Luke (14/2/2002-   )

   6. Judith Gay Luke (14/7/1970-   ) by adoption.

5. David Norman Southwood (19/12/1941-   ) worked for the AMP Society (now AMP), married Margaret Dorothy Bourne (4/1/1944-   ) 1963; had issue.

   6. Stephen John Southwood (30/10/1965-   ) married Jade_____ , later divorced; had issue.

      7. Joshua Southwood (-   )

      7. Natasha Southwood (-   )

   6. Andrew John Southwood (18/10/1967-   ) married Kylie _____ (-   ) lived at Warrandyte; had issue.

      7. Charlotte Southwood (-   ) lived at Warrandyte, Vic.

   6. Katrina Gay Southwood (14/7/1970-   ) married Scott _____ (-   ); had issue.

      7. Rubi Southwood (-   )

      7. Matilda Southwood (-   )

5. Michael Lawrence Southwood (10/12/1943-5/2/1990) married Tessa Stanley (4/11/1947-   );
   had issue.
   6. Troy Southwood (26/9/1972-   ) married Nerida
      _____ (-   ) lived at Glenvold, Sydney; had
      issue.
      7. Dominique Southwood (-   )
      7. Cassidy Southwood (-   )
   6. Natasha Southwood (-   ) married Brett
      _____ (-   ); had issue.
      7. daughter   (-   )
      7. daughter   (-   )
5. Anne Lynette Southwood (3/7/1946-   ) a trained
   nurse;
   Married . . .
(i) William George **White** (9/7/1945-   ) 15/6/1969;
   later divorced; had issue.
   6. Anthony William White (6/7/1971-   ) lived at
      Bayswater, Vic. Married _____ (-   ); had
      issue.
      7. daughter (-   )
   6. Brenden James White (28/8/1973-   ) married
      Kelly _____ (-   ) later divorced; had
      issue.
      7. _____ White (-   )
      7. _____ White (-   )
(ii) Joe **Buckingham** (-   )
5. Marion Kay Southwood (11/4/1948-   ) graduated
   BSc. (Univ. of Melbourne) lived at Watsonia,
   Victoria. Married James **Banbrick** (17/11/1946-   )
   12/7/1980, had issue.

6. Douglas William Banbrick (23/4/1981-   ) married Dianne ———— (-) lived in UK; had issue.
6. Fiona Marion Banbrick (31/8/1983-   )
    partnered _____ (-); had issue.
    7. Maxwell _____   (-)
    7. Bradley Lee _____   (-)
5. Joan Marie Southwood (8/9/1950-   ) married Eric **Hough** (10/8/1952-   ) 16/2/1982. Lived at Hadfield, Vic; had issue.
    6. Timothy Richard Hough (29/7/1983-   ) a police detective. Partnered Rachel Matton (10/8/1984-   ).
    6. Sasha Marie Hough (16/9/1985-   ) married Nathan **Dalton** (-) 10/9/2016.
5. Maureen Lorraine Southwood (2/9/1955-   ) married Steve **Lennon** (-   ) lived at Werribee, Vic; had issue.
    6. Miriam Jane Lennon (3/2/1987-   )
    6. Emma Celeste Lennon (8/1/1992-   )
    6. Declan Patrick Lennon (3/5/1993-   )
4. Nora Johanne Lawrence (27/3/1913-   ) married Ellis **Hancock** (16/11/1913-   ) 1940; lived at South Kingsville, Victoria; had issue.
    5. Barry Ellis Hancock (3/1/1947-   )
    5. Johanne Ruth Hancock (2/6/1949-   ) married David **McKenzie** (-); had issue.
        6. Kylie Heather McKenzie (12/6/1970-   )
        6. Kirk James McKenzie (8/12/1971-   )
    5. Catherine Vallis Hancock (9/4/1954-   ) married Harry **Tjerkstra** (-), 1971.
4. Harold John Lawrence AM, FCIT, FASA, FAIM (18/12/1914-4/11/1997) a transportation consultant and

advocate to the Transport Regulation Board in Victoria. Awarded membership of the Order of Australia (AM) in 1988 for "significant services to secondary industry (esp. transport)". Married Mavis Ella Averill (-   ) in 1940; lived at Balwyn, Vic.; had issue.

5. Raymond Douglas Lawrence AM (17/8/1943-   ) M. Music; Master of Chapel Music (Ormond College, Melbourne, 1982-2001); organist and Director of Music at Scots Church, Melbourne (1984-   ). An internationally recognized organist, musical director and conductor, he performed at many concerts in the world's leading music venues, over many years. Awarded a Membership of the Order of Australia (AM) in January 2020 for "significant service to the performing arts, particularly chamber music". Lived in Melbourne, Victoria.
Married . . .

(i) Rosalie Joan Pollock (-   ) BMus; 17/05/1968; had issue.

    6. Patrick Thomas Lawrence, (23/02/1973-   ), a musician and a business manager, BMus. (Melb. Univ.). Married Rachael Louise Milsom (-   ), BMus. (Victorian College of The Arts), 2011, lived in Melbourne, Vic; had issue.

    7. Hannah May Lawrence (8/5/2006-   )
    7. Will Alexander Lawrence (10/8/2007-   )
    7. James Patrick Lawrence (19/9/2009-   )
    7. Thomas Oliver Lawrence (13/6/2011-   )
    7. Henry Miles Lawrence (7/7/2014-   )

(ii) Elizabeth Sarah Anderson (-   ) MMus.; 17/03/1983; had issue.

6. Jacob Anders Lawrence (08/11/1992-   )
5. Mark Harold Lawrence (8/10/1949-   )
Married . . .
(i) Kate Winmill (-   ) 14/12/1974; had issue.
  6. Joshua Mark Lawrence (17/6/1976-   )
  6. Donovan Joel Lawrence (9/4/1978-   )
(ii) Judith Lander (-   ) 5/5/1990.
5. Neil Thomas Lawrence (21/2/1955-16/7/2015) BA Hons., had a distinguished career in advertising and promotion; married Caroline Francis (-   ) B. Architecture; had issue.
  6. Anna Louise Lawrence (23/8/1987-   )
  6. Thomas Alexander Lawrence (8/7/1991-   )
4. Mavis Bertha Lawrence (1918-1981) unmarried.
4. Frank Ian Lawrence (30/8/1920-5/10/1998) a pastoralist, lived at *Rockvale*, Addington, Vic. until retirement, then moved to Weatherboard Hill, Vic. Married Nancy Ellen Abbott (28/8/1920-21/9/2017) 30/12/1941; had issue.
5. Margaret Anne Lawrence (5/9/1942-   ) now retired. Worked in Sales /Clerical /Small Business. Lived in WA but now in Ballarat, Vic. Married Michael **Blizard** (-2018) 30/4/1981; no issue.
5. Frances Joan Lawrence (9/11/1944-   ) a triple certificated nurse, Maternal and Child Health, also Pastoral Care, LTh. (Melb. College of Divinity. Married David Alan **Starbuck** (23/4/1949-   -   ) a disability carer; 26/5/1973; had issue.
  6. Rachael Ann Starbuck (31/8/1976-   ) an occupational therapist (Latrobe Univ.) in Mental Health. Married Peter David **Gee** (10/7/1977-   )

Bus/Commerce (Monash Univ.) 16/6/2001; had issue.

    7. Ellen Bethany Gee (6/10/2008-   )

    7. Harry David Gee (2/12/2012-   )

6. Rebekah Joy Starbuck (11/8/1978-   ) Bus/Arts (Univ. of NSW), LLB (Univ. of NSW) lived in Sydney. Partner Andre **Haar** (21/12/1976-   ); had issue.

    7. Akira Jackson Haar (21/9/2016-   )

    7. Raine Xenia Haar (6/2/2019-   )

6. Andrew James Starbuck (22/10/1982 -   ) Bus/ IT (Monash Univ.), married Katherine Helen Lambe (1985-   ) 2014; had issue.

    7. Ned Starbuck (2016-   )

    7. Max Starbuck (2019-   )

5. Bryan Hugh Lawrence (14/10/1948-   ) BEcon./ Politics (Monash Univ. 1971), worked in IT, retired, lived in Kew, Vic., unmarried.

5. Richard Armitage Lawrence (4/10/1950-   ) worked in engineering/welding in Ballarat, Vic. Married Debra Richards (-   ) 1983, divorced; had issue.

6. Zacharij Richard Charles Lawrence (26/7/1984-   ) dentist (Univ. of Perth), works in WA.

6. Birahny Anne Lawrence (28/2/1986-   ) a disability carer.

6. Casody Aidan Ian Lawrence (15/10/1987-   ) BEd. Primary (Ballarat Univ.)

5. Rosalind Marie Lawrence (3/4/1954-   ) a specialist continence nurse, married Thomas **Robertson** (26/4/1955-   ) worked in IT, lived in Ivanhoe, Vic.; 22/9/84; had issue.

6. Nicholas Thomas Robertson (28/8/1986-   )
   works in IT.
6. Megan Nancy Robertson (3/12/1988-   ) BEd.
   Primary teacher
6. Timothy David Robertson (3/2/1991-   )
5. Ian Robert Lawrence (6/2/1956-   ) pastoralist,
   lived at *Rockvale*, Addington; married Maureen
   Elizabeth Towns (24/3/1948-   ) a legal secretary;
   11/7/1987; had issue.
   6. Genevieve Claire Lawrence (12/12/1992-   ) BSc.
      (Melb. Univ.) worked in banking.
5. Kenneth John Lawrence (1/2/1961-   ) BSc. (Melb.
   Univ.), dairy farmer at Jindivick, Vic., married Jillian
   Gayle Waterson (30/9/1964-   ) a secondary school
   Music teacher; 10/12/1989; had issue.
   6. Kate Johanne Lawrence (14/4/1995-   ) BEd.
      primary teacher, married Nicholas Alexander
      Watson (21/5/1995-   ) plumber, now a police
      officer; 19/12/2015; had issue
      7. Paige Elizabeth Watson (21/4/2019-   )
   6. Ruth Sydney Lawrence (23/2/1997-   ) a
      registered nurse, married Lance Thomas Newton
      (26/1/1996-   ) an electrician; 15/1/2021.
   6. Benjamin Ian David Lawrence (29/12/2000-   )
      studying Arts/Music (Melb. Univ.) in 2021.
(ii) Margaret Rubina Sherren (28/1/1992-   ) 19/2/1955;
(second wife of George Douglas Lawrence, p. 214). She
was the matron at St. Catherine's School, Toorak, Vic. from
1923-1945, which included the evacuation of the school to
Warburton Chalet in WWII. Sherren House at the school
is named after her. Latterly she lived at Balwyn, Victoria.

No issue.

3. Jessie Katherine (Kitty) Lawrence (30/6/1881-4/4/1955) lived at Grandview Grove, Hawthorn, as a child. Married Rev. Cuthbert Tremayne **Rodda** (20/10/1879-25/6/1963) 19/4/1917 at St. John's Anglican Church, Camberwell. He was the Parish Priest successively at Balranald and Urana in NSW then Myrtleford, Chiltern, Broadford and Violet Town in Victoria. Retired in 1946 to Kilsyth then moved to Brighton, Vic.; had issue.

    4. Elinor Jessie Rodda (4/2/1918-25/7/1991) married Frederick William **Buckland** (25/1/1919-13/9/1993) in 1942, lived at Kailzie, Mansfield, Vic.; had issue.

        5. Lawrence John Buckland (17/2/1944- /6/2006) graduated BCom. and worked in Canberra.

        5. Victoria Katherine Buckland (12/4/1946-   ) married David John **Hobby** (26/7/1946-   ) 29/8/1970; had issue.

            6. Jane Katherine Hobby (12/6/1974-   )

            6. Jill Miranda Hobby (27/1/1978-   )

        5. Clive Frederick Buckland (6/10/1949-   ) married Janice Robertson (28/3/1950-   ) 7/4/1972; lived at Mansfield, Vic.; had issue.

            6. Emma Louise Buckland (4/4/1976-   ) MB, BS (Monash Univ. 1999), FRANZCOG 2014, lived at Bendigo, Vic.; m. Timothy Gerard Brown; had issue.

                7. Alexander James Brown (5/8/2006-   )

                7. Hayley Marjory Brown (28/6/2011-   )

            6. Scott Frederick Buckland (26/1/1979-   )

            6. Rebecca Anne Buckland (26/1/1979-   )

    4. Brenda Katherine Rodda (20/10/1919-26/5/2003) married Rev. William George Alexander **Tooth**

(11/2/1911-27/6/1988) 12/11/1947. She trained at Deaconess House, Sydney, and carried out missionary work in Africa for four years. Following her marriage they lived in parishes in NSW and Victoria. Latterly at St. Clement's Anglican Church, Elsternwick, Vic. died at Kooweerup, Vic.; had issue.

5. David George Tremayne Tooth (16/8/1950-   ) married Karen Grundy (4/3/1950-   ) a precision instrument maker; had issue.

    6. Jonathon David Tremayne Tooth (23/7/1981-   )

    6. Joanna Helen Tremayne Tooth (3/6/1983-   ) married Nathan **Carey** (-   ) 2005; had issue.

        7. Levi Robert Carey (-   )

        7. Jacob David Carey (-   )

5. Philip Charles Tremayne Tooth (16/11/1952-   ) studied at Royal Melbourne Institute of Technology (now RMIT Univ., Melb.)
Married . . .

(i) Susan Mary Riley (-   ) 16/11/1973; had issue.

    6. Daniel Philip Tremayne Tooth (8/2/1978-   )

    6. Megan Katherine Tremayne Tooth (3/9/1979-   )

(ii) Desley Christianson (-   ) 25/3/1989; had issue.

    6. Whitney Colleen Tremayne Tooth (28/3/1990-   )

5. Keren Rosemary Tremayne Tooth (15/7/1955-   ) trained as a mother-craft nurse; married Peter Lyndon **Gillespie** (5/7/1956-   ) 11/8/1979; had issue.

    6. James Arthur Gillespie (22/7/1982-   )

    6. Katherine Jane Gillespie (11/4/1984-   )

    6. Andrew Lyndon Gillespie (24/9/1985-   )

5. Nigel Richard Tremayne Tooth (13/10/1958-   ) married Patricia Gayle Kelly (10/3/1960-   )

10/5/1986; had issue.

  6. Joshua Richard Tremayne Tooth (6/1/1988-)

  6. Nicholas Richard Tremayne Tooth (27/7/1989-)

  6. Kaitlin Patricia Tremayne Tooth (22/10/1991-)

4. Lloyd Tremayne Rodda (11/12/1921-) an engineer and farmer at Mataura, Southland, NZ. Married...

(i) Elizabeth Yenkin (20/7/1924-) trained as a nurse, 11/2/1955; had issue.

  5. Edwin Rodda (13/9/1955-) married Evelyn Flanagan (-) 13/10/1990

  5. Katherine Rodda (29/10/1956-)

  5. Rosemary Rodda (12/4/1958-)

  Married . . .

  (i) Selwyn **Price** (-)

  (ii) Philippe **Gauthier** (-); had issue.

    6. Tomas Frederique Gauthier (30/1/1995-)

    6. Stefan Alexander Gauthier (4/10/1996-)

  5. Jill Rodda (30/3/1959-).

  (i) married Ken **France** (-); had issue.

    6. Timothy Robert France (6/1/1980-)

    6. Daniel James France (7/8/1982-)

    6. Victoria Jane France (4/8/1988-)

  (ii) partnered Peter MacGregor **Keast** (-) 2001. Lived in North Otago, New Zealand.

  5. Bronwyn Keast (14/1/1964-) married Stewart **McKenzie** (6/7/1957-) November 1997; had issue.

    6. Virginia Ellen McKenzie (1/9/1998-)

(ii) Rosita _____ (20/1/1940-) 2/5/1989 (second wife of Lloyd Tremayne Rodda)

4. David Vernon Rodda (14/9/1923-26/7/2012) enlisted in the AIF, September 1941, and after a short period of training was posted to Singapore, arriving there on 24/1/1942. Became a prisoner-of-war of the Japanese after the surrender on 15/2/1942. Served on the construction of the Burma railway from mid-1942 to Dec. 1944 and then was forced to work in a coal mine near Omutu, Kyushu, Japan, until the end of WWII in August 1945. Graduated MB, BS (Univ. of Melbourne 1952); spent two years working in Victorian hospitals; six months at Ridley College, Melbourne, then ten years as a missionary doctor at Murgwanza Hospital, Murgwanza, Tanzania (1956-1965). Worked in General Practice at Berwick, 1966-1968, and then with the Mental Health Authority (Victoria) in Psychiatry. Married Gwendoline Nonie Slade (18/1/1926-30/7/2016) 20/9/1958. Gwen completed nursing training at the Queen Victoria Memorial Hospital, Melbourne, and then worked in Tanzania (with the Church Missionary Society), lived in Melbourne; had issue.

5. Brenda Elisabeth Rodda (9/7/1959-   ) (Rodda-Winden after marriage) married Stephen **Winden** (27/12/1960-   ) 19/2/1995; had issue.

6. Sharni Rodda-Winden (23/12/1992-   )

6. Tessa Rodda-Winden (1/3/1997-   )

5. Marcus Alexander Rodda (27/5/1961-   ) BSc. (Univ. of Melbourne); served four years in the Victorian police force, then twenty years in the Australian army (retired as a Major); now (in 2021) works in IT. Lived in Geelong, Vic.;

Married . . .

(i) Vivian Jean Caroline (2/11/1960-9/7/2015)
18/1/1985; had issue.
6. Thomas Hugh Rodda (2/12/1985-17/1/2016)
6. Nicholas David Rodda (2/9/1988-   )
6. Samuel Ian Rodda (14/1/1994-   )
(ii) Helen Elizabeth Burnell (1/11/1962-   ); had issue.
6. Henry Robert Rodda (2/10/2002-   )
6. Eloise Anne Rodda (22/10/2007-   )
5. Graham Lloyd Rodda (26/11/1962-   ) married
Susan McCarthy (7/10/1958-   ); had issue.
6. Arlen Hazel Rodda (10/2/1992-   )
5. Helen Katherine Rodda (19/7/1964-   ) partnered
Michael **Cawley** (8/6/1964-   ); had issue.
6. Jacob Darcy Cawley (5/12/1991-   )
6. Henrietta Rose Cawley (4/12/1995-   )
6. Alfred Bing Cawley (12/2/2002-   )
4. Muriel Rosemary Rodda (13/3/1925-   ) unmarried;
trained as primary school teacher and missionary. Worked
in Northern Australia and the Philippines, since 1955.
Skilled in linguistics and worked with the Wycliffe Bible
translators.
3. Helen Ruth Lawrence (23/7/1883-21/4/1964).[15] Her
early life was in Melbourne, Victoria; trained as a nurse at
Launceston General Hospital; served in World War I in
a number of Australian Army hospitals including No. 3
A.G.H. in Egypt, then England and France, 1915-1918.
Married Ethelwynne Dearsley **Cobb** (1873-1958), a WWI
veteran, horticulturalist, fruit grower and soldier-settler.
Lived at Red Cliffs, in the Sunraysia district of Victoria and
then in Melbourne (1958-1964); had two daughters, by
adoption.

4. Beverley Cobb (1927-   ) lived at Harare, Zimbabwe, and later Darwin, NT; a trained nurse; married H. **Goslet** (-   ); had issue.
   5. Ruth Barbara Goslet (1958-   ) married Glyn **Williams** (-   )16/8/1980.
   5. Marianne Helen Goslet (1959-   )
   5. Christopher Harry Goslet (1960-   )
4. Geraldine Cobb (1930-1960)
3. Marjorie Muriel Lawrence (1886-1894)
3. Dorothy Rose Lawrence (1889-1948); unmarried.

Notes

Chapter 12

CAROLINE MARIENNE LAWRENCE
(1837-1865)

Caroline Marienne Lawrence was the fourth daughter of W.E.Lawrence and spent her early years in Van Diemen's Land. She married William Henry Barnard FGS on 4/2/1859 at St John's Anglican Church, Launceston. They then lived at Portland, Victoria where William was Receiver and Paymaster for the Colonial Treasury. In February 1865, in the same month as his wife died, he was appointed Receiver, Paymaster, Land Officer and Gold Receiver at Ballarat. Six months later his son Howard died aged one and half years old. From 1878 he was Secretary/Treasurer of the Ballarat Cemetery Tust and was the first Registrar of the Ballarat School of Mines, serving in this capacity from 1872 to 1881.

Ballarat was a major goldfield in Victoria in the 1850s-1860s, and in late 1854 serious unrest among miners had developed over the issue of miners' licence fees, without political representation. This led to open rebellion and the Eureka Stockade was subsequently built. The Stockade was attacked by colonial forces on 3rd December 1854 and demolished with more than thirty deaths, mostly miners. Even 10 years later, Barnard would have found his appointment in Ballarat challenging.

Genealogy

2. Caroline Marienne Lawrence (30/11/1837-13/2/1865) married William Henry **Barnard** (4/2/1831-12/1/1900) 4/2/1859; had issue.

3. Maude Marienne Barnard (6/3/1863-27/3/1864)
3. Howard George Lawrence Barnard (11/3/1864-21/8/1865)

Caroline died at Beechworth, Victoria, after a lingering illness (tuberculosis) and Barnard subsequently had three more wives:
  (ii) Bessie Lynn (1845-3/9/1881) 23/4/1867, had eight children. Bessie died during the birth of her eighth child, Octavia, who also died at the time.
  (iii) Ellen Barnard (1843-1884), his first cousin, 29/8/1883; no issue.
  (iv) Flora Barnard (1845-1929) sister of Ellen, 28/4/1886; no issue.

Notes

Chapter 13

ELIZA MARGARET MILLIGAN
(1844-1891)

Eliza Margaret Milligan was born in 1844 after the marriage between Mrs W. E. Lawrence and Alexander Murray Milligan (bp. 27/2/1812-15/12/1883) on 9/11/1843. Milligan, an immigrant from Scotland, had been in Van Diemens Land since 1835 and had a range of interests; initially a teacher, then town surveyor in Launceston from June 1844, a magistrate and a successful businessman. He was present at the inaugural meeting of the Launceston Mechanics Institute on 8/3/1842, and an office-bearer of the Institute in some subsequent years. The Institute became known as the Launceston Public Library in 1929 and then was part of the State Library of Tasmania from 1945.

The Milligan family lived in Launceston and the family home *Treherne*, an elegant Victorian weatherboard house at 158 Georgetown Road, Newnham, was built in 1870. The house was sold in the 1890s and now (in 2021) has been splendidly restored by the current owners.

Eliza married Charles Gaunt, the thirteenth child of Dr. Matthias and Frances Gaunt of Windermere, Tasmania in 1868.

Charles was one of fifteen siblings, and his family is an example of how life was in some families in the early 1800s. The fifteen Gaunt children were born from 1826 to 1844.

1 Sydney (1826-1900);
2 Frances (1827-1910) married J. E. Lawrence (1828-1874) (p. 131);
3 Jane (1828-1880);

4   Matthias (1830-1843) died from scarlatina at age 13;
5   Joseph (1832-1891);
6   John (1833-1870);
7   Thomas (1834-1854) died from dysentery at age 20;
8   Emma (1835-1854) died from consumption at age 19;
9   Edward (1837-1904);
10 Richard (1838-1890);
11 Elizabeth (1839-1903);
12 William (1841-1841) died at 8 days old;
13 Charles (1842-1916) married Eliza Milligan;
14 Ellen (1843-1844) died at six months old;
15 James (1844-1854) died from a brain tumour at age 10.

(Of the fifteen, six died before the age of 21 years, three of whom died in 1854.).

Charles worked as a clerk in Launceston in the years after the marriage. In 1871 he was convicted of embezzlement of £300 from his employer and served sixteen months in the Hobart Gaol.

Eliza and Charles had eleven children and the family moved to Ulverstone, Tasmania, after her death in 1891, where the younger children finished their schooling. Three sons, Richmond, Sydney and Graeme, farmed at Nietta, south of Ulverstone, and, to this day, Gaunt's Road and Gaunt's Homestead are local features.

The first two later moved to Western Australia and farmed near Kojunup, WA; Sydney leaving a large family of descendants. Graeme died at a young age and his son and family lived in Victoria. Charles Alan Gaunt moved to British Columbia, Canada and his family subsequently lived in the USA. Maxwell and Jack Gaunt moved from the Ulverstone area and their families, many of them farmers, have lived in Victoria and New South Wales.

Genealogy

2. Eliza Margaret Milligan (19/9/1844-15/8/1891) married Charles **Gaunt** (28/3/1842-4/1/1916) (the thirteenth child of Matthias Gaunt and Frances Green from Windermere) 22/4/1868 at St John's Anglican Church, Launceston. Eliza died in Launceston (cause of death reported as "congestion of the liver and gastritis") when her youngest child was only four years old. Widower Charles died in Kew, Victoria (intestate, with assets of £156); had issue.
3. Ethel Mary Gaunt (15/5/1869-7/9/1906) Married . . .
(i) Arthur Henry **Beart** (1866-2/12/1926) in May 1894; lived in Qld; had issue.
4. Alex Graeme Beart (2/2/1896-5/12/1896) died of meningitis.
4. Arthur Maxwell Beart (17/2/1899-19/5/1961). Lived in South Australia; issue unknown
(ii) John Heaton Cooper (-) details of marriage unknown; had issue
4. Dorothy Heaton Cooper Beart (4/8/1906-28/9/2007) later added her father's last name Cooper to be her surname.
3. Alec Lawrence Gaunt (30/9/1870-13/2/1871)
3. Maggie Isobel ("Aunt Daisie") Gaunt (22/8/1871-3/4/1952) adopted, married Carl **Jacoby** (1859-20/6/1940) of Hamburg, Germany in 1896; died in Heidelberg, Vic; had issue.
4. Elsa Jacoby (1896-1966) married Arthur Fraser **Byass** (1891-1971); had issue.
5. Margaret Fraser Byass (20/5/1920-28/9/2017) married Don **Winch** (-), 1946; had issue.

6. Katrina Winch (1947-   )
6. Vicki Winch (1950-   )
6. Penny Winch (1952-   )
5. Joan Fraser Byass (1922-13/9/2017) married Norm
    Hopkinson (1917-1971) 1946; had issue.
    6. Valerie Joan Hopkinson (1947-   ) married S.
        Bristow (1946-   ) in 1969.
    6. Jeffrey Arthur Hopkinson (1950-   )
    6. Gail Elizabeth Hopkinson (1951-   ) married Paul
        Clayton (1949-   ) 1969; had issue.
        7. Tracey Ann Clayton (1969-   )
        7. Brad Paul Clayton (1972-   )
    6. Christine Jane Hopkinson (1956-   )
5. Elizabeth Louise Byass (1/6/1929-18/5/1999) married
   Duncan **McMeekin** (26/7/1924-18/10/1984) 1952;
   had issue.
   6. Terry McMeekin (1953-   )
   6. Simon McMeekin (1955-   )
   6. Sally McMeekin (1960-   )
   6. Louise McMeekin (1964-   )
3. Richmond Lewis Gaunt (24/9/1873-6/6/1936); lived in
   Western Australia, died at Katanning WA.
3. Elinor Grace Gaunt (20/2/1875-1953) lived in Victoria.
3. Hugh Murray Gaunt (6/8/1877-1900) lost contact with
   family; lived in WA, died in Perth, WA.
3. Sydney Harrington Gaunt (15/12/1878-25/12/1958)
   married Mary Howell Cox (11/4/1884-4/5/1971),
   5/5/1909; died in Kojunup, WA; had issue.
   4. James Harrington Gaunt (28/2/1910-26/9/1969) married
      Dorothy Lorden (-   ); no issue.
   4. Mary (Molly) Grace Harrington Gaunt (29/7/1911-   )

married Alex James **Philipps** (-   ), 29/5/1941; had issue.

5. Graeme Alex Philipps (24/6/1942-   ) married Rhonda Marie Radford (5/8/1959-   ) 26/5/1983; had issue.

   6. Sharon Lee Philipps (17/3/1984-   )
   6. Ashley Graeme Philipps (11/4/1986-   )

5. Peter James Philipps (17/3/1944-   ) married Elizabeth Dulcie Wright (7/3/1945-   ) 17/11/1966; had issue.

   6. Mary Jane Philipps (15/12/1970-   ) married Ian **Michael** (-   ) 8/10/1995.
   6. Michael James Philipps (27/11/1979-   )

5. Maxwell John Philipps (24/6/1948-   ) married Julie Pope (4/10/1954-   ) 2/3/1974; had issue.

   6. Richard John Philipps (28/5/1977-   )
   6. Deborah Nicole Philipps (18/6/1979-   )

4. Helen (Nell) Harrington Gaunt (7/10/1913-   ) married Gordon **Hair** (-   ) 20/4/1942; had issue.

5. Donald Gordon Hair (7/1/1943-   ) married Rhonda Fleay (-   ) 6/5/1949; had issue.

   6. Jysae Helen Hair (21/4/1981-   )
   6. Kallen Donald Hair (25/7/1983-   )

5. Michael Ross Hair (1/9/1947-   ) married Carolyn Anne Packard (27/8/1951-   ) 6/3/1981; had issue.

   6. Zebedee Edward Hair (29/12/1981-   )
   6. Asher Benjamin Hair (6/7/1983 -   )

5. Robert Henry Hair (27/7/1951-   ) married Ruth Jocelyn Hunter (13/11/1952-   ) 11/1/1975; had issue.

   6. Brendon Paul Hair (13/8/1979-   )
   6. Glenn Robert Hair (30/8/1983-   )

4. Dorothy (Dosh) Harrington Gaunt (4/1/1918-   )
married Neil Lawson **Loveland** (-   ) 9/6/1954;
had issue.
  5. Brian Frederick Loveland (26/3/1955-   ) married
  Sheryl Wells (14/5/1959-   ) 2/7/1995; had issue.
    6. Nicole Jean Loveland (14/12/1995-   )
  5. Sydney James Loveland (27/9/1956-   ) married
  Jacinta Lee Jolliffe (11/3/1963-   ) 8/4/1989; had
  issue.
    6. Rohan James Loveland (29/7/1991-   )
    6. Jac Robert Loveland (25/6/1993-   )
    6. Joss Neil Loveland (25/6/1993-   )
4. Henry Harrington Gaunt (1/3/1920-22/11/1943) of
Kojonup, WA. A Flt. Sgt., served in Sqn. 31 RAAF in
WWII.[1] He went missing while returning to Coomallie
airfield near Batchelor, NT, after a raid on the Japanese
seaplane base at Taberfane, Aru Islands, Timor.[2]
The wreckage of his Beaufighter A19-145 was eventually
found in 1993 near Junction Bay, NT (west of
Maningrida) along with the remains of his navigator.
Henry Gaunt has never been found.[3] Married Andrie
Lesley Webster (-   ) 3/4/1943.
3. Charles Alan Gaunt (18/1/1882-27/6/1955) brought up in
Tasmania, then emigrated to British Columbia, Canada.
Married . . .
(i) Minna Gertrude Wallace (1879-23/7/1924) from Stratford,
Ontario, 21/11/1906; had issue.
  4. Maxwell Alan Gaunt (18/12/1909-25/1/1965) born
  Vernon, British Colombia: a master mariner, lived in B.C.
  then emigrated to USA in 1951, based in the San Diego
  area in latter years. Married Helen Elizabeth McKinnon

(15/8/1919-   ) from Vancouver, BC, 8/8/1953; had issue

    5. Lesley Helen Gaunt (30/7/1956-   ) B. Arts (Theatre Arts, Univ. of Nevada); a costumier and later a Fire Officer and National Parks Ranger.
Married...

    (i) William Scott **Whistler** (28/9/1960-   ) 18/8/1979; no issue

    (ii) James Le Roy **Collister** (17/2/1948-   ) 19/10/1996; no issue

    5. Debra Ann Gaunt (15/7/1957-25/6/2020) a talented artist, lived in California, unmarried.

(ii) Dorothy Frances Barton (-   ) (second wife of Charles Alan Gaunt)

3. Marcus Graeme (Gray) Gaunt (4/4/1883-28/1/1906) died aged 23 after a lingering illness, lived in Ulverstone, Tas.; the family subsequently moved to Victoria. Married Alice Andrews (1878-1974) 5/10/1904; had issue.

    4. John Graeme Gaunt (18/9/1905-6/4/1981) married Elaine Margaret Dougherty (25/8/1910-   ); had issue.

    5. Yvonne Margot Gaunt (23/9/1933-   ) married Jack **McCall** (7/6/1925-   ) 9/4/1955; had issue.

    6. Kim Amanda McCall (21/3/1956-   )
Married. . .

    (i) Paul **Spencer** (10/7/1952-   ); had issue.

      7. Elly Spencer (10/7/1982-   )

      7. Julia Spencer (8/7/1983-   )

    (ii) Eric **Smith**; had issue.

      7. Jack Smith (14/1/1994-   )

    6. Mark Ernest McCall (25/8/1957- /5/1958)

    6. Phillipa Jane McCall (5/2/1959-5/10/1986)

6. John Linus McCall (23/12/1960-   ) married
Samantha Hunter (-   ); had issue.
7. Thomas McCall (8/12/1995-   )
6. Kate McCall (9/7/1962-   ) married Robert
Corbet (-   ); had issue.
7. Tambo Corbet (18/4/1991-   )
7. Geordie Corbet (10/6/1994-   )
7. Esther Corbet (17/10/1995-   )
6. Julian Edward McCall (19/1/1964-   )
6. Barnaby John McCall (3/1/1966-   )
6. Sophie Heloise McCall (2/11/1969-   ) married
Darryn **McDonald** (-   ); had issue.
7. Cooper McDonald (13/5/1993-   )
7. Riley McDonald (12/8/1995-   )
5. Pamela Margaret Gaunt (3/3/1935-   )
5. Patricia Ann Gaunt (5/4/1940-   ) married Ian
Francis **Rose** (30/10/1934-   ) 24/4/1965; had
issue.
6. Richard Andrew Rose (25/11/1966-   )
6. Rebecca Francis Rose (12/4/1968-   )
5. Graeme Michael Gaunt (17/4/1945-   ) married
Betty Wong (8/11/1952-   ) 20/11/1970; had issue.
6. John Graeme Gaunt (11/12/1972-   )
6. Bryn Edward Gaunt (20/11/1975-   )
6. Dion Michael Gaunt (9/11/1977-   )
3. Maxwell Leigh Gaunt (23/7/1885-30/5/1966) schooled
in Ulverstone, trained as a metallurgist at Ballarat School
of Mines; farmed in Victoria. Married Katherine (Kitty)
Caroline Urquhart (25/8/1884-26/7/1942) 13/3/1907; died
in Northgate, Brisbane, Qld.; had issue.
4. Margaret Jean Gaunt (31/1/1908-1/4/1989) a Bush

Nursing Sister, lived in Qld. then NSW. Married Sidney Fisher **Harriss** (1963-   ) 4/10/1947.

4. Maxwell Duncan Gaunt (7/3/1909-30/1/1969) lived in Victoria. Married Coral Ray[2] (6/7/1922-27/5/2014) 3/10/1942; had issue.

   5. Peter Maxwell Gaunt (4/9/1943-1/4/2009) married Robyn Howlett (16/11/1946-   ) 5/3/1966; had issue.

      6. Andrew Maxwell Gaunt (4/11/1969-   ) partnered Cristel Secaira (21/9/1973-   )

      6. Julie Robyn Gaunt (22 /7/1971-   ) married David **Jolliffe** (1/9/1955-   ) 27/8/2005; had issue.

         7. Hannah Grace Jolliffe (22/7/2001-   )

         7. Nathan Campbell Jolliffe (5/4/2004-   )

      6. Sarah Jean Gaunt (23/11/1974-   )

      6. Mark Peter Gaunt (10/12/1978-   ) lived at Bowral, NSW.

      Married . . .

      (i) Helen Smith (-   ) 4/2/2002; had issue.

         7. Harrison Gaunt (20/4/2003-   )

         7. Helena Gaunt (10/9/2004-   )

         7. Mia Gaunt (23/3/2008-   )

         7. Luca Gaunt (23/3/2008-   )

      (ii) Belinda Verrell (19/1/1983-   )

   5. Edward James Gaunt (9/7/1947-   ) lived in NSW Married . . .

   (i) Patricia Kilkeary (1/8/1949-   ) 6/3/1970; had issue.

      6. Mathew James Gaunt (25/8/1973-   ) married Clair Ngaio Wood (24/6/1969-   ) 1/2/2003; had issue.

7. Nicola Moana Gaunt (14/12/2003-   )
7. Oliver James Gaunt (8/6/2009-   )
(ii) Jennifer Kay Turner (9/1/1955-   ) 22/4/1978.
3. John (Jack) Elliott Ruthven Gaunt (23/6/1887-5/12/1952) married Flora McDonald (12/9/1889-10/10/1962). Born at *Treherne* Newnham, Launceston, died in Cheltenham, Vic.; had issue.
4. John (Jack) McDonald Gaunt (10/5/1909-25/1/1988) married Rita Eileen Lang (12/2/1903-10/5/1994) in October 1938; had issue.
5. Pauline Joan Gaunt (28/3/1940 -   ) married William David **Barber** (-   ) 2/11/1963; had issue.
6. Kerrie Anne Barber (25/4/1966-   )
6. Darren John Barber (13/6/1968-   )
4. David Charles Gaunt (1/10/1911-15/3/1994) married Annie Lavinia Jessie John (21/6/1910-   ) 31/12/1938; had issue.
5. David Michael Gaunt (10/10/1940-   ) married Coral Anne Wheeler (28/3/1942-   ) 25/9/1964; had issue.
6. Andrew David Gaunt (24/7/1966-   )
6. Richard James Gaunt (26/8/1969-   )
6. Stuart Charles Gaunt (14/3/1974-   )
5. Macyll Anne Gaunt (3/12/1943-   ) married Bruce William **Watson** (31/1/1938-   ) 20/12/1965; had issue.
6. James McDonald Watson (16/8/1968-   )
6. Kathryn Anne Watson (18/8/1970-   )
5. Yvonne Gladys Gaunt (12/10/1950-   )

Chapter 14

A Son Remembers ...
... The early life and times of Elizabeth Muriel Lawrence
- wife of Effingham Lambert Lawrence
John Lambert Lawrence, Mandurah, WA (2021)

When I left Tasmania to work as a jackeroo for Noel Dennis at Brolga in the Western District of Victoria in May 1968 I took with me many pleasant childhood memories, some of which would remain with me for the rest of my life – even if I was to not realise this at the time.

During the later years in the life of my mother, Elizabeth Muriel (Betty) Lawrence (1906-1993) (p. 145) I made frequent visits back to Tasmania to spend a week or so at a time with her, along with re-visiting my old home at Billopp. On these occasions I loved to quiz Mum about the "good old days" and to listen to her recollections of happenings during the early days of her life in Tasmania – both before and after her marriage to my father, Effingham Lambert Lawrence (1898-1967) (p. 145). Facts, figures and diary entries; tales of "gathering" sheep in the highlands, and the one occasion when some thousands of sheep were lost due to the first winter snow storms coming early to the mountain run country intrigued me as did stories of some of the old characters Mum came across in her travels. Thankfully, Mum was encouraged by other members of her immediate family to put pen to paper and record for posterity some of those interesting tales. They make great reading, especially for someone who has relocated from Tasmania to Victoria, then on to one of the warmer and more arid states of Australia, Western Australia, as I have, and where my wife Sue, children Cameron, Matthew and Samantha have been living since 1972.

"In 1866 E.B. Lawrence (p. 143) started leasing land around about Arthur's Lakes which was known as Horton's Run and Lawrence's Paddock for some years. This was relinquished in 1871. About 1911 E.D. Lawrence (p. 145) acquired land at the Great Lake between Miena and Arthur's Lakes, stretching along the north shore of the Great Lake and took in the areas known as the South Mountain, Howell's Neck and Boggy Marsh. Two thousand acres was freehold and 24,000 acres was leased from the crown. Public Crown auctions were held every three or five years and leases were bid for at a nominal amount per annum for varying lengths of time. Annual rent was not actually paid, but had to be spent on improvements to the holding, e.g. fencing, roads and buildings.

These days (early 1980s) the Poatina Road traverses most of this country, to link with the Lake Highway connecting Deloraine and Bothwell. This Lake Run was relinquished in 1933 to Messrs. Brazendale and Triffett.

The Lake Country was much later in its pastoral growth, so when the lowlands started to dry off stock was transferred to this high country until about May, when the first heavy snow falls could be expected. Strong 3-4 year old wethers would even be left up there all the year, only being brought down for classing and shearing. Ewes would be taken up in January, as soon as their lambs were weaned, and would stay until May. This allowed the lowland pastures to improve before winter came and the stock returned. A resident shepherd would be in charge of everything in the high country.

In 1915-16 a severe drought caused all the sheep to be sent off *Billopp* to the Lake Run and left there as long as possible.

But in 1919 the first snow came early and fell for ten weeks. This prevented the sheep being brought back down and E.D.L. lost 3,000 of them.

When the Hydro Electric Commission first dammed the Great Lake at Miena in 1912 it raised the level of the lake and the shepherd's house at Howell's Neck had to be moved to higher ground. A roomy house was built of wood with double walls, between which, sod was packed as insulation against the cold. The shepherds and their families were a unique people, peculiar to the Lake Country. Because of their isolation they had to be self-reliant and independent. Bothwell, some 30 miles away over rough tracks, would have been the nearest place providing a doctor and supplying stores to anyone living at Howell's Neck.

Mail and provisions would be collected when someone went for them by horse and cart. Kerosene was the lighting fuel, for electricity was not available to them then. The women would make their own bread, and the men did all boot repairs.

Education for the children was non-existent, for there were no radios even, until the 1920s. Because of their isolation they welcomed the rare visitor, and were most hospitable people. In spite of all the hardships and loneliness the jobs were sought after and shepherds for the Lake Country were not hard to find. How different are their amenities today, with radios, television and a network of good roads, with rugged motor vehicles available to suit the conditions. It never ceased to amaze my husband Lambert, to find himself able to drive a car on a sealed road through the country which in many parts had been too rough to ride a horse over, and where the shepherd had mustered the sheep on foot many times.

This, the Poatina Road, had been constructed by the H.E.C. in the early 1960s traversing the land Lambert's father had rented at Howell's Neck and linking the Poatina power station with the Lake highway leading to Hobart via Bothwell, thus giving us here at *Billopp* an alternative route to the capital city.

Once while mustering, or "gathering the sheep" as it is often called here in Tasmania, a shepherd suddenly pointed to a distant hill with the stem of his pipe and said: "See that 'ill over there? That's Bull's 'ill. Two bulls fought there once - for two days they fought, 'til they killed one another. They was vicious cows they was!"

On another never-to-be-forgotten occasion that Lambert recalled, he and a shepherd had started out very early one morning, and he heard that lovely old Irish song The Mountains O' Mourne being sung by the shepherd . . . who had a good singing voice. The experience was unforgettable in its unusual setting, with the tuneful notes and nostalgic words ringing out in the still, frosty air, over the moonlit snowy landscape".

One of the tales I love to recall involved a sheep "drive" from Billopp to the Lake Country (an annual event) – no mean feat in those days in the best of climatic conditions, let alone when the weather was a bit "off". *

I'll let Mum recount her story:

"Having gone to bed early the night before, I was woken by an officious alarm at 1:30 am. I rose, called Marcus (later Sir Marcus Loane (p. 164), Archbishop of Sydney, Lambert's first cousin and my second cousin through the Thomas family) and finding it raining, crept around to avoid waking Lambert's mother, who I felt would stop me going. I dressed, packed a valise and got breakfast for Lambert, Marcus and myself by 2:15. It was still dark, so we found and caught our horses by the lantern light glinting on their eyes, and left *Billopp* in misty rain. We reached the foot of the Tiers at Blackwood Creek by 5:00 in a misty, grey atmosphere. There we

*Tasmania is in the latitude of the 'Roaring Forties' and has variable weather!

248

found Walter Neale's camp and him ready to count out the 1,300 ewes he had brought ahead from *Billopp* the previous day – on their way to spend the summer at Howell's Neck.

It commenced to rain steadily as we climbed the track up the mountainside with the sheep. Before reaching the top of the Tiers everyone was wet through but the weather was warm. We went over the top at 9:00 am and headed east along beside the Great Lake to Howell's Neck. Every now and then we would all get off our horses and walk for a spell to keep warm. My horse Spider could be turned loose, for she followed me like a dog. Lambert and Marcus had Creamy and Snip, who could not be so trusted.

Later in the morning, with the ground aswim with water, and everything soaking wet (for it was still raining – with no break), Lambert and the shepherd decided to call a break and boil the billy. I looked at them agape. How could anyone get a fire to burn without a dry stick in sight? Nothing daunted, we kept going till we came to a big rotting trunk of a fallen tree. In no time Walter Neale had scooped out the dry interior at the big end, and soon had our billy boiling inside the tree, while we outside in the rain, could not get a sandwich eaten before it started to disintegrate and drop in a sodden mess to the ground.

We arrived at Howell's Neck at 2:30 pm, having been travelling for almost twelve hours. Marcus and I rode on ahead to warn Mrs. Neale of our approach. Rain had ceased by then, but packs and clothes all had to be dried. We had dinner at 3:30 then went for a short walk. We went to bed early that evening to recover. Next day Marcus rode to the fishing camp of Geoff Youl (p. 152) at Tod's Corner and brought back some fish. Geoff was a brother-in-law to Lambert, having married his sister Isabelle.

Lambert drafted the sheep then we left for home at 1:00 pm. We arrived back at *Billopp* having travelled via Arthur's Lakes, without incident except that Spider had cast a shoe and another had to be found and put on, at McCarty's, delaying us so we did not reach *Billopp* until 9:30 pm – in the dark, as we had left it.

On our way home, when pausing at a gateway on top of the plateau, one of Lambert's dogs had sat down to scratch fleas, on the middle of a huge jack jumper ants' nest, which was at least 6 feet (or 1.8 metres) across. He scratched harder and harder, but it was not long before he leapt up thinking he had more fleas than he had sat down with, to our amusement. The ants had become very stirred up and excited, stinging him viciously until he rid himself of them with vigorous shaking.

In spite of rain and fatigue, we were none the worse for our drenching. Marcus and I loved our 50 mile ride and hoped our efforts as assistant shepherds had been of some use. It was an experience we will never forget".

Mum seemed to have a fascination with outdoor activities, especially if it involved rides on horseback accompanying Dad up into Tasmania's high country. All this despite the hardships that could be encountered along the way. The mind conjures up beautiful pictures as I recall the following tale:

"October 7th to 9th 1933 provided me with a memorable experience and insight into this Lake Country (around the Great Lake). For the third time, Lambert and I (then engaged) made an attempt to ride on horseback to Howell's Neck. The first time was a year earlier and was stopped by bad weather.

The second attempt was frustrated by Lambert's sister Barbara (p. 158) developing appendicitis, and Mary, the maid, tried to stop this one by introducing a bad cold into the household, but we at last succeeded in getting away.

We left *Billopp* in the late morning on a lovely sunny spring day taking a picnic lunch with us – Lambert riding the pony Creamy, and I on his black mare Snip – each carrying a change of clothes and things for two nights in valises.

Riding through *Woodside* we passed *Palmerston* and turned off the road, going through *Saundridge* and *Bluegong* paddocks to the foot of the Tiers. Here we stopped for lunch and boiled the billy on the edge of the timber.

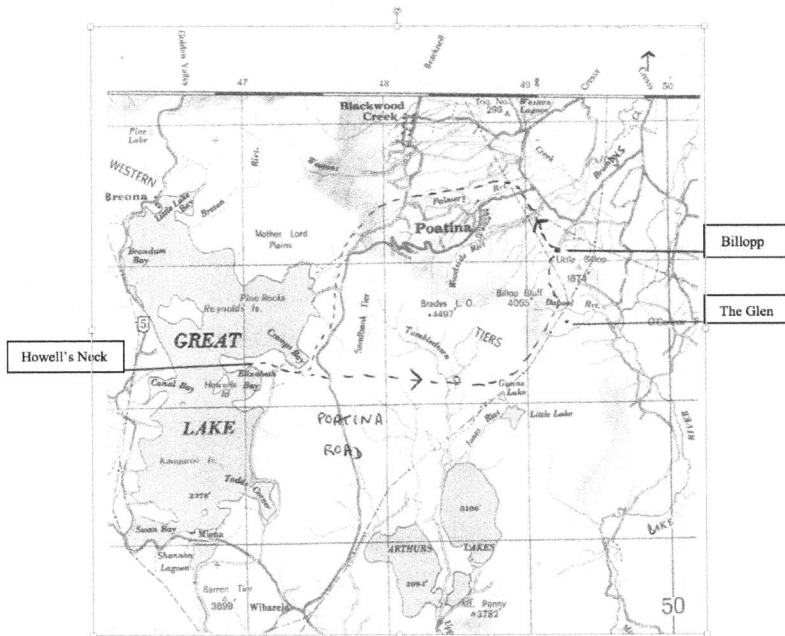

-------- the approximate route of the trip, 7-9 October 1933
(TASMAP, Oatlands, 1:250,000, 1961)
Poatina and the Poatina Road were built in the early 1960s as part of the Poatina hydro-electric scheme.

BILLOPP HOUSE 200m. (660 ft.) asl LITTLE BILLOPP 499m. (1674 ft.) asl
BILLOPP BLUFF 1230m. (4065 ft.) asl (above sea level)

251

Setting off again at 3:00 pm we climbed the Tiers using an old surveyed road for three quarters of the way up, following the valley of Western's Creek. This road petered out into just a trail. We reached the top of the saddle by the Sandbank Tier at 5:00 pm with ten miles still to go across the mountainous plateau to Howell's Neck. Within an hour we reached the shore of the Great Lake, alternately traversing marshes and stony outcrops.

Arriving at the lake we ran into a bitterly cold hail storm, accompanied by thunder, lightning, wind and rain – so different to the weather we had left behind us. The hail was so thick it lay un-melted in a thick carpet of white. We rode through this for an hour, finally arriving at the shepherd's cottage at 7:00 pm as it got dark, nearly frozen and wet through. How my stiffened fingers had held onto reins I know not, and on dis-mounting, my knees felt permanently bent. As I stood on the doorstep, my fumbling, frozen fingers were unable to find the buttons of my wet coat, which I wished to remove before going in, and on looking down I found the front was covered with a large sheet of ice. Lambert's letter to the Neales, telling of our coming, had not been received, but in spite of that we were made very welcome by these hospitable people.

Mrs. Neale would not let me go too near the fire and made me put my frozen hands into a basin of cold water before gradually warming it up, for thawing can be a very painful business.

At the end of a wonderful hot meal I noticed that the wind had dropped, being replaced stillness. Curious, I looked out the door and was thrilled to find it was snowing, a thing I had never seen before. I was too excited to sleep, and late in the night when the clouds let it, a full moon gave me enough light off the snow to read by. Next morning it all looked like fairy land with its snowy mantle covering the ground and loaded on every twig. Its beauty made me forget our cold arrival, but the snow soon melted.

After working with Walter Neale all the morning, Lambert and I climbed Howell's Sugarloaf in the afternoon and got a lovely view of the Great Lake from north to south; east to west; over its whole extent. Scudding snow showers and gleams of sunshine made it constantly change colour. Peak on mountain peak rose on every side, but there was little wildlife to be seen, except for occasional rabbits, black jays and a few wallabies. After a second night we left at 9:30 am to return via Arthur's Lake, descending the Tiers into the back of *The Glen* a slightly longer route than the 25 miles up.

We reached the foot of the Tiers at 5:00 pm having had lunch at Tumbledown Creek. After p.m. tea with the Ray Swans in *The Glen* house we reached *Billopp* via the Back Run and Little Run, then over the Big Hill (Little Billopp), to be home by dark.

It was the end of another lovely trip and a great experience, thanks to the trust and broad-mindedness of Lambert's mother, for this was in the days when chaperons were still considered necessary. Our jaunt together caused various lifted eyebrows and sly digs from our neighbours, but we had been well looked after and chaperoned by Mrs. Neale in her beautifully kept home, in spite of its isolation."

Billopp homestead and lower paddocks from half way up the *Big Hill* (*Little Billopp*) Photo: c. J. L. Lawrence

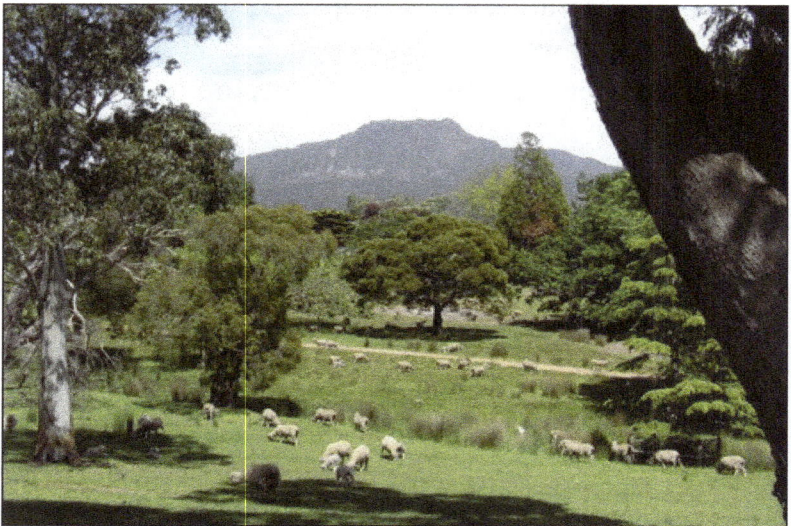

Billopp Bluff, from near the *Billopp* homestead. Photo: c. J. L. Lawrence

Chapter 15

FAMILY MISCELLANY

FAMILY REUNIONS

10-11 March 1973 (photograph pp. 258-259)

The sesquicententenary of the arrival of the family in Van Diemen's Land occurred on 10th February 1973 and a reunion was held to mark the occasion.

Saturday, 10th March – a service of thanksgiving at St Marks Church, Pisa, Cressy followed by a luncheon hosted by Mr. & Mrs. Geoff Lawrence (p. 175) at *Formosa*, Cressy attended by over 100 family members from all parts of Australia and New Zealand.

Sunday, 11th March – a luncheon hosted by Mr. & Mrs. Ian Lawrence (p. 149) was held at *Billopp* and was also well attended by family members.

6-8 March 1998 (photograph pp. 260-261)

Another reunion was held to mark 175 years in Australia involving a programme of events over several days.

Friday evening, 6th March – a cocktail party was hosted by Launceston Church Grammar School at the school, to mark the establishment of the "W E Lawrence Memorial Scholarship".

Saturday, 7th March – a thanksgiving service at St Marks Church, Pisa, Cressy, then a luncheon at *Billopp*, Cressy hosted by Mr. & Mrs. Ian Lawrence. A family dinner commencing at 7pm took place at Jessen Lodge, Longford.

Sunday, 8th March – a morning tea function at *Formosa* hosted by Mr. & Mrs. Brian Lawrence (p.151), then a bus and boat tour of Launceston and the Tamar Valley 12.00-4.00 pm. This was followed by an evening cocktail party hosted by Mr. & Mrs. Lindsay Lawrence (p. 151) at *Fermer*, Westbury.

Attendees in 1998 numbered more than 150 from all states of Australia, New Zealand, South Africa, Hong Kong and the United Kingdom.

Names of attendees: Formosa 10th March 1973 (photograph pp. 258-259)

REAR: Ian Lawrence, Bill Simpson, Martin Lawrence, Graham Henty-Anderson, Max Lawrence, Peter Houghton, Geoff Park, Helen Morris, Kit Morris, Richard Park, Lindsay Lawrence, Spencer Lawrence, Richard (Dick) Lawrence, Mary Ann Silvester, Owen Lawrence, Philippa Lawrence, Seton Synnot, Vernon Lawrence, Frank Lawrence (Vic.), John Lawrence, Anne Liebmann, Kate Lawrence.

MIDDLE: John Foster, Robert Simpson, Gwen Lawrence, Judy Simpson, Blake Lawrence, Monica Lawrence, Jean Simpson, Kate Houghton, Joyce Park, Beth Henty-Anderson, Barbara Gibson, Geoff Lawrence, Lynne Lawrence, Alison Loane, Peter Loane, Les Park, Alan Hobbs, Margaret Hobbs, Dorothy Dennis, Pat Lawrence, Annette Synnot, Noel Dennis, Joan Dennis, Carolyn Menzie, John Menzie, Sheila Dennis, John Mackey, Norman Dennis, Eva Beck, Gordon Beck, Patsy Hawker, Kitty Howson, Hilary a'Beckett, Dennis Lawrence, Tom a'Beckett, Bob Liebmann.

SITTING: Frances Foster, Margaret Lawrence, Gwendolyn Youl, Isabelle Youl, Margaret Foster, Nancy Lawrence (NZ), Lorraine Lawrence, Angela Foster, Vernona Lawrence, Dorothy Park, Betty Lawrence, Beryl Russell, Jean Lawrence, Ardyn Lawrence, Ilma Lawrence, Nancy Lawrence (Vic.), Irene Mackey.

SEATED IN CENTRE: Diana Lawrence, Frank Lawrence (Tas.).

FRONT: Merrilyn Lawrence, Brenda Lawrence, Brian Lawrence, Kenneth Lawrence, Colin Liebmann, John Houghton, Celia Morris, Elizabeth Houghton, Susan Morris, Megan Morris, Rowan Liebmann, Sarah Houghton, David Liebmann, Stuart Liebmann, William Lawrence, Sally Lawrence, Michael Lawrence, Patrick Lawrence.

ABSENT FROM PHOTO: Bea Lawrence, Emma Lawrence

Reunion 10-11 March, 1973 (at Formosa)

Reunion 6-8 March 1998 (at Billopp)

On the following pages find the Number Key to match names in the list of attendees in 1998.

1. Virginia Maunder-Taylor
2. Annette Goble
3. John Goble
4. Alison Park
5. Richard Park
6. Geoffrey Park
7. Diana Targett
8. Joyce Park
9. Robert Maunder-Taylor
10. Rosemary Weatherly
11. Nicholas Targett
12. Robert Simpson
13. James Maunder-Taylor
14. Jean Simpson
15. Stuart Lawrence
16. Sarah Lawrence
17. Emily Lawrence
18. Michael J. Lawrence (NSW)
19. Tim Lawrence
20. Sam Lawrence
21. William (Bill) Lawrence
22. Nigel Borthwick
23. Christopher (Kit) Morris
24. Geoffrey McKinley
25. Griff Weatherly
26. E. Frank Lawrence
27. David Loane
28. Winsome Tong
29. Robert Loane
30. Joan Loane
31. Gwen Foster
32. Leigh Heard

33. William Foster
34. Patricia Lawrence
35. Henry John Foster
36. Lindsay Lawrence
37. Neil Heather
38. Claire Targett
39. Peter Howson
40. Edward Loane
41. K. Hugh Targett
42. Angus Lawrence
43. Joe van der Meer
44. John Hannah
45. Bruce Douglas
46. Colin Liebmann
47. Peter Houghton
48. Cameron Lawrence

49. William (Bill) Gorman
50. Graham Henty-Anderson
51. Lois Strange
52. Francis Henty-Anderson
53. Alec Sylvester
54. Barry Blake
55. Robyn Blake
56. Ian Silvester
57. John H. Lawrence
58. Serge de Kantzow
59. Ian M. Lawrence
60. Elizabeth Simpson
61. Alan Hobbs
62. Viv. Adams
63. Gwen Lawrence
64. John L. Lawrence

65. Maryellen Yencken
66. Peter Tong
67. Robert Tong
68. Roslyn Propsting
69. Alison Loane
70. Philippa Heard
71. Katie Heather
72. Lawrie Heussler
73. Roslyn Lawrence
74. Dennis Lawrence
75. Dinny Lawrence
76. John V. Lawrence
77. Anne Wilson
78. Henrietta Hannah
79. Frances Douglas
80. Katherine Houghton
81. Celia Krawinkel
82. Thomas Krawinkel
83. Elizabeth Gorman
84. Alison Weatherly
85. Lynne Lawrence
86. Gwendoline Adams
87. Sally Gartlan
88. Margaret Lawrence
89. Flora de Kantzow
90. Poppy de Kantzow
91. Jean Estill
92. Lars de Kantzow
93. Margaret Hobbs
94. Kitty Howson
95. Susan Lawrence
96. Mary van Dissell
97. Valerest Yencken
98. Ken Lawrence
99. Pauline Morrison

100. Angela Foster
101. Ardyn Lawrence
102. Eva Beck
103. Percy Lawrence
104. Ilma Lawrence
105. Margaret Foster
106. Barbara Gibson
107. Susan Borthwick
108. Clare Borthwick
109. Beatrice Lawrence
110. Ruth Lawrence
111. Jill Lawrence
112. Patrick Lawrence
113. Geoffrey Heard
114. Kate Lawrence
115. Rosalind Loane
116. Sarah Propsting
117. Marcus Loane
118. Toby Gorman
119. Kate Douglas
120. Fred Gorman
121. Megan Morris
122. Marjie Gorman
123. Celia Lawrence
124. Jemma Lawrence
125. Henry Lawrence
126. Meg Lawrence
127. Harriet Lawrence
128. Michael J. Lawrence (Tas.)
129. Madeline Lawrence
130. Lorraine Lawrence
131. Belinda Lawrence
132. Sally Lawrence
133. Josie Lawrence
134. John Heard

135. Sylvia Tong
136. Barbara van der Meer
137. Kristi Sadler-Wharemate
138. Katrina Sadler-Wharemate
139. Helen Morris

140. Tanis Douglas
141. Andrew Tong
142. Beatrice Harding
143. Susan Estill

THE POLWARTH CONNECTION

W. E. Lawrence was a businessman with various interests, one of which was the pastoral industry. *Formosa* and *Billopp*, near Cressy Tasmania were his first properties but at the time of his death he had several others as well in northern Tasmania (p. 69).

Many of his descendants have continued this interest and some have been significant leaders in the industry. His son, O.V. Lawrence (1836-1915) (p. 181), married Editha Wettenhall (1836-1872) (sister of Holford Wettenhall, see below) and their daughter **Ada Caroline Lawrence** (1861-1892) married **Richard Vinicombe Dennis** (1842-1912) (p. 182) of *Tarndwarncoort*, Warncoort, Vic.

Dennis had a major role in establishing the **Polwarth** sheep breed. He wanted sheep that did well in terrain difficult climatically, and wet underfoot for much of the year. Crossing a Lincoln ram with Merino ewes in 1880 proved to be a successful experiment and led to the establishment of Polwarths (originally known as "Dennis comebacks") as a distinctive breed of sheep. His flock is recognized as one of the three original flocks on which the breed is based. The other two were that of his brother Alexander and of Holford Wettenhall (of the *Carr's Plains* station). Polwarth is a local regional name in Victoria where *Tarndwarncoort* is situated and was adopted as the name of the breed in 1919.

The Polwarth breed celebrated the centenary of its establishment in 1980.[1]

265

Noel Charles Richard Dennis (1926-2010) (p. 197) *Brolga*, Warncourt, Vic.

Bob (1922-2001) and **Dorothy** (1920-2018) **Dennis**, (p. 196) *Lariggan*, Warncourt, Vic.

Geoffrey L. Lawrence (1915-1984) (p. 175) *Formosa*, Cressy, Tas, and **Richard E. Lawrence** (1920-1995) (p. 177) *Rockthorpe*, Cressy, and in West Australia, 1960s-1980s;

- were among the principal breeders, exhibitors and exporters at that time. Tarndwarncoort is stud no. P1 in the stud book of registered Polwarth flocks, 2019-2020 (based on comeback progeny, from 1880) and Formosa is no. P76 (1906).

Polwarths continue to thrive in suitable conditions in Australia and sheep from the blood lines of the above studs are found in a number of overseas countries, especially in South America. Many descendants of W. E. Lawrence have also been involved as breeders of Polwarth sheep over many years, although the flock numbers have decreased in recent years.

FAMILY OVERVIEW

Family groups, in 2021, are found in all Australian states, also in

- **New Zealand**
  - William Lawrence (1823-1898) (p. 113)
  - Leslie Frank Lawrence (1863-1947) (p. 135)
  - Archie Barnard Lawrence (1867-1945) (p. 159)
- **Republic of South Africa**
  - Owen Effingham Lawrence (1881-1956) (p. 171)
- **United Kingdom**
  - Beatrice Helen Isabelle Harding (1925-2009) (p. 153)

Individual members, including the above Polwarth breeders, have become known nationally, and occasionally internationally, for a wide variety of reasons.

Robert William Lawrence (1807-1933) (p. 91) is recognized as the first resident botanist of Van Diemen's Land. He was a significant collector of botanical specimens and sent these to Prof. W. J. Hooker at Kew Gardens, London.[2]

Admiral Sir Anthony Monckton Synnot KBE, AO (1922-2001) (p. 100) had a stellar career in the Australian Navy, becoming chief of the Defence Force Staff 1979-1982.

Donald Hevingham Lawrence (1943-1994) (p. 140) was a highly respected sports journalist (golf and tennis) in Melbourne (1946-1986), and an inductee in the Sports Australia Hall of Fame, 1991.

Prof. Michael John Lawrence (1941-) (p. 163) had a distinguished career as an academic retiring in 2001 as Emeritus Professor of Information Systems, University of NSW.

Sir Marcus Lawrence Loane KBE (1911-2009) (p. 164) was a well-known Anglican clergyman, the first Australian-born Archbishop 1966-1982 and Primate of Australia 1978-1981.

Dr. Octavius Vernon Lawrence (1836-1915) (p. 181) was one of the first graduates of Melbourne University Medical School and first awardee of the degree M.D. from that institution in 1871.

Michael Dennis Effingham Lawrence (1930-2010) (p. 203) took over the family pastoral property *Brantwood*, Avenel, Vic., at an early age. He quickly established a reputation as a progressive and innovative manager and his family eventually had extensive landholdings in Victoria and western NSW. *Brantwood* was one of the very early herds when Murray Grey cattle became established as a viable breed in Australia in the 1960s.

Dr. Herman Fermor Lawrence (1862-1936) (p. 183) had an international reputation as a clinician and researcher in the development of the use of X-Rays and radium treatment.

John Vernon Lawrence (1934-) (p. 214) had a distinguished career as a journalist and is the only Lawrence (known to the author!)

to have been subject to a deportation order (from Kenya, 1994).

Raymond Douglas Lawrence, AM (1943-) (p. 223) is well-known internationally as an organist, musical director and conductor.

Effingham Nicoll Lawrence (1820-1878) (p. 42) (whose father Judge Effingham Nicoll Lawrence was first cousin to William Effingham Lawrence) was a Louisiana member of the 1872 United States House of Representatives serving a record of only one day in that role.

Major General Sir John Thomas Jones (1783-1843) (p. 59) 1st Baronet KCB was a British Army officer with a distinguished career in the Royal Engineers, and brother-in-law of William Effingham Lawrence.

THE "LORD LIVERPOOL"

The *Lord Liverpool* was built at Hasting, Sussex, England in 1814. She was a 73 ton sloop made of spruce and pine. The owner's name was Lawrence, the Captain was Lawrence, and the home port was London.[3] Although, originally listed as a sloop,[*] in Australian waters from 1824-1833 she was listed as 73 ton cutter.[†]

Some sources suggest that she may have seen service in Indian waters for pleasure cruising, possibly before the journey to Australia in 1822-23. It is known that she did do some local trading in Europe, including a trip to Amsterdam. It is uncertain just when her rig was changed to that of a *cutter*.

---

[*] A sloop is a sailing ship with a single mast, typically meaning one headsail in front of the mast, and one mainsail aft (or behind) the mast.

[†] A cutter is a sailing ship, similar to a sloop, but with more sails and a single mast. It is fore-and-aft rigged with two or more headsails and often has a bowsprit. It can carry up to five sails fully rigged (Maritime Museum of Tasmania, Hobart).

The reason for naming the *Lord Liverpool* is unknown, but it is interesting to note that Robert Banks Jenkinson (1770-1782),[4] 2nd Earl of Liverpool (Lord Liverpool) was the Prime Minister (1812-1827) and Master of Trinity House (1812-1827). He had inherited the position after the previous Prime Minister, Spencer Perceval (1762-1812), was assassinated on 11/5/1812 in the corridors of the Houses of Parliament, London. The perpetrator, John Bellingham, within four days was tried, convicted and sentenced to death. He was hanged a week later on 18/5/1812. The Trinity House connection indicates an association, if not a friendship, between William Effingham Lawrence and Lord Liverpool, and he had "offered to give them (WEL & EBL) a letter to the Governor of NSW and recommendation of a grant of land."[5] The War of 1812 with America and the final campaigns of the Napoleonic Wars were fought during his ministry.

In 1822 she commenced her trip to Van Diemen's Land departing London, Deal on 16/5/1822 with Lawrence, his family and crew, with a stopover in Rio de Janeiro from 19th July to November 1822. From there it was a non-stop voyage to Port Dalrymple (Kelso Bay) at the mouth of the Tamar River, VDL, arriving 10/2/1823, as the first privately owned vessel from England. The next day the vessel was ordered to Georgetown[6] on the eastern side of the Tamar River due to the fear of bushrangers where she remained for six weeks. She then made a record 4½ hour passage from there to Launceston with pilot John Cutter,[6] a record which stood for 75 years.

Van Diemen's Land was the official name for the colony until the name Tasmania was gazetted on 1/1/1856 even though Tasmania had been in common use for the previous 20-30 years.

The *Lord Liverpool* in 1822[7] was loaded with merchandise[8] such as ironmongery, furniture, agricultural implements and mechanics tools ready for use in Van Diemen's Land.

The passengers for the journey[8] were
- William Effingham Lawrence, age 41.
- Mrs. Mary Ann George, later to become Mrs. W. E. Lawrence.
- Two children, believed to be Charles (b.1818) and Mary Ann (b.1821), leaving behind Robert Lawrence (b.1807) still at school in England.
- Chas. Roberts, a blacksmith
- James Stone, apprentice, and
- his cousin Effingham Prest (c.1805-1880), apprentice, who married twice, settled in Launceston, and named his firstborn William Effingham Prest (1838-1851).

The crew on *Lord Liverpool* consisted of
- Captain George Coulson (1778-1862), who later became a shipping pilot on the Tamar River. He settled at Dilston where many of his descendants still live in that region, and has Coulson Creek (at Dilston) named after him. Of interest is that after his death, AM Milligan (3rd husband of Mrs WE Lawrence) was an executor of his will.
- Mate Samuel Budge, nothing further known.
- William Carpenter, a carpenter, who was subsequently killed by local natives whilst kangarooing on Dick Sydes's Plains, beyond the Third Basin. This area was the 4th Basin which is today the catchment of the Trevallyn Dam on the South Esk River upstream from the Gorge, Launceston.

and four seamen
- Joseph William Bell, who became an auctioneer, the father of William Thomas Bell (1829-1885) of the firm Bell & Westbrook, Launceston.
- John Jacobs, who in 1824 was listed as seaman on the *Alfred*[9] but later became a pilot with the Van Diemen's Land Co. at *Woolnorth* and Circular Head in north west Van Diemen's Land. A boat harbour near Table Cape was named after him.
- James Raiker, nothing further known
- Andrew Taylor, nothing further known

After arrival, the *Lord Liverpool* was offered for sale to the colonial authorities, but, on refusal to purchase, was sold privately mid-October 1824, and departed for Sydney arriving 27/10/1824.[10] The vessel again became a coastal trader doing the runs between Sydney and Newcastle with passengers and cargo from 1824-1832. The Sydney Gazette 2/12/1824 writes that she left Sydney Thursday morning and returned Saturday morning with cargo, with comment "Quick work this!"[11] She ran aground twice, both on Nobby's Island at the mouth of Hunter River, one of the 200 ships who also foundered there during this period. The first occasion was 10/11/1830[12] after which she was repaired, but the more serious event on 9/5/1831 under Master Taggart fortunately occurred with no loss of life. The vessel was later again repaired, but both she and two other coastal sailing vessels had been superseded by steam vessels and needed to seek cargo further afield. In Feb-March 1832 she was in New Zealand, and a voyage 20/1/1833-12/2/1833 was listed as Cooks Straits, New Zealand, and Eastern Islands (Society Islands).[13] On 4/7/1833 *H.M.S. Imogene* brought news to authorities that the *Lord Liverpool* had sunk in a wild storm off the coast of Tonga with no loss of life or cargo.

FOR QUEEN (OR KING) AND COUNTRY

Family members have contributed in large numbers to the armed forces, including nursing services, in many different ways, over a long period of time. This has included

The Boer War (1899-1902)

World War I (1914-1918)

World War II (1939-1945)

and a number of other conflicts.

Contributors through the nursing services include

Alice Maud Synnott (1864-1951) and **Mary Synnott** (1868-1946) (p. 103), served in Australian Army Hospitals in the Boer War and in France in WWI, also

Helen Ruth Lawrence (1883-1964) (p. 231) served in Australian Army Hospitals in France in WWI and suffered injury as a result. We also find

Joseph Lawrence Milligan (1844-1867) (p. 130) British Army; a Cornet with the 14th Hussars (heavy cavalry), died at York after a fall from a horse whilst on active service in England in 1867.

Bruce Effingham Lawrence (1879-1948) (p. 210) Australian Army; a long serving cavalryman, participated in the historic charge by the 4th Australian Light Horse at Beersheba, Palestine in 1917.

Leonard Arthur Lawrence (1890-1924) (p. 132, 139) British Army; a Captain with the Royal Dublin Fusiliers, served in France in WWI and later in Aden and other places, murdered while serving in Aden in 1924.

Norman Owen Lawrence (1917-1994) (p. 172) South African Forces; a Lieutenant served in North Africa, captured at Tobruk 1942 and prisoner of war in Italy and Germany 1942-1945.

Donald James Alexander Dennis (1920-1997) (p. 192) Australian Army; Lieutenant, captured on New Ireland, New Guinea 1942, prisoner of war of the Japanese in Japan, 1942-1945.

Richard Effingham Lawrence (1920-1995) (p. 177) Australian Army; a Corporal served in 2nd 40th Battalion, captured at Timor 1942, prisoner of war of the Japanese on the Burma Railway in Thailand and Japan, 1942-1945.

David Vernon Rodda (1923-2012) (p. 230) Australian Army; 8th Division Signaller, captured in Singapore 1942, prisoner of war on the Burma Railway and then in Japan, 1942-1945.

Owen Lawrence Loane (1922-1942) (p. 171) Royal Australian

Air Force; Flying Officer, died during a bombing raid over Burma, September 1942.

John Henty McWhae (1917-1943) (p. 108) Fleet Air Arm, Royal Navy; Flight Sergeant, died during active service, February 1943.

Henry Harrington Gaunt (1920-1943) (p. 240) Royal Australian Air Force; died during a bombing raid to a Japanese base in the Timor Sea, from his base in Northern Australia.

Timothy Monckton Synnot (1916-1997) (p. 98) Royal Australian Navy 1930-1960s, retired with rank of Captain.

Anthony Monckton Synnot (1922-2001) (p. 100) Royal Australian Navy 1939-1982, finally Admiral and Chief of Defence Force, 1979-1982.

James Arndell Youl (1928-1953) (p. 154) British Army; served on the Suez Canal Zone, and whilst on active service contracted poliomyelitis and died in Egypt in 1953.

Angus James Effingham Lawrence (1979-2004) (p. 180) Australian Army; a Trooper, died during an Army training exercise from heat exhaustion in Northern Australia, 2004.

Caroline (1892-1943) and **Kenneth** (1892-1943) **McWhae** (p. 108) died in 1943 when the cargo ship they were on as passengers was torpedoed in the Atlantic Ocean, two months after the death of their son (John Henty McWhae – see above).

ST. MARKS CHURCH, PISA

St. Marks Church, Pisa, south of Cressy, Tasmania is a small weatherboard country church much loved by local residents.

It was built in 1864 on donated land and has served the local community well since then, mostly as a place of worship but, in earlier years, also as a venue for a school during week days. These days it is used mainly for family events such as family reunions, weddings and funerals.

W. E. Lawrence was buried in the Cypress Street Cemetery,

St Marks Church, Lake River, Pisa, Cressy
(photo courtesy Duncan Grant)[14]

Launceston, after his death in 1841. This was one of the earliest cemeteries in the town – consecrated for use in 1823, the last burial took place in 1929 and in 1952 remaining headstones were taken away or destroyed. The land became an open space used by Broadland House School in 1962,[15] and subsequently the Launceston Church Grammar School, as a sportsground.

Lawrence's headstone, erected in the late 1800s, was retrieved and has been re-erected in the grounds of St Mark's. After nearly one hundred and forty years it had been eroded badly and has been renovated in 2021 with the assistance of funds donated by the family (see below).

On the 16th November 1975, a service was held at St Marks Church to dedicate two stained glass windows in the church, in thanksgiving for the establishment of the family in Van Diemen's

Land in 1823. Sir Marcus Lawrence Loane (p. 164), Archbishop of Sydney, officiated at the service. The windows were donated by members of the family from Victoria, some of whom were present at the service along with those from Tasmania.

In 2018 the Anglican Church began a process of rationalising church property in Tasmania and St. Marks was one of the properties to be sold. This galvanised action locally and the end result is that the property is to be purchased by a local group and held in perpetuity as a community asset.

Our Lawrence family is one of the groups involved in this process and it is a pleasure to acknowledge the very generous financial support of this project by many family members, not just those in Tasmania, but also from many other parts of Australia.

Funds donated to the project will be used, as indicated by the individual donors, to

- enable the purchase to be completed
- assist with renovation of weathered tombstones, and
- provide a fund for ongoing maintenance needs.

The process of change of ownership has now been completed (Sept. 2021), and celebration of the church as a community asset is likely to be part of the family bicentenary events in 2023.

THE BARNARD FAMILY

In the early years of Van Diemen's Land, because of the low population, there was a shortage of prospective spouses for people of marriageable age. The historical record shows many families where inter-marriage occurred several times between two families. It is with the Barnard family that this occurs most frequently with this Lawrence family.

George William Barnard (1791-1864), born in England and served in the Navy during the Napoleonic Wars. He travelled to

Van Diemen's Land in 1817 and received a grant of land on the River Tamar known as *Landfall*, married Anne Greensill (1809-1879) 1829 and had issue.

> 2. Clara Barnard (1836-1861) married Effingham Billopp Lawrence (p. 144)
> 2. Grace Barnard (1840-1928) married Effingham Billopp Lawrence (p. 144)
> 2. Jessie Barnard (1847-1939, p. 210) married Octavius Vernon Lawrence, MD (p. 181)
> 2. Rose Barnard (1838-1930) married Alfred Green (-   )
> 2. Seven other children

William Henry Barnard (1831-1900) son of John Barnard (1789-1864) and nephew of George William Barnard, married

(i) Caroline Marienne Lawrence (1837-1865) (p. 233)

(ii) Bessie Lynn (1845-1881), married 1867

(iii) Ellen Barnard (1843-1884), his first cousin

(iv) Flora Barnard (1845-1929), sister of Ellen.

Bayard Edgell Barnard (1911-1980) great-grandson of George William Barnard married Gwendoline Lawrence Loane (1913-2005) (p. 170) (his second cousin) in 1938.

THE JOURNEY AS THE FAMILY GENEALOGIST

The long-term interest I have had in the history of our family has been very rewarding, sometimes amusing and unexpected incidents have occurred.

Given that some of our direct forebears lived in **North America** in the years 1635-1780, it has been a long-term challenge to establish contact with members of the family currently living in that region

•Dick and Pat Lawrence (p. 177) after checking the New York phone book, were able to meet Dorothy Cushman (1908-1981) (p. 43) (daughter of Effingham Lawrence, 1878-1956) in New York in 1962 and were given material on the family.

•Notices in the press in Providence, Rhode Island, and in the New York Genealogical Society newsletter in 1995 produced an enthusiastic response from Court and Polly Dixon (p. 41), a very friendly elderly couple who lived in Connecticut. Court was a descendant of John Burling Lawrence (1774-1844) (p. 32), and was fascinated to have relatives in Australia (almost as if it was in another solar system!). He met our tour bus one afternoon at the local pizza parlour in Old Lyme, Connecticut, and took me to their home for a two-night stay (others in the group felt I should not be going off with an unknown American in this fashion!). They were a very hospitable couple but he very firmly would not give the addresses of his two adult children as they "would not be interested", so no long-term contact ensued.

•In July 2021, as this book is going to press, a forty-year process is coming to fruition

– In 1981 Mary and Mike Graham (p. 173), from Durban, RSA, met Richard and Barbara Lawrence in San Maarten, West Indies, whilst on a working holiday. It was felt there was a family likeness, addresses were exchanged and nothing happened until 2001 when letters were exchanged. Richard knew his family history to his Lawrence grandfather, but little else.

– In 2020 Mary tried further contact and this led finally to an exchange of emails in July 2021 with Anne Sallee, eldest daughter of Richard, who happens to be the 'family genealogist' for this family of Lawrences.

– Anne Sallee[16] is also a descendant of John Burling Lawrence (p. 35), lives at Winter Park, Florida and welcomes contact with members of our section of the family.

•2002 saw a fortuitous meeting in Hobart with David and Rosalie Lawrence from Florida, and contact has been maintained since. It is said by 'local experts' that David also has 'the look' of our Lawrence men and DNA testing is underway to assess the likelihood of a family connection.

In 1993, Virginia Maunder-Taylor (p. 153), while preparing for the 21st birthday of her eldest son James, took a closer look at the 1973 family book. She then realized that the village in **Hertfordshire, England**, where she had lived with her family for 20 years, Hertingfordbury, was the village of the three Lawrence brothers who departed England for Long Island in 1635. The view from her kitchen window included the house of the Lawrence family in the early 1600s.

Finding family members with whom contact has been lost can be a project requiring persistence and ingenuity, and is sometimes achieved in interesting ways –

•Contacting everyone with a certain name listed in a particular telephone directory – sometimes successful, sometimes a fruitless activity

•Periodically, over the years, we have received phone calls from unknown persons, who turned out to be family. In one instance, contact was nearly lost as we were definitely not buying anything from the caller!

•'Wanted to contact' notices in newspapers remains, in some instances, a useful means of contacting people

•The internet has, of course, become available to genealogists in recent years and it has been used extensively with the current book. It was not available for use with the 1973 edition

•An approach to people is sometimes met with no response.

People may not wish to be found (quite understandable). In other cases the postal service may be less than efficient.

Finally, the family reunion held in March 1973 produced an interesting incident when half the attendees realized their ancestor was born before W E Lawrence found time to be married in 1826, and half descended from those born after the marriage. Consternation and, in due course, amusement followed (a matter of much less concern in 2021!)

The journey has been very worthwhile and I thank everyone for their contribution to it.

Frank Lawrence 2021

Notes

Notes

REFERENCES

Chapter 1 – Origins of the family

1. *Historical genealogy of the Lawrence family: from their first landing in this country AD 1635 to the present date July 4ᵗʰ 1858* / Thomas Lawrence. - E. O. Jenkins, New York, NY, 1858. https://archive.org/details/historicalgeneal00lawr/

2. https://www.museumoflondon.org.uk/application/files/5014/5434/6066/london-plagues-1348-1665.pdf

3. *A history of epidemics in Britain from AD 664 to the extinction of the plague, Vol.1* / Charles Creighton. – Cambridge University Press, Cambridge, 1891, pp. 282-371 Ch. VI, 'Plague in the Tudor Period'; and p. 692. www.gutenberg.org.

4. https://en.wikipedia.org/wiki/Timeline_of_British_history_(1500%E2%80%931599)

5. *Find a grave memorial* – St Albans district Hertfordshire, England - Lawrence (88 items) https://www.findagrave.com/memorial/search?firstname=&middlename=&lastname=Lawrence&includeMaidenName=true&birthyear=&birthyearfilter=&deathyear=&deathyearfilter=&location=&locationId=county_11355&memorialid=&datefilter=&orderby=&includeMaidenName=true

6. https://www.findagrave.com/memorial/169996915/robert-lawrence citing St Peter's Churchyard, St Albans, St Albans District, Hertfordshire, England; Maintained by Charles Boetsch (contributor 48409474)

7. https://ewww.findagrave.com/memorial/169976355/john-lawrence citing Saint Alban's Cathedral, St Albans, St Albans District, Hertfordshire, England; Maintained by Charles Boetsch (contributor 48409474)

8. https://www.findagrave.com/memorial/169979957/cecily-lawrence citing Saint Alban's Cathedral, St Albans, St Albans District, Hertfordshire, England; Maintained by Charles Boetsch (contributor 48409474)

9. https://www.findagrave.com/memorial/170126141/john-lawrence citing Saint Alban's Cathedral, St Albans, St Albans District, Hertfordshire, England ; Maintained by Charles Boetsch (contributor 48409474)

Bibliographic note: Another record, which this author has discounted in favour of the above record, in which a John Lawrence is 8 years younger but also died in 1609 (the apparent son of William Lawrence and Katherine Beaumont) but his 1st marriage to Elizabeth Knowlton means he was 7 years old, and 24 for his 2nd marriage to Margaret Roberts.
(see https://www.findagrave/163481542/john-lawrence)

10. https://www.findagrave.com/memorial/169946635/elizabeth-lawrence citing Saint Alban's Cathedral, St Albans, St Albans District, Hertfordshire, England; Maintained by Charles Boetsch (contributor 48409474)

11. *Ancestry.com England and Wales marriages 1538-1988.* John Lawrence 1554

12. Baptism dates only and not birth dates are given during this period

13. https://www.findagrave.com/memorial/201719764/john-lawrence citing Saint Alban's Cathedral, St Albans, St Albans District, Hertfordshire, England; Maintained by Linda Wilson (contributor 47594266)

14. https://www.findagrave.com/memorial/170126200/thomas-lawrence citing Saint Alban's Cathedral, St Albans, St Albans District, Hertfordshire, England; Maintained by Charles Boetsch (contributor 48409474).

Bibliographic note: There is another reference to a man of the same name, See Memorial *#124088812/thomas-lawrence* citing St Stephen Churchyard St Albans, with different parents, but *Thomas' 170126200* family history is also attached to this file, Maintained by Robert DeVowe (contributor 48224154). …
Both cannot be right. The author has chosen the 1st record.

15. *Ancestry.com. England, select births and christenings, 1538-1975*

16. https://www.findagrave.com/memorial/170387957/joan-tuttle citing Saint Nicholas Church of Ireland Cemetery, Carrickfergus, County Antrim, Northern Ireland; Maintained by Charles Boetsch (contributor 48409474) .

17. https://www.werelate.org/wiki/Person:John_Tuttle_%2839%29

18. https://www.findagrave.com/memorial/170363582/william-lawrence citing Saint Alban's Cathedral, St Albans, St Albans District, Hertfordshire, England; Maintained by Charles Boetsch (contributor 48409474).

Chapter 2 – The Family in North America

1. *Ancestry.com. New England : the great migration and the great migration begins : 1620-1635, Vol. 4, I-L* / Robert Charles Anderson. - New England Historic Genealogical Society, Boston, 2005:   Specific references –
John Lawrence pp. 254-258, (digital screen 362-366);
Mary Lawrence pp. 258-259 (digital screen 366-367);
Thomas Lawrence pp. 259-263 (digital screen 367-370);
William Lawrence pp. 263-268 (digital screen 371-376).
2.   http://www.olivetreegenealogy.com/ships/planter1635.shtml   'The Planter' passenger list.
3. *Historical genealogy of the Lawrence family: from their first landing in this country AD 1635 to the present date July 4th 1858* / Thomas Lawrence. - E. O. Jenkins, New York, NY, 1858; p. 9, pp. 38-41, pp. 40-46, pp. 51-52, pp. 158-159. https://archive.org/details/historicalgeneal00lawr/
4. *A Complete History of Connecticut, Civil and Ecclesiastical, from the Emigration of Its First Planters, from England, in the Year 1630, to the Year 1764; and to the Close of the Indian Wars: With an Appendix, Containing the Original Patent of New-England, (2 vol.)* / Benjamin Trumbull. - [British Library, Historical Print Editions, 1880], reprint editions in America; Vol. 1, pp. 497-498, Henry Lawrence. Google ebooks.
5. https://en.wikipedia.org/wiki/New_Netherland and Wikipedia entry for New Amsterdam.
6. *Ancestry.com. UK and Ireland, find a grave index, 1300s-current.* https://www.findagrave.com/memorial/124088812 -Thomas Lawrence 1588-1625, includes baptism dates for his children.
7. *Famous families of New York* publ. 1917, resubmitted by W. David Samuelsen. http://files.usgwarchives.net/ny/state/bios/ffny/lawrence.txt
8. *Ancestry.com. Colonial families of United States of America 1607-1775*, Vol. VII, pp. 6-15. Ahles Family, images 4-16: enumerates Lawrence family tree.
9. *Historical society of the New York Courts: John Lawrence 1618-1699.* https://history.nycourts.gov/figure/john-lawrence/
10. https://www.findagrave.com/memorial/36821946/john-lawrence
11. *Ancestry.com. New York, Wills and Probate Records, 1659-1999, Wills Vol. 5-6 (1693-1707)*, p. 298, screen 192, John Lawrence handwritten will 1698/99.

12. *Ancestry.com. New England marriages prior to 1700* / Clarence Almon Torrey. - p. 160, Mary Whittingham.

13. *Ancestry.com. New England historical and genealogical register : genealogical gleanings in England* / Henry F. Waters, Henry Fritz-Gilbert, 1885; p. 173, William & Mary Whittingham; p. 39, G. Saltonstall.

14. *Genealogical and personal memoirs relating to the families of Boston and eastern Massachusetts* / William Richard Cutter. – Lewis Historical Publishing Co., 1908, pp. 355-356. Google ebook.

15. https://en.wikipedia.org/wiki/Gurdon_Saltonstall#Personal_life

16. https://en.wikipedia.org/wiki/Gabriel_Minvielle

17. https://www.findagrave.com/memorial/163787886/thomas-lawrence

18. The Glorious Revolution. http://www.ouramericanrevolution.org/index.cfm/page/view/m0117

19. https://en.wikipedia.org/wiki/Leisler%27s_Rebellion

20. *The History of Long Island: Containing an account of the discovery and settlement, with other important and interesting matters to the present time* / Benjamin Franklin Thompson. – E. French, Long Is., NY, 1839, pp. 421-427. Google books.

21. *The history of Long Island, from its discovery to the present time* / Benjamin Franklin Thompson. – Gould Banks & Co., [NY], 1843, Appendix, p. 395. https://archive.org/details/historylongisla01thomgoog/page/n395/

22. *Our history: Family portrait reminiscent of colonial Queens* / Joan Brown Wettingfeld (article)

23. Footnote: https://www.findagrave.com/cemetery/2623125/william-lawrence-family-burial-ground

24. *Settlers of the long grey trail: some pioneers to old Augusta County ... /* John Houston Harrison. - Genealogical Publishing Com, 1975, pp. 29-39. Google ebook

25. https://www.findagrave.com/memorial/173314636/william-lawrence The author has used the '*New England; the great migration and the great migration begins; Vol 4. . . 2005*' as the authority (William 1656-1720).

26. https://www.wikitree.com/wiki/Rodman-127 Sarah Lawrence.

27. https://en.wikipedia.org/wiki/Philip_Carteret_(colonial_governor)

28. https://www.findagrave.com/memorial/134674186/philip-carteret

29. https://jrm.phys.ksu.edu/genealogy/needham/ search term Elizabeth Smith

30. *Encyclopedia of American Quaker genealogy, Vol. 3, 1867-1947* / William Wade Hinshaw, et. al. - Edwards Bros. Inc., Mich., 1936. <u>Richard Lawrence family, p.200</u>, and <u>p. 178 Stevenus Hunt. https://babel.hathitrust.org</u>

31. *Ancestry.com. Bowne family of Flushing Long Island* /Edith King Wilson. – William Byrd Press [NY], 1948, p. 11, Richard Lawrence.

32. Footnote:- http://blog.nyhistory.org/yellow-fever-hits-1790s-new-york/

33. <u>*The Burling Books : Ancestors and Descendants of Edward and Grace Burling, Quakers (1600-2000), Vol 1*</u> / Jane Thompson-Stahr. - Gateway Press, Inc., Baltimore, MD., c2001, p. 125, John Lawrence. Google ebook.

34 Footnote:- *The Burling Books, Vol. 1*…by Jane Thompson-Stahr, c.2001; p. 29 footnote

35. Footnote:- *The Burling Books, Vol. 1*…by Jane Thompson-Stahr, c.2001; p. 50 footnote.

36. *Ancestry.com. New York historic homes and family history, Vol. I-IV*; Vol 1, pp. 319-320, Family of Embree (images 1-3).

37. <u>*The Burling Books : Ancestors and Descendants of Edward and Grace Burling, Quakers (1600-2000), Vol 1*</u>. - Gateway Press, Inc., Baltimore, MD., c.2001, pp. 149-153, Caleb & Sarah Lawrence: Google ebook

38. *Ancestry.com. 1911 England census Appendix-New York in the Revolution*, p. 418, Roster of state troops (Lawrence),
p. 543 Westchester Company Militia Captain Lawrence.

39. *Ancestry.com. New York historic homes: family history, Vol I-IV.- Provo, UT, USA, 2002. (originally published under a different title in 1907)*; Vol. 1. pp.112, 125, 135, (images 1-26) Family of Schieffelin.

40. Footnote:- Google maps; also source - https://forgotten-ny.com/2007/07/manhattanville-manhattan/

41.https://www.findagrave.com/memorial/12789975/john-burling-lawrence

42. *Ancestry.com. U.S. Encyclopedia of American Quaker Genealogy, Vol 1-V1, 1607-1943* for Alfred N. Lawrence; Extract taken from Vol III, 'New York Monthly Meeting', p.800

43. *Ancestry.com. New York, US wills and probate records, 1659-1999 – Proceedings, Vol 0011-0012, 1849-1850, p. 488. (screen shot 290)*

44. https://en.wikipedia.org/wiki/Frederick_N._Lawrence

45. *Ancestry.com. US Quaker Meeting Records 1681-1935: Philadelphia Pennsylvania; Green Street Monthly Meeting*

46. *Ancestry.com New York, US death index, 1892-1898, 1900-1902* Anna Hough Lawrence 1893.

47. *Newspapers.com.* 'Times Union' Brooklyn, NY; 15 Aug 1928, p. 43; Obituary N T Lawrence

48. *Ancestry.com.* New York. US death newspaper extracts 1801-1890 (Barber collection) in New York Evening Post, 24 Aug 1890 for Isabel Gillet Lawrence death notice.

49. *Ancestry.com. US find a grave index, 1600s-current.* NT Lawrence, d.1968

50. *Newspapers.com.* 'Chicago Tribune', Chicago, Ill; 20 Nov 1968, p. 90; Obituary, Newbold T Lawrence, age 75.

51. *Ancestry.com. US: Enlisted WWII draft cards* – N T Lawrence, age 19.

52. *Ancestry.com. U.S., Consular reports of births 1910-1940* Richard Cromwell Lawrence

53. *A history of Thomas and Anne Billopp Farmar and some of their descendants in America* / Charles Farmar Billopp. – Grafton Press, New York, 1907, pp. 53-57. https://archive.org/details/historyofthomasa00lcbill/page/53/mode/2up/search/major+thomas+billopp

54. *Ancestry.com. London, England, marriages and banns, 1754-1923.* All Hallows Barking by the Tower, City of London. # spelt 'Catherine Farmer'.

55. Footnote:- https://www.nysenate.gov/timeline ; also - https://en.wikipedia.org/wiki/United_States_Congress#History

56. https://en.wikipedia.org/wiki/Effingham_Lawrence -Effingham Nicoll Lawrence

57. http://ancestry-world.com/Townley.html accessed 2/2019 Also *Ancestry.com. https://longislandsurnames.com*

58. *Historical genealogy of the Lawrence family... .* Jenkins, 1858: ..., p. 56 'Three Brothers vessel'

59. *Ancestry.com. NY city marriages 1660-1800*, p. 107, Hannah Lawrence.

60. *Ancestry.com. New England : the great migration and the great migration begins: 1620-1635*, Vol. 4, I-L / Robert Charles Anderson. - New England Historic Genealogical Society, Boston, 2005, p.266, Sarah Lawrence (b.1675-) or Sarah Lawrence (b.1679-)

61. https://www.wikitree.com/wiki/Burnham-34 Thomas Burnum (Burnham).

62. https://www.findagrave.com/memorial/192901119 Thomas Burnham.

63. https://www.wikitree.com/wiki/Lawrence-238#Death
64. *Ancestry.com. U.S. and International marriage records, 1560-1900.* Thomas Burnham.
65. *Ancestry.com. Global, Find a grave index for burials at sea and other select burials locations, 1300s-current.* Thomas Burnham
66. https://scripophily.net/laca18.html - © 2002 T. Mark James

Chapter 3 – Effingham Lawrence

1. *Historical genealogy of the Lawrence family: from their first landing in this country AD 1635 to the present date July 4th 1858* / Thomas Lawrence. - New York, NY, E. O. Jenkins, 1858. https://archive.org/details/historicalgeneal00lawr/
2. *William Robert Chaplin papers on Trinity House relating to the period 1513-1965, compiled 1928-1965* / William Robert chaplin (unpublished) held State Library of NSW. http://archival.sl.nsw.gov.au/Details/archive/110320249
3. https://www.trinityhouse.co.uk/about-us/history-of-trinity-house
4. *Ancestry.com. Rhode Island Vital extracts 1636-1899, Vol. 14: newspapers: Marriages, deaths*, p. 43 notice of EL death.
5. *Ancestry.com. England & Wales Prerogative Court of Canterbury Wills, 1384-1858* for Effingham Lawrence.
6. *Ancestry.com. Post Office Land Directories, London* . - various dates.
7. *Ancestry.com. Genealogies of Pennsylvania families from the Pennsylvania genealogical magazine, Vol. 1 Arnold-Her* . - pp.522- 524 (screen 527-529).
8. *A history of Thomas and Anne Billopp Farmar and some of their descendants in America* / Charles Farmar Billopp . – Grafton Press, New York, 1907, pp. 53-57. https://archive.org/details/historyofthomasa00lcbill/page/53/mode/2up/search/major+thomas+billopp
9. *The ancestors and relatives of William Addams Reitwiesner, Part CCCCXC: the descendants of Thomas Billopp.* http://www.wargs.com/family/0490.html
10. 'Bentley Manor' https://theconferencehouse.org/about/history/
11. *Ancestry.com. London, England, marriages and banns, 1754-1923.* All Hallows Barking by the Tower, City of London. Effingham Lawrence &

'Catherine Farmer'.

12. *Ancestry.com. London, England, Church of England baptisms, marriages and burials, 1538-1812* for Catherine Lawrence. All Hallows Barking by the Tower, 1749-1812. Birth 5/3/1782, baptism 12/4/1782.

13. *Australian Dictionary of Biography, Vol. 2, 1788-1850* / editors: A.G.L. Shaw and C.M.H. Clark, 1967 edition. http://adb.anu.edu.au/biography/lawrence-william-effingham-2336

14. *Ancestry.com. London, England, Church of England baptisms, marriages and burials, 1538-1812* for Catherine Lawrence. All Hallows Barking by the Tower, 1749-1812. -Birth 23/9/1783, baptism 31/10/1/1783.

15. *Ancestry.com. London, England, Church of England deaths and burials 1813-2003* for John Lawrence burial 21/3/1830 St Luke, Finsbury, Islington (possibly JCL).

16. *Ancestry.com. East India Company Penang Civil Service*, p. 351. John Curson Lawrence.

17. *Java : past and present : a description of the most beautiful country in the world, its ancient history, people, antiquities and products* / Donald Maclaine Campbell. – W. Heinemann, London, 1915, p. 639. https://seasiavisions.library.cornell.edu

18. *The family of Sir Stamford Raffles* / John Bastin, Julie Weizenegger. - Marshall Cavendish International Asia Pty.Ltd, 2016, p. 75. Google ebooks, digital image.

19. *Ancestry.com. UK registers of East India Company*; 1810, p. 302, "...commissioner recovery of small debts", Prince of Wales Is.; 1820, p. 351, "...senior merchant (at home)".

20. *Cases heard and determined in Her Majesty's Supreme Court of the Straits Settlements, 1808-1884, in 3 volumes, Civil cases : Vol. 1.* - Singapore, 1883, p. iv. https://archive.org

21. Magelang, Central Java, Indonesia. Google maps.

22. *Ancestry.com. UK register of East India Company and Directory;* "1819... pay master and storekeeper.

23. *The India Office and Burma Office lists.* 1821, p.351 ..."and superintendent of Company's lawsuits John Curson Lawrence (at home)". Google ebooks, digital image

24. *Raffles of the Eastern Isles* / C. E. Wurtzburg. – London, Hodder &

Stoughton, 1954, pp. 56, 61, 63, 66, 82, 185, 248, 312, 323, 368, 385. http://www.archive.org

25. Footnote: - https://www.wikipedia.org

26. Footnote: - *World history at KMLA : History of Java. 'Java within the Dutch East Indies'.* – footnote: https://www.zum.de/whkmla/region/seasia/xjava.html

27. *Ancestry.com. London, England, Church of England baptisms, marriages and burials, 1813-1917.* – Baptism of ACL age 10, HCL age 6.

28. *Ancestry.com. UK Articles of Clerkship, 1756-1854.* HCL.

29. *Ancestry.com. London cemetery registers, 1841-1966.* HCL.

30. *Ancestry.com. London, England, Church of England baptisms, marriages and burials, 1538-1812* for Catherine Lawrence. All Hallows Barking by the Tower, 1749-1812. - Birth 2/5/1785, baptism 1/6/1785.

31. *Ancestry.com. UK England, registers of employees of East India Company and the India Office, 1746-1939*: The East India Register and directory, 1810. (Screen 76).

32. *Ancestry.com. UK England, registers of employees of East India Company and the India Office, 1746-1939*: General register 1790-1842, p. 195, (screen 255). ECL history 1800-1824.

33. *Ancestry.com. England & Wales Prerogative Court of Canterbury Wills, 1384-1858*, for Effingham Calvert Lawrence, (screen 150-151).

34. *Monthly magazine, vol. 39, Part 1, 1815*, p. 367. Notice of marriage.

35. *The Gentleman's magazine, Vol. 206 / F. Jefferies, 1859*, p. 218, Feb 1859.

36. *Ancestry.com. Church of England marriages and banns, 1754-1932*: Westminster, St Marylebone, 1811-1816, (screen 420).

37. *Ancestry.com. India, select births and baptisms, 1786-1947*, Vol 10, p. 108, 'baptism 25 Dec 1816, Dacca, Bengal, India.'

38. *The Register of Tonbridge School from 1820-1893 / ed. W. O. Hughes, 1886*, p. 25. https://archive.org/details/registeroftonbri00tonb/page/24/mode/2up

39. *Ancestry.com. Cambridge University Alumni, 1261-1900: Alumni Cantabrigienses, Vol. 3, K-R / J. A. Venn, et. al.* – Cambridge University Press, London, 1922-1954: 1951 edition, p. 112.

40. *Ancestry.com. England & Wales, Civil registration marriage index, 1837-1915*; '1868, Q1-Jan-Feb-Mar: -Lawrence, Effingham John (Kensington).'

41. *Ancestry.com. Census records – (household occupants)-*
1861, Middlesex, Staple Inn -'EJL 44, sole occupant'.
1871, Kensington -'EJL 54, Sarah wife 62 (b. Kensington), Agnes 13, John 11.'
1881, Kensington - 'EJL 64, Agnes 23 daughter (b. Middlesex Paddington) & servant.'
42. *Ancestry.com. England & Wales, civil registration death index, 1837-1915.* '1877, Q1-Jan-Feb-Mar: -John Effingham Lawrence'.
43. *Ancestry.com. England & Wales, National probate calendar (Index of wills and administrations), 1858-1995*: Registered 16/3/1888, resworn March 1890, £12,378
44. *Ancestry.com. England & Wales, Civil registration index, 1837-1915.* Caroline Elizabeth E Lawrence
45. *Ancestry.com. England & Wales Civil Registration: birth index 1837-1915.* Evangeline Gertrude Cardon.
46. *Ancestry.com. London, Church of England Marriages and Banns, 1754-1932*: Kensington and Chelsea, All Saints, Notting Hill, 1878-1900, (screen 224).
47. *Ancestry.com. India select births & baptisms, 1786-1947, ref.* Vol. 10, p. 618. Charles Harding Lawrence.
49. Sussex House Asylum, London. http://studymore.org.uk.
50. *Ancestry.com. UK Burial and cremation index, 1576-2014* for Harding Charles Lawrence
51. *Ancestry.com. England & Wales, National Probate Calendar (Index of Wills and Administrations), 1858-1995*; 1889. Kaberry-Lywood. - The will of Caroline Effingham Elizabeth Lawrence (1824-1889)
52. *Ancestry.com. London, England, Church of England baptisms, marriages and burials, 1538-1812* for Catherine Lawrence. City of London; All Hallows, Barking by the Tower, 1749-1812. Birth 17/8/1786, baptism 4/9/1786 (image 94).
53. *Debrett's baronetage of England, with alphabetical lists of such baronetcies as have merged in the peerage...(etc)...,*7th ed. / J. Debrett, W. Courthope. - J.G. & F. Rivington, London, 1835, page 436. Google books snippet view.
54. *Oxford Dictionary of National Biography.* – Smith Elder & Co, London, 2004, pp. 141-144. R. H. Vetch, revised R. T. Stearn Jones, 'Sir John Thomas,

first baronet (1783-1843)'. Version 2006 online. https://doi.org/10.1093/ref:odnb/15054 c.2021.

55. http://www.wargs.com/family/1090.html Lawrence-Jones baronets.

56. Footnote: - *Sydney Morning Herald*, 17/10/2010. 'No glory in the saga of the Wren family feud' / Lawrence Money. http://www.smh.com.au/national/no-glory-in-the-saga-of-the-wren-family-feud-20100216-o917.html

57. Footnote: - *Australian Dictionary of Biography*, Vol. 12, 1891-1939. - Melbourne University Press, Melbourne, 1990, pp. 580-583. James Griffin, 'Wren, John (1871–1953)'. https://adb.anu.edu.au/biography/wren-john-9198/text16247.

58. *Ancestry.com. England, Andrews newspaper index cards, 1790-1976.* Elinor Wren.

59. Extracts from *UK Decennial census, 1851, 1861, 1871, 1881, 1991* and some *1901*

60. *Ancestry.com. London, England, Church of England baptisms, marriages and burials, 1538-1812* for Catherine Lawrence. City of London, All Hallows, Barking by the Tower, 1749-1812. Birth 29/7/1790, baptism 26/8/1790

61. *Hackney Archives; M3923/1*, 1863; business transactions between " Edward Billup Lawrence, Effingham John Lawrence and Charles Monro father & son". https://discovery.nationalarchives.gov.uk

62. *Ancestry.com. England & Wales, death index, 1837-1915.* reg. 1a295

63. *Ancestry.com. England, select deaths and burials, 1538-1991.*

64. *Ancestry.com England & Wales, National probate calendar (Index of wills and administrations), 1858-1995.* Wills 1861. (screen 41)

65. *Ireland; calendar of wills and administration, 1858-1920.* Wills 1861. http://www.willcalendars.nationalarchives.ie/reels/cwa/005014884/005014884_00095.pdf

66. *State records New South Wales, Colonial Secretary Index 1788-1825, Lawler-Lawrence, N.*; Reel 6021; 4/1094, pp. 259-262. http://colsec.records.nsw.gov.au/l/F32c_la-10.htm#P4533_146953

Chapter 4 – William Effingham Lawrence

1. *William Sorell in Van Diemen's Land, Lieut. Gov. 1817-1824* / Leone Mickleborough. – Blubber Press, Hobart, 2004, pp.31-32.
2. *Australian Dictionary of Biography, Vol. 2, 1788-1850.* – Melbourne University Press, [Melbourne], 1967, pp. 93-95.
Bruce Wall, 'William Effingham Lawrence 1781-1841'.
https://adb.anu.edu.au/biography/lawrence-william-effingham-2336
3. *Governor Arthur's convict system, Van Diemen's Land, 1824-1836* / W. D. Forsyth. - Sydney University Press, [Sydney], 1970.
4. *Backsight : a history of surveying in colonial Tasmania* / Alan Jones. – Institution of Surveyors, Australia (Tasmanian Division), Hobart, 1989, pp. 41-45.
5. *The story of Port Dalrymple: life and work in Northern Tasmania* / Llwelyn Slingsby Bethell. - Blubber Press, (fac. ed.) January 1980, pp.72-73.
6. *Colonial Time*s, 11 May 1841, p. 2. Obituary, William Effingham Lawrence.
7. *Ancestry.com. London, England, Church of England baptisms, marriages and burials, 1538-1812.* Mary Ann Smither
8. *Ancestry.com. Australia. Marriage Index 1788-1950.* No. 952
9. *Ancestry.com. London, England, Church of England marriages and banns, 1754-1932* for William George, Westminster, St Martin in the Fields, 1817-1819 (No. 549)
10. *Ancestry.com. Australia. Marriage index 1788-1950.* No. 192
11. *LINC Archives. Names Index. Launceston Census, 1828, p. 70.* WEL household
12. National Archives, Kew, UK – Public Records.
Chancery pleadings – 10 entries for Edward Effingham Lawrence, and one entry - Divorce Court file, # 9727, 1884.
https://discovery.nationalarchives.gov.uk/results/r?
q=edward+effingham+lawrence

Chapter 5 – Robert William Lawrence

1. *Journal of R. W. Lawrence.* – QVMAG, CH553-33/2.,

8 Oct-11 Nov 1830. (Service in the Black War)

2. *The Black War: fear, sex and resistance in Tasmania* / Nicholas Clements. – University of Queensland Press, St. Lucia, Qld, 2014, pp. 128-144.

3. *Flora Tasmaniae : Tasmanian naturalists & Imperial botany*, 1829-1860 / Eleanor Cave. – Eleanor Cave, Hobart, 2012, Chapter 2.
http://eprints.utas.edu.au/14747/2/whole-cave-thesis.pdf

4. *Flora of Australia*, Vol. 1, Introduction, 2nd ed. – ABRS/CSIRO, Melbourne, 1999, pp. 11-104,
A. E. Orchard, 'A history of systemic botany in Australia' .

5. *Van Diemen's Land correspondents, 1827-1849* / T. E. Burns and J. R. Skemp. – Queen Victoria Museum, Launceston, 1961.

6. *Pathfinders in Tasmanian botany: an honour roll of people connected through naming Tasmanian plants* / Dick Burns. - Tasmanian Arboretum, Devonport, Tas., 2012.

7. *The diaries of John Helder Wedge.* – Royal Society of Tasmania, [Hobart], 1962.

8. *Early pioneer families of Victoria and the Riverina : a genealogical and biographical record* / compiled and edited by Alexander Henderson. – McCarron, Bird & Co., Melbourne, 1936, pp. 22-24, 'Monckton Davey Synnot 1854-1938'.

Chapter 6 – Mary Ann Lawrence

1. *Australian Dictionary of Biography*, Vol. 1, 1788-1850. - Melbourne University Press, Melbourne. 1966, pp. 531-534, Marnie Bassett, 'Family of Thomas Henty 1775-1839'
https://adb.anu.edu.au/biography/henty-thomas-2179

2. *The Hentys : an Australian colonial tapestry* / Marnie Basset. - Melbourne University Press, Parkville, 1962.

3. *War beneath the sea: submarine conflict 1939-1945* / Peter Padfield. – Hodder & Stoughton General Div., 1995.

Chapter 7 – William Lawrence

Chapter 8 – Eliza Lawrence

1. *Australian Dictionary of Biography*, Vol. 2, 1788-1850. – Melbourne University Press, [Melbourne], 1967, pp.230-231. W. G. Hoddinott 'Joseph Milligan 1807-1884'.
https://adb.anu.edu.au/biography/milligan-joseph-2456
2. *Vocabulary of the dialects of some of the Aboriginal tribes of Tasmania* / Joseph Milligan, Royal Society of Tasmania Papers, [Hobart], 1859.
3. *The Cornwall Chronicle*, Saturday 28 December 1867, p. 2. Notice of death of Joseph Lawrence Milligan.

Chapter 9 – John Effingham Lawrence

1. *Citation*, Sport Australia Hall of Fame, induction 12 Nov 1991. (Don Lawrence) https://www.sahof.org.au/hall-of-fame/member-profile/
2. *The Margaret Smith story* / Margaret Smith as told to Don Lawrence. – Stanley Paul, London, 1965.
3. *Greg Norman – my story*, by Greg Norman and Don Lawrence. – Aurora Press, Sydney, 1983.
4. *Victoria Golf Club 1903-1988* / Don Lawrence. – Lester-Townsend Publishing, Sydney, 1988.

Chapter 10 – Effingham Billopp Lawrence

1. *Appointment wrongfully terminated? : the appointment and termination of Lieutenant Colonel G. A. D. Youl, MC as Commanding Officer, 2/40th Battalion, 1940-41* / Douglas Morris Wyatt. Self published, Tasmania, 2017.
2. *Doomed battalion : Mateship and leadership in war and captivity: The Australian 2/40 Battalion, 1940-1945 (2nd edition)* / Peter Henning. – [Exeter, Tasmania], 2014.
3. *Ada M a'Beckett – a profile* / Frances Douglas, BEd., MEdSt. - Monash University, Melbourne, June 1989.
4. https://thehenryjones.com/artist/angus-douglas/
5. *This our fathers did for us : the story of a pioneering family in Tasmania* / Derrick Loane. – Self published, Sassafrass, Tas., 1991.

6. *Marcus L. Loane, a biography* / John. R. Reid . – Acorn Press, Sydney, 2004.

7. *From strength to strength : a life of Marcus Loane* / Allan M. Branch. – Australian Scholarly Publishing, Australia, 2015.

8. *Australia in the war of 1939-1945, Series III, Air No. 1: Royal Australian Air Force 1939-1942* / Douglas Gillison. - AWM, Canberra, 1962, pp. 403, 513, Owen Lawrence Loane.

9. Angus Lawrence inquest Coroner's Court Darwin, file D0194/2004. https://justice.nt.gov.au/__data/assets/pdf_file/0003/208362/angus-lawrence.pdf

Chapter 11 – Octavius Vernon Lawrence

1. *Medical Journal of Australia*, 13 Feb 1937, pp. 270-272. Obituary, Dr. H. F. Lawrence.

2. *The doers : the history of surgery at St. Vincent's Hospital, Melbourne, 1890s-1950s* / Ivo Vellar . – Publishing Solutions, Richmond, Vic., 2002.

3. *How and when to use radium therapy* / Herman Lawrence. – Stillwell & Co., Melbourne, 1911.

4. *Australian Journal of Dermatology*, Vol. 2, 1953-54, pp. 99-103. 'Herman Lawrence, Doyen of Dermatology' by W. W. Lempriere.

5. *Therapeutics, dietetics and hygiene: an Australian textbook* / John William Springthorpe. - James Little, Melbourne, 1914. 'Radiotherapy' section contributed by Dr. H. F. Lawrence.

6. *Early pioneer families of Victoria and the Riverina : a genealogical and biographical record* / compiled and edited by Alexander Henderson. - McCarron, Bird & Co., Melbourne, 1936, pp. 49-59. The Dennis family.

7. *Dennis family journey West Penrith to Warncoort, Victoria* / Wendy Tuechler, 2017. Privately held papers. wtuechler@bigpond.com

8. *Six generations: Tales of the Dennis family in Western Victoria* / Alexander W. Dennis. – A. W. Dennis, Colac Vic., 1963.

9. *The old ewe* / Noel Dennis. – Shoestring Press, Wangaratta, Vic., 1988 (for children).

10. *Polwarth sheep 1880-1890: a resume of the first 100 years* / Noel C. R. Dennis. – Polwarth Sheep Breeders' Association of Australia (Victorian Branch), Ballarat, Vic., 1982.

11. *Murray Greys: Australia's own beef cattle* / ed. T. Hewat, photographs M. Stephens. – Studmaster Press, Berwick, Vic., 1972, pp. 54-55.

12. *Salt of the earth : stories of families surviving the rural crisis in Australia* / Marjorie Johnson . – Collins Dove, Melbourne, 1988, pp. 132-141.

13. *Beersheba, a journey through Australia's forgotten War* / Paul Daley. – Melb. Univ. Press, Carlton, Vic., 2009

14. *Ring the Chief Justice* / John V. Lawrence. – Arcadia, Nth. Melb., 2020.

15. *Helen Ruth Lawrence (1883-1964): an account of her life as an army nurse and thereafter* / a presentation to East Melbourne Historical Society, 7 Jan 2016, by Janet Scaife. https://emhs.org.au/biography/lawrence/helen_ruth

Chapter 12 – Caroline Marienne Lawrence

Chapter 13 – Eliza Margaret Milligan

1. *Beaufort, Beaufighter and Mosquito – in Australian service* / Stewart Wilson. – Aerospace Publications, Fyshwick, ACT, 1990

2. *Australian War Memorial Roll of Honour located on panel 102 in the commemorative area.* https://www.awm.gov.au

3. *Dicing with destiny* / Coral V. Gaunt. - Pedder Press, Camden, NSW, 1997

Chapter 14 – 'A son remembers'

Chapter 15 – Family miscellany

1. *Polwarth sheep1880-1890 : a resume of the first 100 years* / Noel C. R. Dennis. – Polwarth Sheep Breeders' Association of Australia (Victorian Branch), Ballarat, Vic., 1982.

2. *Van Diemen's Land correspondents, 1827-1849* / T. E. Burns and J. R. Skemp. - Queen Victoria Museum, Launceston, 1961.

3. *Lloyds register of British and foreign shipping, 1826.* – Lloyds, London.

4.https://en.wikipedia.org/wiki/Robert_Jenkinson,_2nd_Earl_of_Liverpool ; also - *Encyclopedia Brittanica, Vol. 17.* - Encyclopedia Brittanica, [London]. 1966, p. 595

5. Personal letter from histographer Wm. R. Chaplin, Trinity House, London to author, received 5/7/1973.

6. *Shipping arrivals and departures-Tasmania, 1803-1833* / Ian H. Nicholson. – Roebuck Society Publication No. 30, Canberra, 1983, pp. 86 (1823), p. 99 (1824).

7. *Flotsam and jetsam : floating fragments of life in England and Tasmania* / Henry Button. – A. W. Birchall, Launceston, 1909, (Simpkin Marshall & Co, London. fac. 1993), pp. 392-396.

8. *Launceston Examiner (Tas. 1842-1899)*, Saturday 18 Apr. 1885, page 3 – Obituary for Mr. William Thomas Bell, also *Tasmanian Dictionary of Biography*. https://tdob.org/John%20Jacobs%20and%20Barbara%20Hay accessed 6/5/2020

9. LINC Archives Tasmania, search term *Lord Liverpool*

10. *Shipping arrivals and departures, Sydney 1788-1825* / John S. Cumpston, 1977.

11. *Sydney Gazette*, 20 Nov 1830, p. 3. 'Domestic industry: Lord Liverpool' (ship)

12. *Shipping arrivals and departures, Sydney, 1826-1840* / Ian H. Nicholson. – Roebuck Society Publication No. 23, Canberra, 1977, pp. 81 (1832), p. 93 (1833).

13. http://oceans1.customer.netspace.net.au/pacific-main.html   Lord Liverpool Tonga

14. St Marks Church Lake River, Pisa, Cressy (photo courtesy Duncan Grant)

15. The Examiner, 27/1/2019: '*Our history: resting place for pioneers*', Dianne Cassidy, L'ton Historical Society

16. Ann Sallee contact details are as follows *aesallee@gmail.com* Tel: (954) 25308501

Index of Names

Notes – (birth-death) given whenever possible
　　　– if marriage date is only available (- m.date -)
　　　– partners or children without surnames or dates are not indexed
　　　– group photographs are not indexed
　　　– square bracket denotes [specific event] as recorded in the manuscript, or an estimated birth year [est.b.year -]
　　　– surnames before marriage are used, where applicable

Index of Events and Places

About the Author

Effingham Frank Lawrence grew up on the Lawrence family property, Billopp, in Northern Tasmania. He was educated at the Launceston Church Grammar School and later graduated from the Medical School of the University of Adelaide, South Australia. After post-graduate training in Canada and Melbourne he returned to Southern Tasmania where he was a local General Practitioner at Taroona for 35 years. During that time, he also gave special service to diabetes, family planning and sexual assault services. In 1995, he was one of 20 GPs across the country who were acknowledged for services to the community.

Away from medicine, he has also had a long-term membership of Lions Clubs International, has twice been awarded a Melvin Jones Fellowship for "dedication to humanitarian services" (the premier award of that organisation) and later a Life Membership. In 1997 the municipal council of Kingborough awarded him a special Certificate of Appreciation for service to the community.

Frank first developed an interest in the Lawrence family genealogy in the 1950s with the encouragement of his father and an older cousin. In late 1972, he published a family history "1834 Before and After". That book was widely distributed amongst the family at that time and was used as a basis for this book.

Frank has been married for 54 years and has three children and six grandchildren.

Bea Lawrence OAM
(Long-suffering wife!)